Library of
Davidson College

THE EUROPEAN DEFENCE INITIATIVE

By the same authors

EUROPE OR THE OPEN SEA?

CRISIS IN EUROPEAN DEFENCE

Also by Geoffrey Lee Williams

THE PERMANENT ALLIANCE: The European–American Partnership, 1945–1984

GLOBAL DEFENCE: Motivation and Policy in a Nuclear Age

DENIS HEALEY AND THE POLICIES OF POWER (*with Brian Reed*)

THE EUROPEAN DEFENCE INITIATIVE

EUROPE'S BID FOR EQUALITY

Geoffrey Lee Williams
and
Alan Lee Williams

Foreword by
Lord Home of The Hirsel

St. Martin's Press   New York

© Geoffrey Lee Williams and Alan Lee Williams, 1986

All rights reserved. For information, write:
Scholarly & Reference Division,
St. Martin's Press, Inc., 175 Fifth Avenue, New York, NY 10010

First published in the United States of America in 1986

Printed in Great Britain

ISBN 0-312-26932-3

Library of Congress Cataloging-in-Publication Data
Williams, Geoffrey Lee.
The European defence initiative.
Bibliography: p.
Includes index.
1. Europe—Military policy.   2. North Atlantic
Treaty Organization.   I. Williams, Alan Lee.   II. Title.
UA646.W53   1986   355'.0335'4   85-26187
ISBN 0-312-26932-3

To our father Alfred Edward Williams

Contents

Foreword ix
Acknowledgements xi

Introduction 1

PART I THE PAST
1 Britain and the Third Force Syndrome 15
2 The Growth of the Strategic Dichotomy 28
3 The Rise of Europeanism 43

PART II THE PRESENT
4 The Fragmentation of Alliance: the Need for a New Military Strategy? 61
5 European Defence: How Real Is the Soviet Threat? 78
6 The Transformation of the Soviet Navy: the Threat to Europe and NATO's Response 102
7 National Perspectives within the Alliance: Impediments to Defence Integration 113
8 Differing Priorities: the Lesson of the Siberian Pipeline Drama 132
9 The British Nuclear Defence Option 140

PART III THE FUTURE
10 The Unilateralist Threat to Peace: the Rise of the Peace Movement 163
11 The Dual Track Decision: the European Dimension 172
12 The Limitations of Arms Control: the Need for a New Beginning? 186
13 European Defence and the Strategic Defence Initiative 200
14 Conclusions 213

Notes 220
Selected Bibliography 232
Index 233

Foreword: The European Defence Initiative: Europe's Bid for Equality

This book, written by the Williams brothers, is an important and timely contribution to the debate about the future of the NATO alliance.

They have a premise and a theme. The premise is that NATO must be based firmly on two pillars, Europe and America, and that nothing must be allowed to divide that partnership. In that they must be right, because the lesson of this century has been that to defeat a first-class military power it was necessary to mobilize both Europe and America. One or the other will not do to deter a country as powerful as the Soviet Union, it has to be both.

Their theme is the need to strengthen the European pillar. Certainly that is desirable – it ought to be possible to organize a more effective performance from the European members than has been available up to now.

They do not belittle the difficulties, and more important, they do not fudge the issues. They come down firmly on the side of Britain's adoption of Trident, arguing that if Britain is to retain a nuclear deterrent then it should be the best available.

They canvass all the possibilities for strengthening European NATO from the standardization of equipment from Europe's resources to the controversial conclusion that the German Federal Republic should at some future date be allowed to lease nuclear weapons under NATO rules.

Their analysis of Russia's attitude to disarmament over the last 40 years leads them to the conclusion that the formula of mutual and balanced and verified disarmament has no attraction for Russian leaders, and they will strive to maintain and to add to their superiority over the whole range of weaponry.

Therefore they conclude that Europe and America will have to sustain their determination to maintain forces which will carry conviction to the Russian leaders that the price of aggression will always remain too high.

They pose a challenge to the people of Europe to maximize the defence of their own continent, so that the twin pillars which support the NATO edifice may be equal in power.

No one will agree with all the arguments which the authors advance, but this is an analysis in depth of the problems of the defence of free peoples everywhere, and anyone who reads this book will be stimulated and rewarded.

LORD HOME OF HIRSEL

Acknowledgements

We should like to thank Julie Parsons who typed the book in its entirety and we are also grateful to Penelope Ford for her assistance in reading the manuscript. Finally, we should like to acknowledge the encouragement given by both Nicholas Sherwen of NATO and Peace through NATO (PTN). The views expressed are entirely our own.

GEOFFREY LEE WILLIAMS
ALAN LEE WILLIAMS

Introduction

This study will seek to examine the increasing interest in and relevance of the so called 'Europeanist' strand in NATO's defence thinking. This aspect of NATO's defence planning could encourage the recasting of the strategic priorities established by the so called 'Atlanticists' over the last 36 years.

We argue that the Europeanist element in NATO would actually weaken the political stability of the Western Alliance, unless and until a clear rationale for the rise of a 'second centre of deterrence' is defined and established in terms which enable it to be genuinely reconciled with the need to retain the indissoluble link with the United States.

The need to maintain the Western Alliance is examined against the background of the growing, yet by no means inevitable, clash of economic and political as well as military priorities between Europe and America, as they are likely to develop over the next decade.

The 'Europeanization' of NATO's defensive posture must include a major revision in the local strategy of NATO on the critical central front. This will place greater emphasis on the need to exploit the real military resources of Britain and West Germany, together with that of France, within a new arrangement compatible with NATO, but encapsulated within this new European political dimension. The mechanism as well as the military doctrines required to achieve this are examined with reference to the military capabilities and defence structures of Britain, Western Germany and of France and the minor members of NATO as they might develop during the 1990s. The logic of the so called air–land battle and the follow-on force attack which NATO is considering are assessed as positive contributions to Europe's defence. But since NATO's new 'forward' strategy has its origins in atlanticist thinking, rather than in a rediscovery of a genuine continental tradition, we shall seek to demonstrate that a 'Europeanized' NATO, with America as its irremovable strategic centrepiece, will need to establish a distinctive identity based on the separate British and French and possible West German nuclear perspectives.

The need to raise the nuclear threshold through heightened conventional force capabilities are examined in the context of the British, French and American versions of deterrence. Also, we have critically examined the contradictions inherent in the twin pillar concept of NATO, given the vulnerability of Europe to Soviet pre-emptive strikes directed at specifically designated European targets. That still remains the critical deficiency for NATO.

This study attempts, then, to set out what European defence could look like in the 1980s and beyond, given the political pressures to modify the existing 'Atlanticist' connection. This modification – if it were to succeed – of NATO's present strategy is palpably inspired by the notion that the rich and highly developed states of Western Europe should be capable of playing a primary role in their own defence, (as opposed to their present undignified and less-than-necessary military dependence upon the United States).

We seek to show that this 'Europeanized', as well as largely conventionalized posture involves a profound, but not necessarily fundamental change in the nature of the Western Alliance. This process of Europeanization however could prove exceedingly dangerous to the European powers themselves, if the political basis of the European–American relationship were weakened or ruptured by such a development.

We aim in this study to isolate the variables, such as the political and economic as well as strategic pressures, which favour the rise of a genuinely European defence effort designed to face and negate the military power of the Soviet Union.

As far as we can, we seek to examine the critical issues at stake in a 'Europeanized' NATO consisting of a strong European dimension. This can only succeed if it is reconciled with the global strategic interests of the United States. Moreover, such a 'Europeanized' and increasingly denuclearized NATO must be seen to be compatible with arms control measures, and the overall stability of the balance of power in Europe, as well as being consistent with the strategic nuclear balance itself.

Clearly, the acid test of a viable all-round defence of Western Europe lies in its contribution to the integration of Western Europe. Yet such integration is paradoxically perhaps also the central weakness of an alliance based upon a more equal relationship between America and Western Europe. There remains a basic antithesis between unreformed Atlanticism and latent Europeanism in NATO, which only a more equal relationship between their respective pillars can diminish.

Introduction

We argue that the 'Europeanization' of NATO, through the emergence of an increasingly separate second centre of deterrence, based on a degree of strategic autonomy, carries both enormous opportunities and incalculable dangers which must be properly assessed. Nevertheless, it is an urgent task whose contemplation should not be indefinitely delayed.

The supreme paradox we find is that until and unless NATO is 'Europeanized' in some manner which captures the overwhelming support of the peoples of Western Europe, then the fatal attractions of neutralism and one-sided disarmament will grow into an irresistible force which no Western European government will be able to resist. And yet such a 'Europeanized' NATO, if not handled properly, could shatter the link with America and drastically diminish the security of Europe as a whole.

The question is: 'Will the historic rise of 'Europeanized' defence in the 1980s bring a lasting peace or not?' We seek to pose and hopefully answer that question in the affirmative.

This book looks at the broad alternatives that face Europe in regard to defence as embodied in the three schools of thought: they are encapsulated in the concepts of Atlanticism, Europeanism or Neutralism. We have argued that the two former options can be reconciled with each other and hence with the security of the states of Western Europe but that the latter – that is neutralism – would place Western Europe at the mercy of the Soviet Union by creating an imbalance within the security structure which the existence of both NATO and the Warsaw Pact have hitherto made impossible.

We have therefore not bothered to examine the non-option of neutralism in great detail, since we do not believe that neutralism is for Britain or for Europe a serious proposition. Be that as it may, this study includes an update of Soviet military thinking in relation to a war in Europe, as well as a reasoned assessment of the impact of technological change on Soviet military planning. Clearly the United States and its NATO allies face a serious challenge in defending Western Europe, given the close physical proximity of the Soviet Union, and its superiority in conventional forces; (a 3 to 1 advantage in tanks, a 2 to 1 advantage in armoured personnel carriers, a 3 to 1 advantage in conventional artillery and at least a 2.4 to 1 advantage in tactical aircraft). These factors, together with the Soviet achievement of strategic parity with the United States, have enhanced the importance of theatre nuclear forces as a component of NATO's overall defence strategy.

This book, then, will seek to place the issue of theatre nuclear forces into the doctrinal perspectives of either the 'Europeanist' or 'Atlanticist' strategies for NATO in the years that lie ahead.

We attempt to think through the problems of European defence in relation to clearly defined expositions of the 'Europeanist' and 'Atlanticist' solutions to security.

This book is, then, about the defence of Europe over the next ten years, which could prove to be a period of great danger. The perception of this danger lies in the changing relationship between the United States and the European members of NATO. The somewhat confused and contradictory response to the Soviet military build-up since the mid-1970s has induced a crisis of confidence within the Alliance which threatens its very existence. There is the distinct prospect of a split between the advocates of a totally separate European defence effort, and the more cautious Atlantists who fear that the United States could quit Europe if such a development were to become a reality. The crisis is therefore a growing one, as the respective protagonists line up to do battle over which option to pursue. However it is already clear that the question of how best to remake the defence of Europe has become the issue of the day.

This book, however, seeks to show that this debate over strategy is not what it appears to be. Why? Because the choice between the Europeanists and Atlanticists is neither new nor as irreconcilable as the contemporary debate implies. The Europeanist solution to European security represents a distinct tradition which reflects the European way of warfare: it is the past reasserting itself over the future.

This study therefore begins with an examination of the historical development of Europeanism, before turning to its more recent evolution and future prospects. We then come to a number of conclusions broadly in favour of both the Europeanization and conventionalization of NATO, in which a more equal relationship between Europe and America becomes possible. Nevertheless, the West will still have to depend upon nuclear deterrence indefinitely. In this study we therefore recognize the importance of the strategic nuclear balance, but it is important to realize that the central military balance with the Soviet Union has changed a great deal since the Cuban Missile Crisis. At that time, the preponderance of US strategic might eventually convinced the Soviets that an incursion into Cuba was not worth the destruction that a US nuclear attack would bring upon the Soviet Union. Hence, the Soviets withdrew their missiles from Cuba vowing, 'Never will we be caught like this again.'[1]

This statement foreshadowed events, for in 1979, President Carter asked Moscow to remove its 'training' brigade from Cuba. President Brezhnev, with a greatly improved war machine at his disposal, refused. While these incidents are not strictly analogous,[2] it is essential to note that the military balance of the 1960s has been redressed by the Soviets, with serious policy implications for the US administration.

Upon examining the facts, one can conclude that while the US was committed to a policy of detente with the Soviet Union (a policy initiated by the Nixon Administration), the USSR had embarked upon the greatest militarization programme in its history:

Weapons Production from 1973 to 1982[3]

US		USSR
350	ICBMs	2,000
3,000	Combat aircraft	6,000
72	Warships	85
27	Attack submarines	61
11,000	Tanks	54,000

While this build-up did not go unnoticed within the US defence establishment, the pervading atmosphere of *détente* coupled with the disgrace and distrust of the military as a result of Vietnam, severely limited the capability of the United States to respond. It was not until the Soviet invasion of Afghanistan in December, 1979, and the failure of US forces in extricating the Iranian hostages, that Western support began to mount for a renewed investment in US defence capabilities. It is for these reasons that in this study we define the current Soviet threat in terms of the post-Carter administration.

Aside from the threat of sheer numbers of Soviet weapons, a threat identified at this time was the vulnerability of the US ICBM force to a disabling first-strike by the Soviet SS-18. In this missile's most recent mode (Mod 3) an accuracy of 1200 feet CEP (Circular Error Probability) has been achieved.[4] This means that half of the time a warhead from the SS-18 would fall within a circle measured 1200 feet from an ICBM silo, thereby destroying the missile within that silo. The improved accuracy of the SS-18 poses an even greater threat to the US ICBM force when one considers that the monster SS-18 can carry up to 40 warheads.

Another Soviet threat was that posed to America's West European allies by the mobile SS-20 Intermediate Range Ballistic Missile. (Up to 441 of these missiles have been deployed in Eastern Europe and the Soviet Union at the time of writing.) The only comparable US system in Europe was (prior to 1984) the ageing Pershing I missile, with a much shorter range than the SS-20. With this new missile the Soviets had the capability to threaten every NATO member in Europe, without resorting to its huge stockpile of strategic nuclear missiles.

It was also discovered that Soviet research and development into anti-satellite weapons had far exceeded US efforts in that field. Intelligence reports indicate that the Soviets have successfully disabled satellites in low orbit under test conditions. This presents a serious threat to the US Space Shuttle programme (which has assumed increasing importance in long range defence plans), as well as the existing early-warning and communication satellite network.

Moreover, Intelligence sources have collected evidence of Soviet violations of the Arms Limitation accords. While the US did not ratify the SALT II treaty, both the US and the USSR agreed to abide by the treaty's terms while re-negotiation took place. However, the Soviets have violated the spirit if not the letter of their agreement by:

(1) practising rapid re-loading of ICBM silos, thus circumventing limits on missile launchers;
(2) developing a second new ICBM even though SALT II limited both sides to only one new system;
(3) encryption of ICBM test flight results; and
(4) developing an in-depth Anti-Ballistic Missile defence while the standing ABM treaty restricts both sides to only a perimeter defence network.

It is therefore, clear, then, that the Soviet strategic threat is both real and pressing. Consequently, policy options have been developed for consideration by President Reagan in an attempt to keep pace with Soviet defence growth.

Based on the Scowcroft Commission's Report on Strategic Nuclear Forces (initiated by the Reagan Administration), the land based leg of the strategic triad (i.e. ICBMs) will continue to be vulnerable to a first-strike but not to the degree that would warrant the development of elaborate basing modes such as the Carter Race-Track proposal.[5]

However, the basic need to update the ageing US ICBM Force cannot be overemphasized. While the Minuteman ICBM has been greatly modified, an entirely new missile is required to exploit recent developments in both guidance and propulsion. It is therefore clear that President Reagan will go ahead with the deployment of the MX missile in existing silos but in limited numbers. It is believed that a force of 100 MX missiles would provide a credible deterrent against the Soviet SS-18. Moreover, a limited deployment of the MX would reduce the missile's first-strike capability by limiting the number of sensitive Soviet targets that could be attacked. It is obvious that the lead time for ICBM development and deployment is too long to permit cancellation of the MX in favour of the Midgetman single warhead ICBM which is still in its earliest conceptual stages. A move to cancel the only ICBM that the United States could field by the turn of the century would certainly be interpreted by the Soviets as a lack of American resolve.

It is also clear that development of the Trident II submarine-launched nuclear missile will continue, and that it will be deployed (though deployed in small numbers), until it has been demonstrated that US land-based ICBMs have become less vulnerable. In any event, deployment of the Trident II aboard invulnerable submarines (barring any unforeseen breakthroughs in Anti-Submarine Warfare technology) will enable the US to accurately target Soviet ICBM silos and thus maintain its strategic deterrent.

Regarding the third leg of the strategic triad, it is desirable that deployment of the B-1B bomber be continued as scheduled, and that funding for the development of 'Stealth' technology should be increased. The standing fleet of B-52s will have completed their third decade of active service and despite new cruise-missile technology, the high integrity of Soviet air defences have made the bomber threat negligible. The B-1B bomber, which incorporates state of the art electronic countermeasures, combined with the deadly accuracy of the cruise missile will restore a measure of credibility to the threat of retaliation from the air. Furthermore, the importance of the manned bomber cannot be overlooked because unlike missiles, they can be recalled after they have been sent aloft. With the addition of in-flight refuelling, bombers can remain on station for hours, as well. (Noting the Vietnam experience, strategic bombers can provide a means of responding to any distant conventional threat as well.)

In the realm of tactical nuclear forces in Europe, it is both necessary and desirable that deployment of Cruise and Pershing II missiles continue, subject to an arms control trade-off with the Soviets. Such deployment will underscore the set-back to the Soviets as well as demonstrate the unity of the NATO alliance. In a strictly strategic sense, deployment of these missiles will nullify the Soviet advantage in

SS-20s. This means that the United States will not have to immediately resort to its ICBM if Europe is threatened. Instead, the Cruise and Pershing II missiles stand as a deterrent and thus restore faith in the American commitment to NATO through the strategy of flexible response. Now that these weapon-systems have been deployed they should not be relinquished without considerable Soviet concessions with the respect to their own deployment of the SS-20s.

As far as air-defence of the continental United States is concerned, it is suggested that ABM research continue but at a more realistic pace. Despite the patent shortcomings inherent in the Reagan 'Star Wars' defence doctrine it offers some hope of marginal gains in laser and particle beam defence technology before the turn of the century. Yet in the short term the US defence budget should be providing more F-15 fighters for air defence in light of the new Soviet Blackjack bomber. While US defence planners should always continue to look ahead, budgetary constraints suggest that the US should make careful use of defence funds.

Finally, it is also clear that funds should be allocated to improve the Command–control–communications (C^3) structure. Rigid control of nuclear forces lessens the risk of accidental war occurring and also helps to control escalation of conflicts. Moreover, if the Soviets know that they cannot decapitate the American command structure, US retaliation being then imminent, the value of deterrence is increased. This knowledge must increase European confidence in the American extended deterrent system upon which their own security continues to rest.

While the Soviet Union will continue to suffer economic setbacks and political instability, the threat of an outright strategic attack upon the United States will remain highly unlikely. However, we can expect Soviet adventurism in various quarters in an effort to divert domestic opposition. The likelihood of a superpower conflict through proxies (e.g. Cuba) is a real possibility – though the probability of this diminishes provided America maintains a high-profile in its defence preparations at all levels. It is for these reasons that the US President should continue the restoration of the Armed Forces initiated by the first Reagan Administration. If a confrontation with the Soviets (in any form) seems likely, history teaches us that the Soviets respect only great power and therefore, they should be denied any decisive strategic advantage. Moreover this consideration is vital in the context of the European-American relationships, because the American readiness to honour its commitments to NATO is rendered suspect in a situation where the Soviet Union is perceived to have an outright strategic lead over the United States.

The sheer magnitude of this defence programme has understandably raised new calls for greater restraint of nuclear weapons and rightly so. It is important to keep in mind, however, that the US nuclear arsenal is being upgraded, not necessarily expanded.

At the present time, the Soviet Union is not interested in effective implementation of arms control measures as opposed to the conduct of endless negotiations about arms control. We attribute this fact to the leadership crisis within the Politburo and the Soviet desire to maintain their lead in first strike weapons (SS-18s and SS-19s), intermediate range nuclear missiles (SS-20), and anti-satellite technology.

Moreover, previous arms accords teach us that future agreements must be negotiated very carefully if we are to avoid future destabilizations such as the current proliferation of warheads aboard ICBMs. As the Scowcroft Commission concluded, a multi-warhead ICBM presents a much greater threat than a single warhead missile, and a country is more likely to adopt a first-strike or fire-on-warning strategy rather than lose up to 10 warheads per missile from the 'threat' of incoming fire. (It should be noted that the United States does not and will not adhere to a first-strike or fire-on-warning doctrine, because the initiation of nuclear war by plan or accident is inherently incompatible with the ideology that the defence establishment seeks to preserve.)

Frankly, it is our belief that an arms control agreement is not likely to be easily achieved, and may in the event of agreement be less than satisfactory, especially when the Soviets have demonstrated non-compliance with earlier agreements. This is not to say that negotiations should not be pursued. In fact, the number of US nuclear systems that will be due for retirement provide the US with concessions that will lower the total number of US weapons, without actually weakening its ability to deter Soviet aggression.

In the meantime, to demonstrate America's sincere wish to make nuclear war less likely, it is worth considering a US initiative to create a joint Soviet-American tracking station (perhaps under UN auspices) in Europe. Creation of such a facility might lessen Soviet fears of the Pershing II as a first-strike weapon, as well as helping to allay the fears of America's European allies. Obviously, a great deal of planning would be necessary to make such a facility feasible.

Furthermore, it is essential that America resist pressure (Soviet and domestic) to limit the US developing anti-satellite capability, at least until such time as she can pose a similar threat to Soviet satellites and

Space Shuttle (currently under development) as they pose to her systems.

Once these policy prescriptions have been reconciled within the current and projected political–economic framework, it is reasonable to assume that the US strategic deterrent will be restored to a credible level. While such a re-armament programme will undoubtedly provoke a negative Soviet reaction, the relative strength of the American economy and the frailty of the Soviet economy places the West overall in a stronger position should a new arms race ensue (although one should bear in mind the considerable capacity of the Soviets to sacrifice domestic development in the name of defence).

Nevertheless, the overriding concern for President Reagan's second Administration must be the restoration of the US strategic threat at least to a level in excess of parity (in terms of capability) with the Soviets. Only then can the United States effectively deal with the Soviets in an attempt to prevent war and thereby regain the confidence of its allies. We believe that only on the basis of a restored American military power on the lines discussed above can we envisage the growth of an increasingly Europeanized and conventionalized NATO, which has the renewed self-confidence to assert a truly European consciousness and separate identity. The twin pillar concept of NATO is an idea whose time has come. It can only be achieved if America attains or successfully regains military superiority over the Soviet Union. The notion of strategic parity with the Soviet Union is a dangerous delusion. This arises from the fact that America remains responsible for the maintenance of global security which means that parity with the Soviet Union is a euphemism for American military inferiority.

The case for a more Europeanized NATO, then, rests on a division of labour within the Western alliance which would enable America to accept its wider global commitments. However the acceptance of parity (in the sense that America and Russia are genuinely equal in military power) must and can only mean that the doctrine of extended deterrence lacks credibility. Given that situation, then NATO Europe would be forced to reject the twin-pillar concept of NATO for a totally separate defence effort based on an attempt to construct a superpower Europe. This book argues against such a desperate remedy and therefore argues for a different and far less radical course. We have divided the book into three interrelated parts dealing with the past, present and future. We start with an attempt to trace the evolution of the twin-pillar concept of European defence as revealed in the tension between 'atlanticism' and 'Europeanism' through the vagaries and contradictions inherent in British defence thinking since the second world war. There we consider the growth of the Western alliance with regard to its response to technological and strategic changes which have threatened its unity and cohesion before finally turning to consider those factors which favour the rise of a real 'European' defence effort.

Part I
The Past

1 Britain and the Third Force Syndrome

In the debate over the kind of international environment in which Britain should seek a suitable role for herself there has for long been a division between adherents to vague concepts of 'Atlantic interdependence', and those who attached prime importance to similarly vague concepts of 'European unity'.

The battle was joined when Britain's first application for membership of the European Economic Community (EEC) was made by Mr Harold Macmillan in 1961 and rejected by President Charles de Gaulle in January 1963, on the occasion of one of his bi-annual press conferences. The French veto of the British application, together with the subsequent French decision taken three years later to withdraw from the North Atlantic Treaty Organisation (NATO), was part and parcel of the same bid to destroy the twin-pillar concept of Atlantic interdependence. France was determined to destroy the presumed Anglo-Saxon domination (symbolized by the European Recovery Programme) of European economic and political institutions which had followed the historic Marshall Aid programme. The French veto came hard on the heels of their rejection of the United States version of the 'flexible response', which had been outlined by the then US Secretary of Defence, Mr Robert McNamara, in the summer of 1962 as a rational means of avoiding an all-out nuclear war. President de Gaulle, with his *force de frappe*, simply favoured the retention of the concept of 'massive retaliation'.

Then came the second British attempt to join the EEC by negotiation – or perhaps on this occasion, by stealth – which, after the initial moves by Mr Harold Wilson in November, 1966, predictably came to nothing within a matter of weeks. The situation left Britain in a dilemma since the economic and political case for entry to the EEC had never been exhaustively studied. This was plainly the case with the abandonment of Britain's role East of Suez, which, in the context of the country's strategic interests was not consciously related to the pursuit of a Eurocentric policy.

The relationship, however, between strategic and economic issues, which are so obviously inter-twined, was underlined when in Washington in August 1965, Senator Jacob Javits, of New York, advocated an Atlantic free trade area. Some six months later this idea was furthered in Britain by Professor Edward English, of Carleton University, Ottawa, in an article which attracted considerable attention in the City of London.[1] The completion of the Kennedy Round, the devaluation of sterling and the international monetary crisis all combined, in a logical progression, to induce an attempt at least to rationalize the economic, political and strategic issues involved.

Crisis within the Western world over strategic issues, as well as a crisis of confidence between it and the Third World, over trade and aid were further symptoms of growing dichotomy and disintegration. There was a widespread feeling that part of the malaise in Western Europe stemmed from Britain's exclusion from the Common Market and that, in the light of the so-called Luxembourg compromise of January 1966, the supra-national tendencies of the Treaty of Rome no longer constituted an impediment to British entry. It was within that context of thought that British defence policy evolved. The Europeanization of the defence posture of Britain came about in stages. But whatever Britain's role within the EEC, NATO still remained at the centre of Britain's strategic interests.

The conflict, however, between the so-called maritime and continental schools of strategy must be seen in its new setting of the nuclear–missile age; that is, between, essentially, the Europeanist and Atlanticist versions of security. The shift, however, towards a greater committment to the defence of Europe had always carried with it the seeds of greater political and military integration with those European powers already committed, consciously or not, to a diminution of national sovereignty. But for Britain the maintenance of national sovereignty had been best asserted beyond Europe.

Between 1950 and 1966 Britain was involved in 85 military operations. They fell into four categories: counter-insurgencies, interventions, deterrent deployments and United Nations (UN) operations. These collective endeavours were the stuff of British influence and power in those areas where Britain's interests were imperilled. The loss of such a role in the world outside Europe was reckoned on the balance sheet of influence in which Britain acted both as a consumer and a producer of security. Britain, by virtue of her past great power status, and a resultant general disposition to play a substantial diplomatic–military role, had a privileged relationship to, and between, the two super-powers. To be counted among the nuclear oligarchs, at least as a potential adversary or close associate, was the basis of Britain's position as a great power.

But what happened when that relationship to the super-powers became degenerate? This occurred in two distinct ways: through the renunciation of a role external to Europe, on grounds of domestic economy; by the process of adjustment to a customs union which, as a concomitant of economic and commercial policies, could ultimately involve British integration in Europe. This aspect of the dilemma was obscured, however, because joining or not joining the Common Market was presented, at the level of the man in the street, either as an economic package deal or a political manoeuvre designed to prevent a Franco-German domination of Western Europe.[2] In neither case was it apparent that membership of the Common Market involved the progressive abandonment or at least diminution of Britain's individual role in world politics. The logic of that situation was not apparent; and indeed by the early 1980s Britain made it clear that her capacity to act alone – as the Falklands campaign demonstrated – remained undiminished. But like the earlier Suez crisis it was a melancholy example of independent action which in no way diminished the importance of NATO to Britain. Of course NATO is essentially an international body and not a potentially supranational one as is the case with the EEC.

Defence policy under Mr Wilson's Labour Government in both its phases – that is, the earlier phase, Atlanticist in origin and purpose (1964–66), and the latter phase (1966–70), Europeanist in origin and purpose – seemed to confirm the reality of the basic dilemma in which the British now found themselves.

Being partly provoked by loss of self-confidence, the dilemma produced uncertainties. Britain still hoped to deploy a military presence in certain trouble spots in which she was involved without the support of allies. The need to do so was imperative: as with the Beira patrol and the Icelandic fishery dispute. Also confrontation with Indonesia during the period 1963–66 over the Federation of Malaysia involved a relatively massive British defence effort in the Malacca Straits and the Borneo territories. These limited but large scale operations were important demonstrations of Britain's independent power and crucial evidence of its effectiveness. Indeed, the clash with Argentina over the Falklands in 1982 in which British naval power was demonstrated was further evidence of the capability. But in any confrontation with the

Soviet Union, the UK's part in it would essentially depend upon having an ally of commensurate rank, namely the USA.

The containment, then, of Soviet power was properly the concern of NATO. But what, in this context, was a worthwhile British contribution? The answer, inevitably, was that it must be a qualitative one. Yet even this qualitative contribution could not overcome the clear fact that Supreme Headquarters Allied Powers Europe (SHAPE), and with it British military deployment, had become an increasingly inward-looking policy based upon a continental strategy with its concept of static linear defence.

The committment then, was to a continental strategy par excellence in which a purely naval strategy, as opposed to a maritime one, was not feasible or meaningful. Since a maritime strategy uses the sea to exploit geography to the advantage of a country and seeks to deny its advantages to the enemy it was clear that in the nuclear–missile age the UK could not rely exclusively on such a strategy. Britain therefore contributed maritime forces to an alliance in which interdependence was the order of the day. What type of naval contribution, then, could Britain make in the changed circumstances of her deployment in the years ahead?

These changed circumstances, in fact, related to the fact that a long-term commitment to a continental strategy involved the sensible diminution of a commitment to a comprehensive maritime strategy.[3] In future, it appeared, strategy must be European-centred and in this situation the unique contribution that Britain alone had made to Western defence outside of Europe was considered a declining asset. Britain's maritime input became however increasingly difficult with SHAPE an inward-looking continental army and air force, CINCAFMED (Commander-in-Chief Allied Forces Mediterranean) abolished and SACLANT (Supreme Allied Commander Atlantic) based firmly in the USA.

Britain until 1971 then, offset continentalist preoccupations, by exploiting her assets. Malta for a time became a valuable contribution to the defence of NATO's southern flank where alliance unity was rent over the Greco-Turkish dispute *vis-à-vis* Cyprus and the Arab–Israeli wars. Italy, a significant naval power in the Mediterranean, inclined towards a pro-Arab view of Middle East issues.[4] On the other hand, Britain's position, as guarantor of the domestic peace in Cyprus, and her ambivalent stance over Arab–Israeli questions, meant that if she wished to contribute to both alliance unity and a diplomatic settlement in the Near East, her naval presence in the Mediterranean needed to be substantially increased. But such an increase was perceived to be a function of Britain's act of withdrawal from the Indo-Pacific theatre and implied no such policy commitment.

The northern flank profited as well from a British naval presence in seas susceptible to the use of amphibious forces, of which Britain had unrivalled experience. This helped Britain to apply pressure – or what Professor Laurence Martin once called 'non-belligerent' pressure – in a variety of crisis situations against the Soviet Union.[5]

The slow Europeanization of British policy was not accompanied by any readiness of the West European powers to assume a major maritime role outside of the European theatre in defence of sea communications. At the same time the development of intra-European trading reduced Britain's global position and diminished the need for a sizeable navy. Geopolitical events pointed however to an opposite tendency as far as Russia was concerned. She became a global power with world-wide trading interests.[6] Within a few years her merchant fleet became the largest in the world. This ominous development came at a time when Britain withdrew from the Levant and from the Persian Gulf.[7]

The British also pulled out of Singapore, which, timed to coincide with the withdrawal from the Persian Gulf, implied that the strategic case for either commitment was of equal validity and importance in the maintenance of British interests. This was never so. There remained though the problem of what the UK should now undertake to do. Mr Edward Heath, when Leader of the Opposition, declared in the autumn of 1968 that a Conservative government would consider maintaining a British presence East of Suez if returned at the next General Election. Subsequent speeches by Mr Heath hardened this tentative undertaking into something near a firm promise. This promise died when the Conservatives came into power in 1970. Mr Heath's Government looked to Europe for Britain's future role, yet even then, Britain still remained in an imperial posture.

Far apart from the politico–strategic importance of South-East Asia, the Malacca Straits remained an important crossroads for merchant shipping. About a dozen British ships a day passed through them. UK investments in the area were also still considerable. It was such business considerations as these that largely accounted for the Conservative Government's interest in the issue.

But Britain intended to conduct a big military reinforcement exercise from the UK to the Malay peninsula in 1970. This was agreed at the five-power defence conference (between Britain, Malaysia, Singapore,

Australia and New Zealand) in June, 1968. This air-lift by Strategic Command and Air Support Command was to be the last of its kind and representing the earnest of British future intentions, taken together with important undertakings on joint defence between Malaysia and Singapore (on the fulfilment of which it depended). It was seen as a step towards Commonwealth co-operation in the area's defence. But the exercise never took place. Commonwealth defence now became a declining asset. Britain's defence policy was now avowedly Eurocentric.

After 1971, Britain, then, no longer accepted that she was necessarily committed to Malaysia and Singapore should they require military assistance. Hence Australia and New Zealand thus became more reluctant to define their relationship to Malaysia and Singapore. Although this four power arrangement still remained a declaratory commitment, there was a disposition, however, to reappraise the whole situation and divisions of opinion developed, for example, in Australia over defence options, with interest being expressed by some in what would have amounted to a Fortress Australia policy. This version of security, a reaction to Britain's decision to stand down East of Suez, was a mirror image of what is thought to be the neo-isolationist sentiments of some American advocates of a similar policy. For policy-planning purposes, Australian assessments were based on the belief that Britain had opted out of the Indo-Pacific theatre and was not to be expected back. Canberra also accepted the possibility that, because of US domestic political pressures, American intentions in respect to East Asia could prove to be no more trustworthy than British intentions have been.[8]

A credible system of international security had to be built. One could hardly emerge, though, if an isolationist wave swept away the resolve of Australia and New Zealand, as well as the resolve of their super-power centre-piece, namely the USA.[9] The possibility of the latter occurring was soon seen to depend to some extent on what Britain did in the determination of her basic choice between an Atlanticist and Europeanist solution to her security. Britain was at a cross-roads. Subsequently British defence policy attempted to relate this basic choice to the strategic imperatives of the UK. The question of the importance of the Anglo-American alliance and the advanced weapons connection between them, together with overseas security, were stressed as the ingredients of past strategic imperatives. Looking ahead, the problems of NATO's future and a new strategic environment were again, related to the national dilemma over how far Britain should become a continental power.[10]

Moreover, the brutal Soviet invasion of Czechoslovakia in the summer of 1968 dramatically confirmed the crucial nature of the choice about to be made.[11] Obviously the Soviet interest in a detente was circumscribed by an extraordinary fear that her East European empire was about to fall to NATO – inspired counter – revolutionaries. The Soviet Union had shown herself to be led by frightened men. This made her a potential menace to international stability as well as a repressive power bent on the total domination of all those unfortunate enough to have a people's democracy thrust upon them. So the basic questions were now clear.

Could Europe still less Britain withstand Russia without the political and military support of America? Could Europe provide that degree of security which NATO offered with its promise of continued American interest in the military defence of the area? A politically united Europe would have to face the basic security problems of the future. It was clear that for the time being there could be no substitute for NATO.

Yet participation in a Third Force had always animated Europeanist enthusiasm in Europe. The impetus behind Third Force aspirations was based on the belief that Europe should play a role independent of the two super-powers and on equal terms. By bonding West European countries together, the Russian threat to dominate Europe, as well as actual American domination, could be countered and genuinely European interests preserved. Russian fetters on the growing independence of East European satellites highlighted this particular concern. America's concern was evident in the 'isolationist' interpretation put on the EEC's Third Force pretensions. America perceived that geographically, Europe remained more vulnerable than the two super-powers; the latter were both better placed to overcome, and recover from, a large-scale nuclear war. Even a limited nuclear war in Europe would be totally ruinous, therefore an all-out nuclear war could serve no political or military purpose. Russia was itself vast. Her internal lines of communication spanned nearly half the land surface of the northern hemisphere. For the most part she was land-locked. The Allies she dominated in Europe were of crucial importance. The USSR relied upon them for her world position and their existence enhanced her security. The loss of Cuba or North Korea would not fundamentally undermine Russia's power position. But the loss of East European satellites would be a crucially different matter. Hence the intense and violent efforts to keep Czechoslovakia within Moscow's orbit and the desperate efforts to keep Poland from collapsing into chaos. The Soviets feared that the collapse of the cordon sanitaire provided by the

East European communist states might precede their own collapse. Hence Soviet expansionism was both an internal and external necessity. This necessity became even more evident as the Soviets perceived that the correlation of forces appeared to be moving in their favour after signing the SALT I in 1972.

The Soviet Union's main strategic purpose was to deter a direct invasion of her own territory. But with the advent of nuclear missiles, the achievement of a high degree of invulnerability against surprise attack became important. Interest therefore developed in ballistic-missile defence, although the deployment of anti-ballistic missiles around Leningrad and Moscow did not mean this course was yet credible.

Russian deterrence of the USA at first, then, depended upon the existence of a credible threat to both European and American cities. For this purpose the USSR maintained a strategic force capable of striking at these targets. Such a capability initially involved a large force of medium-range bombers for striking both cities and military complexes in Europe and a longer range force for the purpose of exposing the great open cities and industrial complexes of the USA to a nuclear attack. This capability was augmented in 1957, and more particularly since 1962, with a strategic missile threat of increasing magnitude, both in relation to Europe and to North America. Russia's desperate quest for strategic parity forced her to continue to challenge the built-in strategic superiority of the USA, in strategic delivery vehicles. Soviet achievement of 'strategic parity' *vis-à-vis* super-power America was achieved by the early seventies. Soviet strategy was only in part based upon a second strike retaliatory system. They developed a capability, if required, to pre-empt the USA. This threat became increasingly real because the presumed assured destruction capability that both super-powers possessed in respect of each other, was eroded by technological change. The Soviets acquired the theoretical capability to remove at least a third of the US's ICBMs on first strike by the late 1970s.

The USA had acquired a vast alliance system covering 42 countries spread over four continents. Her allies accepted the American nuclear umbrella as the most certain means of deterring the Soviet Union. The Atlanticists recognized that the integrity of many uncommitted countries, such as Sweden and India, was tacitly underwritten by the USA.[12] Such a maritime alliance based on extended deterrence conferred on the USA immense responsibility and power. By the same token, though, it threatened constantly to undermine her own security. For this enormous coalition required a system capable of deterring an attack on scattered allies. The Vietnam War illustrated the point because the terms of the settlement of that war put in doubt both the American readiness and ability to run risks to defend her more vulnerable allies. Thus the credibility of the US commitment to sustain global security was greatly undermined. America's doctrine of extended deterrence was found to be deficient because of the build-up of Soviet power in Europe. The USA felt the need to augment her security system with the strategy of flexible response. This took the form of the deployment of long-range theatre nuclear systems.

By now it was clear that US strategic nuclear power was insufficient to maintain the independence of allies vulnerable to a wide variety of threats. Balanced strategic forces, equipped to deal with any contingency, were accordingly advocated.

A dispersed maritime coalition inevitably maintained greater active manpower resources than a centralized land power. Yet the global commitments of the USA, Britain and to a lesser extent France, greatly diminished the number of men available for the defence of Europe.

Mr McNamara, when he was US Defence Secretary, was thus provoked to say in New York in November, 1963, that it was time to change the assumption of 'a Communist Goliath in conventional strength facing a Western David almost naked of conventional arms, but possessed of a nuclear sling. We should not think of ourselves', he said, 'as forced by limitation of resources to rely upon strategies of desperation and threats of vast mutual destruction'.[13]

But in assessing the prospects of nuclear war and its consequences, the Atlanticists recognized that two super-powers had an advantage in possessing very large land areas for the use of land-based strategic systems. They had attained a high level of applied technology in the field of long-range weapons and vast experience in building them.[14] This had hitherto imposed a permanent handicap on any would-be rivals because the supreme determinants of military capacity – demography, geography, industry, science and technology – lie in absolute favour of the super-powers.[15]

Yet the rising school of Europeanists perceived that in Western Europe, technological resources were available for developing a European deterrent system which could become the possible basis of a Third Force Europe. The ability of British, French, German and Italian industries to meet the technological challenge could not be doubted. Even without American assistance, European technology could design and construct the aircraft, nuclear submarines and land-based missiles and all the necessary military hardware that, in greater measure, the two super-powers now possess. The construction of a credible second strike retaliatory system based, say, upon 500 to 1000 sea and land-based strategic missiles equipped with 10 000 nuclear warheads could no doubt be achieved.[16] Even in present circumstances a combined Anglo-French deterrent system, with four British and five French ballistic submarines and land-based systems are capable of dispatching thermonuclear missiles carrying a combined payload of some magnitude, which could no doubt inflict millions of casualties on the Soviet Union. This capacity (to be augmented by the British Trident system in the 1990s, together with the new echelon of French land-based missiles capable of reaching targets over 13 000 miles distant) appeared to have long-term implications. The basis, then, of a genuine European deterrent already existed. It has long been advocated.

The idea of a marriage between British warhead and guidance experience and French solid-fuel experience has had many advocates. Among them had been Mr Edward Heath, when Leader of the Opposition. But the arrangements for a European nuclear command and control of such a partnership would be formidable. Three components would be required: first, agreement on general strategy; secondly, the necessary means of safe and speedy consultation in times of crisis; and thirdly, undisputed location of executive authority to give the go-ahead for the actual use of nuclear weapons. Then there remains the question of defence against the ballistic-missiles which a West European deterrent system might also require. Western Europe is for example, faced with numerously lethal Soviet IRBMs and MRBMs deployed for the purpose of subduing West European resistance in the event of war. Western Europe's 75 major cities are in relatively close proximity to each other; even if the Soviet Union distinguished between military targets and non-military ones, the casualty rate could hardly fail to be extremely high. Thus Western Europe would require some form of strategic missile defence of the sort envisaged by the United States under the strategic defence initiative (SDI). The ability of Western Europe to protect its missiles immeasurably strengthens its powers to deter. The 'point defence' of its missile silos and submarine bases would not, however, be enough and in time strategic space-defence would have to offer some defence to the cities of Western Europe as well. Such sophisticated capabilities could only be acquired from the Americans if and when they have themselves solved the formidable problems associated with the strategic defence of both area and point targets. But whatever system of deterrence is adopted by the

European powers – whether based on second-strike retaliation, with or without some residual strategic defence – it is clear that the business of control requires a new political framework.

Thus, a Europe wishing to possess an independent nuclear force must also be close to becoming a super-power. Moreover, the Treaty of Rome provides the framework for such a functional federation. The process of economic and political convergence within the Community would eventually necessitate, if all went according to theory, an integrated foreign and defence policy, together with the means of promoting it. Europe could not remain solely a civilian power.

The Atlanticists foresaw that, apart from the alarm that would develop in the Soviet Union, given this slow build-up of strategic nuclear power by the Europeans, the risk of war would be greatly heightened in a situation where the role of pre-emptive strike would in the early years be a difficult one for the Warsaw powers to eschew. In addition to the military risks there were the appalling uncertainties created by Western Europe's self-divisive political tendencies. It was clear, then, to the Atlanticists that the EEC was as yet no more than a pragmatic system for co-ordinating certain economic policies and an even more slender (paper-thin) series of political agreements. This was especially so in the light of the Luxembourg Agreements of 1966. Total European integration in the economic sense was not likely to be achieved in the foreseeable future, doubts were therefore cast on the 'dynamic' spill-over benefits of membership of the Common Market. Neither Mitterrand's France, which was opposed to supra-nationalism, nor Kohl's West Germany, which was opposed to breaking with the USA, could agree on a policy which could make a Third Force Europe remotely possible. Only a unilateral American withdrawal from Europe could facilitate that and the Atlanticists perceived, of course, that Britain had no interest in supra-nationalism. Mrs Thatcher's Government made that plain for all to see as it adhered to a sturdy defence of British national interests.

The idea of a federal Europe was remote and the prospect of a super-power Europe was dim, even though the possibility of a European-owned nuclear force was feasible and perhaps desirable. In short, the dichotomy between the Atlanticist and Europeanist solutions to Europe's security could not be pursued to the point of a complete rupture with the USA. A Europeanist policy in the 1980s based on any premise other than that of 'partnership' or 'interdependence' with America was likely to have dire and unintended results for Western Europe. Europe could not expect to play a role entirely independent of the USA.

Yet though Western Europe, and France in particular, possessed what is apparently an unwanted strategic dependence on the USA, the existence of the North Atlantic Alliance did not displace the need for some national nuclear capacity.

This was President de Gaulle's position: he attempted to restore to France a greater capacity to determine her own destiny and at the same time to ensure that the US nuclear guarantee became more meaningful. He feared that US attempts to transform the independent deterrent of Britain and France into an adjunct of the American deterrent, largely successful in the former instance, could result in strategic policy becoming increasingly an American, as opposed to a European, concern and much to the sub-ordination of specifically European interests.

The Gaullist argument revealed that, whatever interest some French politicians had in federation, the concept of a super-power Europe had never appealed to President de Gaulle nor to his erstwhile successors. His interest was in France and in a European block led by France in close association with West Germany.

The re-emergence of Europe – the apex of civilization – meant, in the French analysis, not a United States of Europe but a united Europe of closely-oriented sovereign states. The concept of a super-power Europe, supported by the federalists, ran counter to the French vision of Europe. There were practical reasons, however, for supposing a super-power Europe to be impossibly remote. To achieve super-power status required a tough transitional period similar to but obviously shorter than the USA's first hundred years. Clearly, economic coordination and political consultation was one thing; the creation of a new nation-state, and a super one at that, was quite another. The basic objection to trying to achieve a super-power in Europe, in order to transform the present balance of power, was to do with considerable military risks involved for the powers concerned during the long interregnum between its conception and realization.

Yet by the beginning of the eighties there arose, as we shall see, a renewed interest in Europeanism. This version of security, however, viewed the attainment of a totally separate European defence effort as a chimera. The Europeanism of the eighties was more realistic: the twin pillar concepts of NATO were about to be rediscovered. In 1980 the Greenwood-Davignon Report gave qualified support to the Klepsch Report which two years earlier had urged greater European-wide 'defence' and military–industrial cooperation. It was clear that collaborative arms acquisition would permit the more effective use of research, development and production capacities of Western Europe. This pointed towards the 'internalization' of the European arms market in which Europe's military-industrial supply potential was now roughly equal to Europe's demands in the defence market as revealed in total defence – related sales by individual countries' could become the basis for a single market for defence equipment. Europe for the first time could become the equal of the United States in its capacity to meet most of its defence needs from its own high technology industries. The United States was now only primus inter pares with its European allies except in its nuclear military capacity. An alliance within an alliance was now possible.

2 The Growth of the Strategic Dichotomy

The strategic dichotomy dividing America and Europe was evident when the consequences of nuclear war became potentially as serious for the USA as they had been for the USSR since World War II. This increased the USA's strategic dependence on Western Europe for deterring the Soviet Union and diminished Western Europe's faith in the reduced credibility of the American nuclear umbrella. The new strategic environment forced a re-alignment of interests within the Western alliance system. States were obliged to choose between the two contending strategies in the circumstances of a delicate balance of terror; that is, between massive retaliation and flexible response. Neither was mutually exclusive, for some degree of massive retaliation is even implicit in the flexible response doctrine.

As the 1968 Reykjavik Conference made clear, NATO's members were determined to maintain the alliance, which had experienced difficulties. In particular, the prospect of a Greco-Turkish war did much to dislocate alliance unity. But the Warsaw Pact invasion of Czechoslovakia did much to restore NATO solidarity, even though Western Europe was not directly threatened. Yet a growing source of disunity was the nature of American equivocation about the alliance's future. The statement of Mr Dean Rusk, as Secretary of State, in December 1967, that the USA would welcome a new form of European defence organization seemed to indicate a certain degree of growing indifference over the existing structure and deployment of NATO forces.[1] Such fears were not justified in view of subsequent Congressional hearings which indicated a marked and continued American interest in the alliance. It was made abundantly plain at the hearings, however, that alliance unity was adversely affected paradoxically by the need expressed to reduce force-level ceilings which would consequently increase dependence upon nuclear weapons. This became even more evident over the next two decades; but at the outset in an attempt to shore up the alliance, NATO's Defence Planning Committee sought to give guidance to military authorities on strategic concepts. Such guidance constituted the second comprehensive review of NATO's strategy since 1956. Yet the economic and political vitality of West European states made a cohesive alliance next to impossible. A number of considerations bearing on this were soon to manifest themselves.

The future strategy of the North Atlantic Alliance still depended on US nuclear capacity or, in its absence, upon Anglo-French nuclear capabilities. Deterrence was increasingly defined as the use of latent military power as a form of political persuasion. A deterrent nexus was also related to intentions as well as to capabilities. The changing nature of the threat posed by the Soviet Union presented complex issues. Alliance policy was not based, however, solely on a political assessment of intentions or on a military assessment of capabilities. That was much too simple.

NATO in fact continued to seek the capacity to deploy, within a given period of time, forces strong and balanced enough to dissuade the Soviet Union from choosing any form of armed conflict. That was not easy either. For the calculus of nuclear conflict, or its avoidance, imposed a new and revolutionary impact on international politics. In short, the dynamics of escalation had to be reckoned with.[2] Moreover, an aggressor could become involved in types of warfare of which neither side had experience. NATO sought therefore to deter by being capable of offering resistance at the level at which the threat was posed.

But as defence planners in NATO began to perceive the calibrations of deterrence were complex. Yet the essence of deterrence continued to be uncertainty. It was this which proved to be of crucial importance. The uncertainty, however, must be absolute and this related to the usability of weapons-systems. The distinction often made between deterrence and defence was thus misleading. For the former depended on the threat to use utterly destructive and unusable weapons; and the latter on the use of usable weapons. But a weapons-system which could not conceivably be used did not, indeed cannot, deter. NATO therefore sustained a policy of deterrence in the hope that it would never be challenged.

Deterrence and defence were considered part and parcel of the same coercive instruments at the disposal of NATO. Since both superpowers habitually tested and evaluated their weapons systems it was assumed by the mid-1960s that they possessed an assured destruction capability *vis-à-vis* each other. The USA it was presumed could take out a quarter of the Russian population and half their industry on any day of the week. The reverse was also palpably true. The situation had produced for the time being a stable balance of power. Massive retaliation had seemingly become a relic of the past. This balance was, however, threatened in the mid-1970s by ballistic-missile systems armed with multiple individually-targeted re-entry vehicles. The balance once again became menacingly unstable under the impact of* technological change.³ Of relevance to the Europeanists within the Western alliance was whether the deterrence of the USSR could be accomplished by anything other than a super-power. NATO without America could not be the same as NATO without France even if (with Britain involved) the latter would be theoretically able to inflict unacceptable damage on the Soviet Union without the commitment of American strategic power. The fact remained, though, that even the French deterrent – or the Chinese and, indeed, the British – was bound to increase the complexity of deterrence and hence its uncertainty.

NATO without America could, with an Anglo-French deterrent force, deter perhaps the Soviet Union against initiating a massive land invasion of Western Europe. But in the 1980s it was increasingly perceived that the threat to European or American interests could lie beyond the central power balance in those parts of the world where the technology of Armageddon neither deters nor defends. The strategic nuclear balance it was recognized, had actually encouraged conflict in areas where the great powers were reluctant to intervene. This became crucial to alliance policy because Soviet intervention increasingly occurred outside Europe where the use of nuclear weapons did not arise. In Europe though the risk of nuclear escalation was devastatingly real, providing a vital element in the alliance's deterrent posture.⁴ Nuclear strategy in NATO, wedded to the flexible response, provided a realistic deterrent; but few understood what nuclear escalation meant. For the use of tactical nuclear weapons in NATO had become a necessity in NATO planning. The resort to first-use – as opposed to first-strike – reflected the asymmetric relationship between NATO and the Warsaw Pact.

Precisely what, though, was a tactical nuclear weapon in this context? A strategic nuclear missile capable of carrying several megatons and aimed at targets outside the 'tactical area' of conflict seemed straightforward enough. A tactical weapon fired a short distance, or a land mine with a small nuclear device attached used in the tactical area, also seemed straightforward. But in fact neither distinction could now be taken for granted. A short-range atomic 'battlefield missile' despatched from Western Europe which hit a target in a populous area would be deemed a strategic weapon. With '7000 Hiroshimas' deployed in West Germany, as Mr McNamara once put it, the conventional distinctions between tactical and strategic nuclear weapons appeared entirely academic. Some 7000 tactical nuclear weapons stored in Europe – under American custody – were readily available for use by allied ground and air forces in seven countries, together of course with the American NATO-committed fleets in the Atlantic and Mediterranean.

Whether the distinction between tactical and strategic nuclear weapons was ever entirely clear or not, the uncertainty created by their existence had contributed to deterrence. It had also contributed to alliance disharmony. To meet growing disquiet the American, British, German, Italian and Turkish defence ministers formed in February 1966, the so-called McNamara Committee. Canada and the Netherlands joined later when the North Atlantic Council established the NATO Nuclear Planning Group.[5] The Europeanization of NATO had begun as the realities of nuclear war now needed to be carefully examined. The traditional idea that starting a nuclear war was a political decision and what followed was simply a matter for military commands was now sensibly abandoned. Political control would be necessary throughout.

A tactical nuclear war in Western Europe it was recognized (particularly by the West Germans) would be generally ruinous. Millions of people would be affected within the first few desperate hours and the area of near or completed devastation could be enormous. The Gaullist view – which had received official support from the Bonn Government- – that any massive attempt by Russia to invade West Germany must be countered by the early use of nuclear weapons, could not be one that offered the people of Western Europe much hope of avoiding a major disaster.[6] Those who were suggesting the early use of nuclear weapons would soon regret it, especially if they were used after the threat to use them had not in fact prevented war. Nothing less than the collapse of the whole strategy of deterrence was involved. Any Soviet belief that NATO's local strategy was incredible and an unlikely means of preventing a forward move – like, say, the annexation of Berlin – would confront the NATO alliance with the choice of accepting a *fait accompli* or initiating a ruinous nuclear war. The first task of NATO's planning group was therefore to consider this whole question of the use of nuclear weapons in Europe where there was a rough balance between NATO and the Warsaw Pact. NATO nuclear policy could only be credible where the Soviets were genuinely uncertain about the stage at which NATO political authorities would authorize the use of nuclear weapons. There remained indeed a disquieting if not a desperate element of bluff about NATO policy in this respect. What, then, of the Soviet threat at the level of conventional warfare? The Russians and their allies had the capacity to conduct limited operations with regard, for instance, to Berlin or in the East Mediterranean. They had achieved a high degree of strategic mobility which the invasion of Czechoslovakia dramatically underlined. The issue over local conventional balance was forced to the fore in the spring of 1968 by General Sir John Hackett in a controversial letter to *The Times*. His argument was compelling. General Hackett, then Commander of NATO's Northern Army Group in West Germany, challenged the supposition, based on the distinction between 'intentions' and 'capability', that though the Russians possessed a formidable military capability, they had forgone expansionist ambitions. He suggested that Britain and some of her allies were over-inclined to let NATO's army diminish in size at a faster rate than the diminution of the threat justified. The general said that 'reduction of Western forces to a very low level might offer the USSR temptations to military adventure which would be hard to resist, or at least that this might open the possibility of political pressure which the West would find difficult to accept'.[7] General Hackett had in mind the US decision to withdraw from Europe another 35 000 men over and above those withdrawn under an earlier agreement. This made the US advocacy of flexible response seem inconsistent and perhaps dishonest. The Australian-born scholar-soldier had raised a highly pertinent question. Even the additional commitment of 20 000 British soldiers (as proposed in May 1968, by Britain) did not offset the US withdrawal of her forces and it was the Warsaw Pact's superiority in Central Europe that was General Hackett's concern.

The Soviet Union had at that time 26 divisions in Central Europe (twenty in East Germany, four in Hungary and two in Poland) which, together with the 200 000 Soviet troops in Czechoslovakia, formed a formidable threat. With a sudden build-up, Warsaw Pact forces could be increased to 70 divisions within a month. But how long would it take to get into position the additional 20 000 British soldiers, which then comprised the new European-oriented Strategic Reserve, and the two US 'rotating brigades' that comprised the American reinforcement capability? How much time would it take to get back the two divisions whose equipment had been stored in West Germany? The airlift of a US division into Bavaria in January 1969, was conducted with a reasonable efficiency, but bad weather affected flight schedules which could have been serious in an actual crisis situation.

Besides the 26 Soviet divisions in Central Europe, 14 of which were armoured, a realistic scenario of war in Central Europe could not be entertained without considering the commitment of some of the Warsaw Pact forces provided by 'Northern tier' members. These made possible a first-wave assault of at least 40 divisions against NATO's 22 divisions (which could perhaps be increased to 24 once the reserve brigades returned to Europe). With 12 NATO divisions in West Germany (some of which were reckoned to be 30% below strength) the total number immediately available for action was probably equivalent to 20 divisions. The deployment of the 2 French divisions remained problematic. Their absence, however, did not basically affect a Russian superiority in divisions of two to one. This committed NATO to the early use of nuclear weapons. Tactically this was inescapable in a situation where the Warsaw Pact have a three to one superiority in tanks which, with a four or five to one superiority in tactical combat aircraft, made any conflict favour the attacking side.

Whether a Soviet attack deploying such power could be held was a debatable question. A superiority of three to one was thought to be necessary in order to overwhelm a defensive deployment. This could be overcome though by concentration of effort increasing the ratio considerably in favour of the attacker. Such an effort could produce a quick tactical victory where, as General Hackett put it, 'the concept of a swift advance to the Rhine, where the Russians would sit like the Israelis on the canal, is at least interesting'.[8] General Hackett's view was a soldier's; he therefore dealt, quite properly, with possibilities arising from the known capabilities of an adversary.

Given the kind of threat posed by the Soviet capability to punch a sizeable hole in the Central front, was there a real prospect that the strategy of the flexible response could prove inadequate when based upon a mere twenty divisions? Crisis diplomacy, which was part of the flexible response concept, depended on the success of NATO in delaying a Russian move long enough for the politicians to threaten a nuclear riposte. Could the Russians be held for more than six days by NATO forces using conventional weapons only? What would be the effect of using tactical nuclear weapons? It would seem that the fewer NATO ground forces available for immediate battle the less time there was before the conflict became nuclear. At the point at which the war went nuclear, the character of the US President would become crucial.

The integrity and courage of the man in the White House was therefore a matter of concern when the military situation in NATO Europe manifestly favoured the numerically stronger side.

In certain circumstances, given the premium in favour of the local use of conventional forces, the Soviet Union might, possessed of some Khrushchev-like boldness, seek to exploit its conventional strength by making a limited move. It was perceived that, following, say, the occupation of Czechoslovakia in 1968 in a desperate effort to reassert Warsaw Pact unity, the USSR might have deliberately created an incident involving the NATO powers. Reduction, then, in Western military strength at the conventional level must never be allowed to fall below the irreducible level. In a speech which attracted wide attention at the time, Mr Healey, then Labour's robust Defence Secretary, made a clear reference, in February 1969 to the local military imbalance in central Europe that posed a danger to European security.

But much depended on the nature of the US commitment to the defence of Western Europe. In the twentieth year of its existence, then, the major Western alliance system stood uncertainly at a crossroads. As events were to prove over the succeeding fifteen years NATO faced unprecedented challenge to its existence. Indeed by the mid-1970s the position of super-power America in relation to the defence of Europe was perceived to be uncertain. It was feared that the US Administration had persuaded itself that a choice existed between a continuing commitment to Western Europe's defence, on the one hand, and a switch to a major maritime role external to Europe, on the other, and deeming the former as less desirable. But the course, to which all West European governments so readily agreed combined alliance growth at the European level with an accommodation with America over the nature of her nuclear guarantee to Europe.

By the mid-1970s, then, three crucial issues had emerged within NATO. These issues encapsulated the perceived need for the European members of NATO to move from a primary dependence on the United States for their own defence to the assumption of their determination to principally defend themselves against a possible Soviet attack. The first issue related to a well-established and hoary question: what relative emphasis should be put on conventional defence as opposed to nuclear deterrence in NATO's future war-planning. The second issue was hardly less complex though no less insoluble: how far should NATO proceed towards a more rational division of effort, especially since adequate conventional forces remained so much more expensive than nuclear forces. The third issue related to the classic question of

America's extended deterrent relationship to Europe: how far could the United States move from its Eurocentric strategy towards a kind of explicit global unilateralism and a more overt maritime strategy.

These issues arose against a changing strategic background which is today much less favourable to the West. Thus the growing friction to which these issues gave rise undermined alliance cohesion. The need for alliance unity was never more pressing and yet never had agreement over such basic issues been more difficult. The search for new solutions to Europe's security, then, was seen to be at two levels: the *global* level and the *alliance* level; that is, the search for security at the world level (as embodied in the 'Atlanticist' concept of extended deterrence with America as the centrepiece of the alliance) and at the regional level, with security (as defined by the 'Europeanists') being principally concerned with a European balance of power. At the first level (the world or global level) the situation was affected by four factors which had all emerged by the end of the 1970s. The first factor was the perceived instability of the overall balance of power: a nuclear balance which had been rendered permanently unstable was inimical to the concept of international security. The basic orientation of the West's security policies was destroyed: this was itself based on the proposition that neither side could defeat the other on first-strike. Now it was increasingly perceived that mutual assured destruction in a nuclear war could not now be relied upon: there could *actually* be a winner or loser in a nuclear war (at least in theory) given advances in technology. The possible defensive utility of outer space was perceived by both superpowers. This in its turn destroyed the basis of the strategic arms limitations talks (SALT I and II); and with it the presumed commitment to a super-power political stalemate based on equally stable strategic nuclear relationship.

The second factor related to the dramatic re-emergence of European insecurity, and thus its growing vulnerability as new weapon-systems were deployed, such as dual-capable missiles and aircraft with extended ranges and augmented payloads. The Soviet deployment of SS-20s (for use against European targets) and the NATO response as embodied in the Cruise–Pershing II deployments were cases in point. The issue appeared to be about the local balance of power in Europe. The Soviets claimed that the SS-20s had restored a balance while NATO argued they had destroyed it. However the 572 new NATO systems were not to be seen as positively contributing to a restored balance because they were too few in number to genuinely offset the 370+ three-headed SS-20s.

The perception of what constituted a balance was variously interpreted in Moscow and Washington with predictably contradictory outcomes. The result was to induce a crisis in NATO as deterrence and reassurance (to use Professor Howard's distinction) diverged.

The third factor came in response to the variables referred to above: this involved specific changes in the strategic doctrines of the superpowers. These changes were not limited to questions of the grand nuclear exchange; they included practical implications for extended theatre operations.

On the American side, the redefinition began in 1974, when Mr James Schlesinger, then US Defence Secretary, elaborated a new counterforce rather than a city-busting strategy as the basis of mutual assured destruction (MAD). This slight but important modification left it unclear to the Europeans as to whether this was consistent, or at variance with the hitherto presumed commitment to mutual societal vulnerability (upon which mutual deterrence rested). In essence the cities-only doctrine was dead: US defence-planners apparently sought a re-orientation in doctrine towards a capacity to conduct a limited but prolonged nuclear war. European opinion became bitterly divided and agitated. President Ford in 1976 brought forward this new thinking under the rubric of national security memorandum 242 (NSC). This laid down the philosophical basis of President Carter's refined Presidential Directive 53 (PD53). This directive was designed to improve US telecommunications in time of crisis, for such an improvement was essential to any kind of extended nuclear war. In short, was America seeking a more credible threat than all-out attack on the Soviet Union given the expanding Soviet capacity to wage nuclear war?

In any event, the way was clear for a further evolution in strategic doctrine: this came with two classified directives from the President, namely, directives numbered 57 and 58. These drew up plans for emergency mobilization and provided for heightened protection for administration officials in the event of nuclear war. These developments further alarmed the European members of NATO. Was America planning a limited nuclear war?

This impression was confirmed with the issuing of Presidential Directive 59 (PD59) that appeared to confirm memorandum 242 which had already established the parameters of possible limited nuclear war scenarios. These included a definite shift towards counterforce strikes on missile silos and military command posts. The need to strike at Soviet military complexes (rather than at cities), was the inevitable outcome of three interrelated factors: the complex and destabilizing advances in technology: acute American domestic pressures: and the inevitable American response to the protracted Soviet arms build-up. Directive 59 *inter alia*, then, called for operational plans for pinpoint attacks on military targets and political leadership groups in the Soviet Union.

The motivation behind American thinking was clear: that of how best to maintain mutual deterrence. For if an extensive war with the Soviet Union was to be avoided, then America must be able to wage a long but limited nuclear war. Clearly, in the light of growing Soviet strategic nuclear capability, the US threat of all-out nuclear retaliation was frankly incredible. This official admission meant that Robert McNamara's mutual assured destruction (MAD) doctrine was now recognized to be grossly inadequate. Of course, the Soviets had never entirely accepted MAD: they had themselves opted for limited nuclear war scenarios; that is, war-fighting and war-winning strategies.

This thinking reflected the undeniable importance that Moscow attached to preventing or responding to a first strike. Their anxieties reflected a real ambivalence in relation to strategic nuclear war: they appeared at the declaratory level to emphasize that a conventional phase followed (rather than preceded) an outright nuclear exchange between the super-powers. Europe, it appeared, was regarded by Soviet defence planners as worth preserving for Soviet military occupation after the successful prosecution of a major global war! NATO rejected this rather curious idea: no such limited war was possible given its own commitment to deliberate and controlled nuclear escalation as embodied in the doctrine of flexible response (introduced by NATO in 1967). Apart, then, from the validity or otherwise of American thinking about nuclear war, the European members of NATO responded with a mixture of alarm, frustration and anger. Yet one thing was clear: should deterrence fail, the Soviets would seek military victory. Were the Americans now about to do the same?

It was this consideration which led to US Congressional hearings on Presidential Directive 59 commencing in the autumn of 1980. These hearings provoked an official dismissal of the view that the United States was considering a limited nuclear war of any kind. It was emphasized – correctly in our view – that PD59 was an attempt to update American strategic thinking within the context of flexible response.

Another not inconsiderable factor affecting European perceptions related to a parallel development: the growing belief that new conventional technologies would make possible a defensive war in Europe.

This would help to avoid the use of nuclear weapons on the grand scale. Again this increased speculation that NATO could re-order its priorities and achieve a higher nuclear threshold. The revolution in precision-guided weapons was the precursor to the evolving technologies of the 1980s. This led to the imaginative concept of the air–land battle as well as the so-called follow-on strategies (discussed in following chapters).

Yet for all this talk of new and additional strategies, the fact remained that NATO was likely to still remain inferior at all levels to the Warsaw Pacts war-making capabilities. The certainty was that the West's presumed technological lead in the new weaponry would not persist. Of course, much of it will never be developed and still less deployed. But evolving technologies do have their part to play in transforming the nature of warfare by holding out the ultimate prospect of a greater European non-nuclear input to NATO. The new technologies were seen as possible solution to NATO's historic weakness: its over-reliance on the early use of nuclear weapons.

For some twenty years successive American administrations had urged their recalcitrant allies to downgrade their nuclear dependency. Now that the Soviet Union possessed escalation dominance in Europe – and perhaps even at the strategic nuclear level as well – this in-built weakness made NATO's strategy on the central front based on the pause and the forward strategy, a totally inappropriate one. Allied governments espoused deterrence because they had no wish to fund conventional forces for the only alternative strategy likely to prove feasible, namely, a large-scale conventional response to Soviet aggression in Europe. Belatedly (and for the reasons already discussed) key NATO governments now had to contend with much popular and elite opinion which perceived the growing risk of nuclear escalation. Moreover, this anxiety (and not all of it entirely rational) also induced a serious disfunction between deterrence and reassurance – the twin objectives of NATO. The chief beneficiaries of this were to be the Soviet Union and the European peace movements.

Yet the American urgings did not bring the conventionalization of NATO but instead raised questions about the viability of the coalition itself. Still worse, American power was on the decline and, as a result, the case for a greater European share of the defence burden through greater burden-sharing by its allies was seen as a device to compensate for that decline. Moreover, since the alliance was created, the more robust West Europeans have developed positive interests in Europe and elsewhere that were perceived to be different from American interests. The Middle East, Southern Africa and the Persian Gulf became cases in point. Could these conflicting interests be reconciled? More specifically, if only the United States could credibly defend the Persian Gulf oil access would Europe do more to offset the inevitable over-stretch that this imposed on the United States, by contributing more to NATO's defence? To the extent imposed by such an exigency given the political constraints that Europe itself faced, would it be possible to assist America's extended deterrence by achieving more effective defence outlays within NATO? Because doubts persisted that NATO had the political will and sense of unity to accomplish such a division of labour this tended to reinforce Washington's latent shift away from its traditional commitment to NATO-Europe.

The facts spoke for themselves. While US policy still enunciated the priority of its NATO commitment and contribution at the declaratory level the greater share of the US's non-nuclear defence expenditure was going into a vast 600-ship carrier-heavy navy. Why? In part, no doubt, this change in strategic emphasis had much to do with the slow disintegration of the Third World and the resultant Soviet opportunism in exploiting its aftermath. For example, no fewer than seven 'Third World' countries have had pro-Soviet regimes installed by force since 1973; South Vietnam, Laos, Angola, Ethiopia, South Yemen, Afghanistan and Kampuchea.

This explained America's growing interest in an expanded maritime strategy. But even if the United States intended no switch in its strategy it was drifting towards a high-profile maritime strategy at NATO's expense. The converse was also true: the European drift from the alliance was also evident (including, incidentally, the as yet unrecognized need for an extended maritime strategy beyond European waters), as Western Europe as a unit found itself an economic power able to cope with the US as an equal. This coincided, as we have seen, with the emergence of differing perspectives on how to conduct East–West relations at a time of growing schism and conflict between the superpowers. It therefore accentuated the strains and tensions within the alliance.

This also exhibited itself in widespread opposition to the logic of certain American-inspired policies. There was widespread scepticism in Europe, for example, about economic measures, such as economic sanctions, that had been implemented to try and influence or coerce the behaviour of hostile powers, including the Soviets. Afghanistan was a case in point, for although a consensus painfully emerged after 1979 that the Soviet incursion of Afghanistan constituted a serious threat to the Western World as well as the Third World, and that the West as a whole needed to constrain Soviet ambition in South West Asia, disagreements had also arisen over the extent, nature, timing and type of the response to that threat. The long-drawn-out Polish crisis also replicated this experience on a minor scale.

Thus a perception existed in Western Europe that US policy and its policy makers from the President down were greatly constrained by domestic politics, which played an over-dominant role in shaping the goals and objectives of American foreign policy. This appeared to be the case with the growing American anxieties about events in central America and in the Caribbean.

There emerged the belief that geopolitical considerations had by the early eighties made the European–American relationship less viable and coherent, and therefore less central to the course of international politics. Such a perception was not yet widely shared at the level of intergovernmental relations within NATO, because as the crisis of confidence deepened, the US and its European allies made efforts to mend fences. The immediate fence mending led to speculation that a division of labour within the alliance as a whole was possible; given an agreed consensus on what constituted the nature of the Soviet 'threat', as well as an agreement about how best to use the diverse capabilities already available to the alliance, together with prospective resources available, to meet the challenges of the future.

Therefore at the declaratory level at least NATO regarded the crisis between the advocates of renewed Atlanticist and Europeanist solutions to the defence of Europe as less than fundamental, and though serious, capable of being resolved given a renewed commitment by principal powers concerned. This official response proved in the event to be inadequate because the analysis upon which it was based was patently superficial: the crisis of confidence was at once more profound and systemic than had proved to be the case over, say, the collapse of the European Defence Community (EDC) in the mid-1950s, or the Suez crisis in 1956 which saw Britain and France defy America and go it alone in a war with Israel which actually provoked recessional collaboration between the superpowers.[9] Even the protracted crisis of confidence induced by the abortive multilateral force (MLF) proposals between 1961–65 cannot be realistically compared with the aftermath of the political decision taken by the NATO council to back (in November 1979) the twin-track decision to deploy 572 Pershing IIs and cruise missiles in face of the Soviet emplacement of its SS-20s. The in-depth consultation over this deployment decision through the frequent contacts over the West's negotiating position at the INF talks in the period during which a trade-off with the Soviets appeared possible was a tribute to alliance solidarity and commitment. And yet at the same time a sense of endemic crisis persisted; but in part this was due to the nature of the central strategic relationship which remained basically unstable.

Clearly, America's perceived military weakness had not been the occasion for alliance unity. The slogan to negotiate from a position of strength was therefore just as valid within as between alliance systems.[10] East–West relations had deteriorated in part because of American weakness. Fundamentally, this meant that Soviet military power was perceived to be equal to (and this perception was not entirely erroneous either), and perhaps more usable than overall American power. Soviet policy therefore became or was regarded as aggressive and inflexible as indeed the temporary abandonment of the INF negotiations testified.

This development was compounded by the growing confusion and uncertainty (to which reference has just been made) in the West over how to deal with the USSR in an era of nuclear parity. This led to two broad schools-of-thought: the European and the American schools of thought. The American analysis ran rather like this: the Soviet Union had entered into a unique period of decline. It was characterized by two contradictory features: the incipient collapse of the Soviet imperium in Eastern Europe on the one side and the arms build-up on the other. These developments revealed an obsessive Soviet fear that the current favourable correlation of forces would be upset. While the objectives of Soviet foreign policy remained fairly constant, Moscow sought to compensate for its growing vulnerability by seeking to assume a global role in which they perceived new opportunities in redefining their relations with China and the Third World. It was clear to the US that President Reagan's visit to China in the spring of 1984 was not an unqualified success insofar as it failed to undo the perceptible shift in Moscow and Peking towards a more stable and perhaps friendlier relationship.

Thus the American analysis foresaw growing opportunities for Moscow to construct a more durable and even more favourable correlation of forces, despite structural weakness in Eastern Europe, and the American arms build-up which should in theory progressively negate Soviet military power. American policy should therefore aim to weaken the Soviet power-structure in Eastern Europe. It should also attempt to reassert American military power *vis-à-vis* the Soviet Union and the Warsaw Pact.

The decision to deploy the new long range theatre nuclear weapon systems was seen as a necessary modernization of NATO's capabilities as well as a striking demonstration of the linkage between NATO – Europe and America. The policy was designed to unite the Western alliance. Clearly, the American deployment decisions in Europe were seen in Washington as a response to West German demands for a NATO response to the SS-20s. Moreover the American negotiating stance at the INF talks received general endorsement by NATO. So did America's rejection of a no first-use strategy for NATO. And yet American policy, taken as a whole constituted only a minimal basis for alliance unity on these and related issues.

The European analysis was not confined to a different perception of Soviet intentions and capabilities. It revealed a different view of global politics and of relations with Third World countries. This was manifest in relation to the Middle East, the Persian Gulf in particular and more dramatically over East–West economic relations. The Europeanist strand of thought articulated the possible beginnings of a new strategy for NATO based on the greater utilization of European military power. But the idea of a limited war in Europe or even a limited nuclear war in general was rejected. Peace like war was considered to be indivisible.

3 The Rise of Europeanism

After three and a half decades of existence under peaceful conditions in Europe, the North Atlantic Treaty Organization (NATO) finds itself the focus of attention of academics, military strategists, statesmen and peace movements from both sides of the Atlantic. Since 1967 when the strategy of flexible response was formally adopted by NATO, the alliance has been more or less stable. However, during this period, as we have argued, new social, political and economic realities have emerged, indicating that now is the time for NATO to seriously consider its strategy and structure and the future direction the Atlantic alliance should take. Currently, four problem areas exist within the alliance that threaten its unity and consequently its effectiveness.

(1) As we have argued, NATO's flexible response strategy, which emphasizes the threat of the use of nuclear weapons in response to Soviet conventional aggression is both precarious and dangerous. Additionally, American academic strategists such as Richard Pipes and Colin Gray who talk about the waging and winning of nuclear war do not make Europeans feel any safer.

(2) The Europeans and Americans hold different views on how to deal with the Soviets in particular and East–West relations in general. Europeans opt for the policy and fruits of detente as seen by their support for 'Ostpolitik' and the building of the Soviet gas pipeline; meanwhile, their American counterparts as evidenced by the Reagan Administration during its first term, took a confrontationary stance towards the Soviets and referred to them as an 'evil empire' in its rhetoric.

(3) The third problem area lies outside of the alliance, that of Third World relations. Again, here deep divisions exist between both sides of the Atlantic.

(4) Fourthly, and perhaps most important, long-standing disputes

over trade plague the alliance, made even more important because of the continuing recession. Underlying all of these alliance problem areas has been the perpetual alliance problem of the need for centralized American control versus the need for independent European control. These recurrent problems do not necessarily indicate the collapse of the alliance, just that a better policy path must be taken.

In terms of policy direction, NATO can follow any one of three paths, although one clearly emerges as being most preferable. The *first* policy direction would entail a continuation of the present NATO structure and strategy with dependence on American nuclear force and the strategy of flexible response. The *second* policy path would be that most favoured by the neutralists, consisting of unilateral steps such as a nuclear freeze, disarmament and declaring a nuclear-free zone. The *third* and most desirable policy direction is that of the conditional Europeanization of NATO, which has been acquiring a broad consensus amongst those most interested in the defence and future security of Western Europe. In essence, the Europeanization of NATO would consist of Europeans taking on a greater responsibility for its security with respect to all aspects of its defence: nuclear and conventional forces in Europe, strategic planning, arms control negotiations and, of course, leadership.

Let us keep in mind, however, that there is no quick, easy solution to the problems which the alliance faces and providing security entails. So, whatever policy path the Atlantic alliance chooses to undertake will have several obstacles along the way. One of those major obstacles is the multiplicity of weapons systems within the alliance. Thus, standardization will have to be a priority of NATO's overall strategy and structure even though it will not prove to be a panacea.

Let us now consider the three policy paths before NATO, beginning with the current policy of flexible response under American dominance. Then the exposition of a neutral Europe coexisting with the superpowers' struggle, but remaining aloof from it will be considered. The third policy proposal, the conditional Europeanization of NATO plus recommendations for increased standardization, will follow. Moreover, the political and economic feasibility of implementing this proposal and the likely reaction of the major actors affected by it will also be considered.

The current NATO structure and strategy depend as we have seen on the American pillar of the alliance. The United States maintains a virtual monopoly over the alliances' nuclear forces, contributes significantly to the ground defence of central Europe and devised the strategy of flexible response. Europe and America, who played the pivotal role in the reconstruction of war-torn Europe with the formation of NATO and the implementation of the Marshall Plan, prospered under this close relationship, however unbalanced it may have been.

However, we reiterate, two crucial factors undermined this preferred relationship:

(1) the Soviet Union's attainment of nuclear parity with the United States; and
(2) Europe's development and partial integration, which has led to its questioning of its unbalanced relationship with the United States.

With respect to the first factor, flexible response was, we repeat, effective as a deterrent while the United States held a substantial advantage in strategic nuclear forces over the Soviet Union, and NATO held a similar advantage in tactical nuclear forces over the Warsaw Pact.

Now, although the Soviet achievement of nuclear parity may still render the waging of a nuclear war unthinkable, the NATO deterrence against Warsaw Pact aggression is dramatically weakened because the threat of nuclear war by the West runs the risk of self-annihilation. As a result, NATO's flexible response strategy based on the threat of nuclear suicide and the maintenance of inadequate conventional forces becomes a much less credible deterrent and has a dangerously low nuclear threshold, the theoretical point at which the political and military leaders decide to go nuclear.

The second factor is intricately related to the first factor which has helped to undermine current NATO policy. In rather crude terms, the rising spectre of Soviet military power and Europe's military dependence on the United States has led to 'Europe's schizophrenia: a fear that the U.S. might not be prepared to risk its own population on a nuclear defence of Europe, coupled with the anxiety that America might drag Europe into an unwanted conflict by clumsy handling of Third World issues or East–West relations.' This deserves more comment as it illuminates some of the divisions within the alliance itself arising from a number of issues, including the so-called 'star wars' controversy.

In essence, Europeans fear not only communist aggression but also the waging of a nuclear war, whose most likely zone would be on their soil. Moreover, many Europeans do not have much confidence in the Reagan Administration's ability to handle sensitive East–West and Third World issues peacefully and effectively. On the other hand, American leaders do not favour any attempt by Europe to play the role of mediator in East-West relations or approve of certain European measures with respect to the Third World and to trade. Additionally, the Western allies have not agreed on the perception of the Soviet threat, an agreement which has to be reached in order for NATO to be effective in providing security against any possible Warsaw Pact aggression. Thus, disunity, which has been a recurrent problem of the alliance, weakens the alliance to the benefit of the Soviets.

Firstly, with respect to the handling of Third World issues, the ramifications of the handling of these issues have repeatedly affected NATO adversely. For example, the United States' invasion of Grenada, a former British colony that still recognizes the British monarch as its symbolic head of state, without prior consultation with the British government angered many Europeans and even led them to question America's adherence to the 1962 Athens' NATO guidelines concerning European Theatre of Nuclear Forces (TNF): 'The ultimate decision for use resides with the nuclear power (the United States or Britain) which is committed to consult with its allies about nuclear employment times and circumstances.'[1] On the other hand, Britain's involvement in the Falklands/Malvinas war compromised the United States' position with its Latin American neighbours. Also the American mining of Nicaraguan ports with the subsequent French offer to remove the mines exemplifies the growing dissension in the alliance over Third World issues.

Secondly, differences over the handling of East–West matters exist on both sides of the Atlantic. In this area many of the differences arise because America, as a superpower, is involved in a global struggle against the Soviet Union, while Europe is not. With this fact in mind, previous disagreements over Europe's decision to participate in the 1980 Olympics, to provide the East with technology, and to help construct the Siberian gas pipeline to America's chagrin are likely to re-emerge in the future. Tensions will continue to increase as long as Europe chooses to practise *détente* while America continues to take a confrontationary stance with the Soviet Union.

The third impediment to Western solidarity involves trade, which is made even more urgent because of the recession. In addition to the aformentioned disputes over East–West trade, American frustration can be observed over the protectionist policies of the European

Economic Community. All in all, these causes of dissension within the alliance are not fatal to NATO but do indicate the urgency for the alliance to address these short-term and long-term problems. Yet, the insufficiency of the present NATO structure and strategy cause a lack of unity, a most important, unquantifiable factor in any alliance.

The lack of unity and the inadequacy of the flexible response strategy give fuel to European calls for neutralism. Over the past several years peace movements have emerged as a vocal actor in the increasingly polarized European defence debate. Leaders of these movements have organized marches of hundreds of thousands of people to protest against the reliance on nuclear weapons, almost all of which are American under American control, in Europe. Their concerns are legitimate and to dismiss them as part of an overall, communist plot, as the first Reagan Administration has attempted to do in past official statements, is foolish. However, neutralists' and pacifists' advocacy of a nuclear-free Europe, a unilateral freeze or disarmament would be desirable in a future world where universal peace was reality and no longer a dream; unfortunately, such a world is not likely in the foreseeable future. Clearly, risk, danger and conflict remain endemic to international politics.

Strategic, psychological, and political considerations render the policy of a neutral, nuclear-free Europe as being irresponsibly dangerous. Firstly, a neutral Europe would still be vulnerable to Soviet domination and possible blackmail, as hundreds of SS-20s would still be targeted in Europe. Secondly, there are psychological reasons that call for Europe to be able to defend itself. Politically, Europe does not want to slide into being a second-rate international actor. And in this vein, the cries of opposition parties against the deployment of nuclear weapons arise as much from the fact that they are out of power, as from their disdain for nuclear weapons. Let us keep in mind that when these opposition parties were in power they did not renounce nor denounce nuclear weapons to guarantee the territorial integrity and value-system of Western Europe. For the present, a neutral, nuclear-free Europe is an undesirable and unfeasible policy aim. To that extent it is deeply disturbing that both the West German SPD and the British Labour Party have committed themselves to an absolutist anti nuclear stance (see Chapter 10).

Professor Michael Howard has sagely provided us with a new and extremely relevant concept to complement deterrence, that of reassurance, the restoration of public confidence in the state's or alliance's deterrence policy. Howard notes the negative and positive role of deterrence. For the potential aggressor, the goal is for the costs of aggression to outweigh the benefits of launching an attack. For the populace, the goal is to reassure that the benefits of maintaining the security arrangement outweigh the social and economic costs of providing defence.[2] The major determinant of the adequacy of the alliance's deterrence policy is the structure and strategy of the alliance. Therefore, neither the current NATO policy nor a neutralist European policy are desirable, because with respect to the former, it has an extremely low nuclear threshold by virtue of the fact that it relies on inadequate conventional forces and a rather incredible threat to use nuclear weapons, and with respect to the latter, it has no deterrence posture whatsoever. Furthermore, neither policy reassures the populace of Western Europe; the current NATO policy has not assuaged most Europeans' fears of a possible war being waged in Europe, while a neutralist Europe would assuage the fears of only a potential aggressor considering invading Europe.

Another important factor in determining the adequacy of a defence arrangement involves who is providing the defence. With respect to NATO, the United States has been the major actor in providing Western European defence.[3] Although this has been adequate for the past three decades, social changes and changes in the military balance between the super-powers have led the new generations of Europeans to question the dependent relationship on the United States. The rising tide of European anti-Americanism is mainly a reaction to the unbalanced alliance relationship, which leaves Europe dependent on an external power for its defence. However, an increased role for the European members of the alliance would help to restore the balance, which by the way never existed, or had the likelihood of existing until the present time, and simultaneously would help to strengthen the alliance. First of all, Europe is confident in its ability to deal effectively with the Soviets. For example, West Germany and France, the two countries most threatened by Soviet military power, are the most confident in dealing with the Soviet Union through political and economic intercourse. Furthermore, the Europeanization of NATO or in other words, the emergence of an alliance would achieve one of NATO's long-standing goals and would reverse some of the adverse trends which pose a potential threat to the alliance. It is salutary to recall that in 1952, the alliance members adopted the 'Lisbon Force Goals', which called for greater European responsibility for its defence, but Europe never attempted to achieve these goals because it chose to concentrate on its economy in lieu of paying for the heavy social and economic costs of conventional forces. Thus, Europe opted to obtain defence on the cheap by relying on American nuclear forces. The 1952 goals of NATO can now be achieved in an attenuated form by implementing the Europeanization process. With regard to the second goal, pacifism and neutralism are much weaker in France than in Germany, chiefly because France has its *force de frappe*, while Germany maintains no nuclear forces of its own.

In short, the Europeanization of NATO would accomplish the two objectives of providing an effective deterrent by deterring a potential aggressor with the strengthening of European conventional forces and by reassuring the European populations with the European control and responsibility of its own defence. Let us now consider in greater detail the policy proposal for the Europeanization of NATO. We make no secret of our general support for this option but like Professor Hedley Bull we do not wish to disguise the complexities involved.

To begin with the major reason generally given for the desire for a greater European role in NATO is misleading; the burden-sharing argument. For example, the United States, which accounts for approximately 55% of the total allies' national income, contributes $138 billion out of the $263.2 billion spent per year on the defence of central Europe, or 52% of the NATO total.[4] Also, the burden-sharing argument becomes less convincing when one realizes the narrowness of using just quantifiable factors such as:

(1) per capita Gross Domestic Product;
(2) defence expenditure per capita; and
(3) the ratio of defence expenditure to Gross Domestic Product.[5]

Most analyses based on using these stricly quantifiable factors to measure burden-sharing within NATO never take into account the following factors, whose costs are borne almost entirely by the European members of the alliance, such as: real estate, the lower personnel costs due to conscription (e.g. the average German soldier earns only $100 per month), the rising dollar exchange rate and the likelihood that Europe could be the potential battlefield and hence risks its civil infrastructure and population, which are tremendous and unquantifiable costs. And lastly, the United States tends to spend more than its European counterparts because it is involved in an unavoidable global confrontation with the Soviet Union. Clearly global security cannot be purchased on the cheap.

However, there exists a myriad of complex and valid reasons for the

Europeanization of NATO. The new social, political and economic realities which NATO face, such as those involving trade, East–West and North–South relations, the growing ineffectiveness of the flexible response strategy, and questioning of the American dominance of the unbalanced alliance call for Europe taking on a greater role in NATO. This need is made even more urgent when one acknowledges the increasing American calls for neo-isolationism and the European calls for pacifism and neutralism, coming mostly from the peace movement and certain opposition parties. In the United States, where there is always the undercurrent of isolationism due to its political history and geographic location, the calls for isolationism are coming from rather lofty circles. For example, Senator Theodore Stevens of Alaska, the chairman of the Senate Subcommittee on Defence Appropriations, advocates retaining a mandate for US troop reductions in Europe.[6] In actuality, troop additions, not reductions, by Europeans, not Americans, are called for.

The first priority for the alliance concerns the strengthening of conventional forces by increasing the European involvement in this vital area of defence. A broad consensus with respect to this subject has been formed already. McGeorge Bundy in his controversial article, which called for NATO's adoption of a policy of no first-use of nuclear weapons, also advocated the improvement of the alliance's conventional foces: indeed 'this cause is argued by such men as Christoph Bertram, Field Marshal Lord Carver, Admiral Noel Gaylor, Professor Michael Howard, Henry Kissinger, Francois de Rose, Theo Summer, and General Maxwell Taylor'.[7] Improvement in NATO conventional forces would strengthen deterrence which relies on the following three factors:

(1) determination to resist blackmail;
(2) reaction at every level of aggression; and
(3) the flexibility to choose between nuclear and conventional forces.

Furthermore, the strengthening of conventional forces would lower the alliance's dependence on nuclear weapons and thus raise the nuclear threshold.

In more specific terms let us now see what the strengthening of NATO's conventional forces would entail. Currently, the Warsaw Pact deploys 173 divisions to NATO's 84 divisions and is generally assumed to be conventionally superior to NATO.[8] To correct this gross unbalance would require a doubling of NATO's strength in this area roughly, along with a similar increase in areas where the forces of the Warsaw Pact have a convincing superiority over those of NATO such as:

(1) anti-tank guided weapon launchers;
(2) artillery/mortars; and
(3) armoured personnel carriers and infantry fighting vehicles.[9]

To accomplish this improvement in NATO's conventional strength the Western allies would have to increase their targeted contribution of 3% real growth in military expenditure to approximately 4–5% per annum over a period of five years. The strengthening of the alliance can occur with only a $1\frac{1}{2}$% increase in NATO's targeted contribution because of standardization, which we will consider later, and the fact that currently none of the allies has attempted to achieve the 3% target and have settled for only a 2% rate of growth per annum on average.

A re-allocation of European resources into NATO expenditures would impose costs on European standards of living, but Europe must confront its problems directly. With regard to the Western European states, stronger European conventional forces would imply moderate social and economic costs. With regard to the functioning of the military apparatus, it most likely would imply continued conscription and longer service.

Britain abolished national service in the early 1960s. However, these costs are bearable and must be borne in order for Europe to move away from its dependence on American nuclear weapons and to provide Europe with deterrence and reassurance. For example, the total gross national product of all of the Western European NATO members equals that of the United States. Furthermore, Europe, which has one-and-a-half times the gross national product of the Soviet Union and twice the population, is superior to the Soviet Union with respect to its economy, population size, technology and military potential. Thus, European strengthening of NATO's conventional forces is well within the realm of possibility and feasibility.

The NATO committed ground forces of the United States, which consists of approximately 350 000 troops, play an important, supporting role in the alliance. For the foreseeable future US ground forces, along with its nuclear forces, will still be required. As the European conventional force deployment increases, the US may choose to decrease some of its conventional forces stationed in Europe; however, present air force, naval and nuclear deployments should be maintained.

These forces link the defence of America and Europe, and to withdraw them would run the risk of European fragmentation and consequent Soviet gain. The United States would respond favourably to the strengthening of European conventional forces and to maintaining current US deployment of its forces in Europe for the purposes of linkage, which is recently reaffirmed by deploying its intermediate-range weapons in Europe instead of at sea.

Structural reform within NATO would also be required to complement the strengthening of conventional forces. First, we agree with Dr Kissinger that the Supreme Allied Commander of Europe (SACEUR), which previously has always been an American, could well be a European in the future to signify the greater responsibility Europeans will take in NATO.[10] Meanwhile, the Supreme Allied Commander of the Atlantic, who commands the ship and submarine fleets, as well as the Secretary-General, who runs the political apparatus of the alliance and who heretofore has always been a European, should be both held by the person best suited for the position. With regard to the position of Secretary-General, Henry Kissinger suggests giving this position to an American, who most likely will be the person best suited for the post because of the need for political and strategic coordination between the United States and Europe. These administrative changes in these important positions would facilitate the Europeanization process of the alliance.

Another structural change within NATO needs to occur in the area of the control of the alliance's nuclear forces.[11] Presently, the ultimate American control of nuclear weapons based in Europe causes European anxiety, which is manifested by the opposition parties' and peace movement's protests over the deployment of the Pershing II and Cruise missiles. To alleviate this cause of anxiety, which adversely affects the alliance, Professor Hedley Bull's policy proposal for the establishment of a European nuclear planning committee within NATO should be implemented.[12] Moreover, this committee will oversee the European control of European-based nuclear weapons. In the area of arms control, the European nuclear planning committee would take over or at least oversee the negotiations on INF, intermediate-range nuclear missiles, in an attempt to mitigate tensions with the Warsaw Pact and to reduce the social and economic costs of nuclear weapons' deployment. However, the realities of arms-control negotiations, given their time-consuming nature and the virtual impossibility of substantial disarmament do not engender great expectations in this area. Remember the SALT I talks took six years until a final accord was reached and

SALT II, although it is being observed, was never ratified. Yet, however difficult the fruits of arms control may be to reach, they remain goals worthy for attainment in the long-term (perhaps only fully realizable in the twenty-first century).

Also, within this area of the alliance's nuclear forces in Europe (TNF), the major European powers need to become more fully integrated into the alliance's nuclear forces. Thus, France, Britain and even Germany, which at present does not possess nuclear weapons of its own, should establish together their own *force de frappe*, as France did in response to the inadequacy of the American nuclear forces to provide France with both deterrence and reassurance. Currently there exist three powerful impediments to the formation of this European nuclear pillar in NATO:

(1) the anti-nuclear mood in Europe;
(2) the lack of cooperation so far between Britain and France in the research and development and production of nuclear technology; and
(3) the possible adverse world-wide reaction to the thought of having a nuclear-armed Germany.

However, these potential barriers to the creation of a European nuclear force are not as formidable as they may appear to be at first sight.

A sizeable but indeterminate portion of the anti-nuclear sentiment in Europe emanates from the American control of these weapons. Moreover, joint French and British cooperation (with the inclusion of Germany if the alliance members see the merit of strengthening the German deterrent capabilities) would have the political incentive of taking on greater responsibility for Europe's defence and the economic incentives of standardization, specialization, bigger economies of scale and lower costs. Thirdly, present-day Germany is vastly different from pre-1914 and pre-1940 Germany; today's Germany is fully integrated into the European community, thriving and a strongly committed member of the Western alliance. Fears of a resurgence of a bellicose Germany are completely unrealistic, for Germany would lose if any war were waged in Europe, and it is her best interest to see that deterrence is as effective as possible. Therefore, the elimination of the discriminatory arms control measure, in effect against Germany since 1954, would be a positive and long-overdue step for NATO to take. The creation of a German nuclear deterrent would augment the existing British and French independent nuclear forces, of which

France alone has the capacity to destroy 40% of Soviet industrial capacity and threaten 70 million Soviet citizens.[13] Meanwhile, British forces are even more lethal than the French ones and together they total 162 missiles, which will increase with the modernization of French nuclear forces and the addition of the Trident systems to the British force.[14]

In short, the building of an Anglo-French and eventual German deterrence system would create a stronger European pillar of NATO and help to offset the unbalanced relationship, which Europe presently shares with the United States.[15] Clearly, considerations about the merits of standardization, which will play an important role in the Europeanization of NATO, must be given renewed attention by NATO's defence planners.

As Professor Pierre has eloquently argued, 'One of NATO's major weaknesses has been its multiplicity of weapons systems',[16] which has resulted in a loss of military effectiveness and a tremendous and appalling waste of money.[17] The findings of a study by Hans-Peter Schwarz illustrates this problem area for NATO, noting that the alliance has:

- 23 different kinds of combat aircraft
- 7 different groups of combat vehicles
- 22 different anti-tank systems
- 36 different models of radar guidance and targeting systems
- 8 different kinds of ground-to-air missiles
- 6 different classes of torpedo and
- 20 different calibres on weapons up to 30 mm[18]

The stupendous waste resulting from such multiplicity of weapons and weapons systems, however, can be substantially reduced through increased standardization. For example, the Callaghan report found that increased standardization could lead to 10 billion dollars per year in savings, and augment military effectiveness by 40% without any increase in military expenditure.[19] Although we believe that this figure is an inflated one, clearly tremendous savings are possible. One major cause of this lack of standardization has been the reaction by European firms in the defence-related industries and their governments to the continuing American dominance of the NATO market. The Europeanization of NATO, which would result in all likelihood in increased opportunities for the European defence industry, would help to alleviate this situation.

Fitting in with the overall scheme of Europeanization, standardization would imply greater collaboration and cooperation for the European members of the alliance. Alexander H. Cornell's study of six jointly-developed weapons systems:

(1) Breguet Atlantique's Long-Range Maritime Patrol aircraft;
(2) the Hawk ground-to-air missile system;
(3) the F-104 G Starfighter aircraft;
(4) AWACS
(5) the Roland ground-to-air missile; and
(6) the F-16 All-Purpose combat aircraft

found that systems that were high pay-off, market-sharing and longer-planned achieved standardization and increased combat readiness.[20] Keeping these findings in mind, NATO should adopt the following guidelines to encourage standardization and arms cooperation:

(a) apply the principles of specialization and comparative advantage to collaborative ventures (e.g. co-production, research and development, manufacturing and work-sharing);
(b) entice firms to select partners on a voluntary basis using commercial and competitive criteria; and
(c) make European governments more efficient in the military market place by having them circulate information to foreign producers about contract opportunities and by removing entry barriers to markets (i.e. protectionist tariffs and preferential purchasing policies).

The last guideline will be harder to implement than the previous two because of the recession, which makes trade liberalization policies virtually impossible to implement.[21] However, the above policies if implemented will encourage collaboration and standardization and increase military efficiency and savings, results which individual governments, Europe and the alliance could surely use. Britain, France and Germany have already felt the benefits of standardization with their joint-production of the Tornado aircraft, which saved them an estimated 2–3 billion dollars.[22]

Of the three policy paths that the Atlantic alliance can take, the path that leads to the Europeanization is by far the most preferable. The present NATO policy of flexible response and structure, which is dominated by the United States, has been confronted with new social, strategic, economic and political realities which render it undesirable as the continued NATO policy, Firstly, as we have constantly emphasized, the flexible response strategy which relies on the threat to use nuclear weapons at an early stage by maintaining inadequate conventional forces, does not provide Western Europe with adequate deterrence or necessary reassurance. Secondly, recurrent and deepening problems between Europe and America with respect to trade. Third World issues, the East–West relationship and the deployment of intermediate-range weapons bring the American dominance of the alliance into question. The third policy path leading Europe into neutralism through the advocacy of a nuclear-free Europe, and world for that matter, of a unilateral freeze or of a unilateral disarmament remains a goal whose achievement does not lie in this century, but could only lead in present circumstances down a blind alley. A more or less neutral Europe would still be targeted by SS-20s and subject to Soviet domination. In short, Europeanization, which does provide Europe with an impressive deterrence posture by strengthening conventional forces in central Europe, and with reassurance by giving Europeans a credible deterrent under European control, will produce a more effective NATO and a stronger Atlantic alliance. The case for the Europeanization of NATO appears to be incontrovertible given the prospective international environment which must worsen before it gets better.

To sum-up then, the Europeanization of NATO must consist of strategic and structural changes in the direction of giving Western Europe greater responsibility for maintaining its own defence. *Firstly*, the conventional forces of NATO are widely and quite properly believed to be inferior to the forces of the Warsaw Pact and thus NATO must strengthen these forces by greatly increasing the European forces in this regard. This strengthening of European conventional forces must imply an increase to $4\frac{1}{2}$–5% real growth in defence expenditure over a five-year period from the present NATO target of 3% real growth. The United States would have to maintain its present air force, naval and nuclear force deployments, although the allies may decide to a redeployment of some of America's ground forces in central Europe. There is much evidence that American army units are wrongly deployed on the central front. *Secondly*, SACEUR should, as we said earlier, become in the future a possibly rotating European position. Meanwhile, the Supreme Allied Commander of the Atlantic and the Secretary-General of NATO should go to the person best suited for the positions, although the political position of Secretary-General should most likely go on a rotational basis to an American, in order to facilitate the strategic and political coordination between both sides of the Atlantic alliance. *Thirdly*, we repeat, a European nuclear committee should be established within NATO to oversee and co-ordinate the European control of nuclear-based weapons on the continent, including the participation in INF negotiations, and to co-ordinate the erection of a European nuclear force as another pillar in NATO. *Fourthly*, we repeat, much of the discriminatory arms control, if not all, should be lifted against West Germany in order to further strengthen the alliance. And *lastly*, the long-standing NATO problem of standardization must, we repeat, be addressed by having NATO adopt definite guidelines to foster greater arms collaboration.

In sum, in our judgement, these policy recommendations will resolve some of the seemingly long-standing alliance problems. NATO's Europeanization will provide deterrence and reassurance, in addition to increasing standardization, which will substantially augment savings and military effectiveness.

Overall, the Europeanization of NATO will receive widespread approval from the various major actors likely to be affected by the implementation of these policy recommendations. The Western European nations will have to invest more into the alliance in terms of money and personnel but they will respond favourably, if not enthusiastically, to this proposal. However, some voices such as the French, may not welcome the idea of a stronger Germany, but it is at least an issue worthy of serious consideration. The United States will gladly accept Europe's taking on a greater responsibility within the alliance, although it will not respond too favourably to its loss of control of the alliance. The United States will still play a vital role in the alliance and lend the much needed support it provides to the defence of Europe. Outside the alliance, the Soviet Union is likely to respond favourably to a diminished American role in Europe, although it will not respond similarly to the thought of a much stronger Europe on its allies' borders. However, much of the possible tension can be mitigated through diplomatic and economic channels as both Western Europe and the Eastern bloc continue to practise *détente*.

In order for the Europeanization of NATO to be successful, unity is required. Although the alliance is actually a coalition rather than a homogeneous group, unity can be achieved, for the Western European states have the same interest in providing for the future security of their political structures and have achieved greater cooperation within the past few decades than they have ever achieved in history. Moreover, industrial and economic integration in addition to the political and structural reforms recommended in this policy proposal will generate further cooperation and unity.[23] Two forums, in which to implement the alliance's Europeanization to restore the alliance's bi-partisanship, currently exist in the EEC's European Council and NATO's Eurogroup. In these forums, the alliance members can live up to their 4 April 1949 charter, 'to defend a way of life not only by military means but also through cooperation in political, economic, social and cultural fields'.[24] Finally, the Europeanization of NATO would be a positive step not only towards preventing a nuclear war but towards preventing any war.

Part II
The Present

4 The Fragmentation of Alliance: the Need for a New Military Strategy?

The debate within the Alliance as to whether defence should be primarily nuclear or conventional is not new.[1] In the 1960s Henry Kissinger summarized the issues of the debate by pointing to the advantages and disadvantages each alternative entailed.[2] His conclusions are still greatly relevant today.

The advantages of a nuclear strategy are that:

(1) it would require smaller mobile units because the dispersal of troops would be necessary to avoid providing an easy target for the highly destructive nuclear weapons;
(2) nuclear war would complicate the aggressor's calculations and therefore limit the likelihood of victory;
(3) the threat of nuclear war would be an easy way to limit and weaken Soviet control over Eastern satellites;
(4) nuclear weapons are the West's most advanced technology; and
(5) nuclear deterrence is the cheapest form of defence available

The advantages of a conventional strategy are that:

(1) it would provide the best chance to limit any conflict that might break out;
(2) it would use the West's industrial potential to its best advantage because of the production effort that the relatively less destructive weapons require;
(3) conventional defence may provide the best means to prevent occupation of threatened countries; and
(4) if nuclear weapons had to be used as a last resort, the onus of initiating such a conflict would lie with the Soviet Union.[3]

These considerations, though useful and educative, provided the wrong approach to the problem. The strategy that NATO actually acquired was not either totally conventional or totally nuclear. It combined both. It is obvious that either strategy pursued independently would be suicidal: the first, because opposing the nuclear arsenal of the Soviets with conventional weapons would be like fighting guns with swords; the second because the appalling choices available would involve the decimation of the human species or surrender. Thus NATO tried consistently but not entirely successfully to move away from a stressed dependence on nuclear weapons, to a greater reliance on conventional weapons for its defence. Conventional weapons were however not seen as a substitute for nuclear weapons. Rather, they were considered complements. The strategy that NATO formally espoused, flexible response, has evidently failed to achieve this worthy objective. It is for this reason that it has failed to provide an adequate deterrent. Thus, if the conventional rungs of the escalation ladder could be strengthened, the policy of flexible response could become more operative.

It is clear that a more operative strategy would present a more credible deterrent thus reassuring the peace movements that there would be peace. NATO must therefore continue to emphasize the argument that deterrence is, at the moment, the most likely method to maintain peace. At least, it could be argued, it has helped to maintain the peace for the past thirty years. As long as the deterrent is unreliable because it is suicidal, it is not a position likely to encounter great popularity. But, a conventional war can be kept within limits only if the prospect of nuclear war seems more unattractive. Therefore by strengthening the conventional leg of the defence triad–strategic, tactical, and conventional forces–and maintaining the other two at the same time, NATO may hope to keep a conflict limited to the lower levels of escalation. This will be possible only if NATO is capable of matching or at least effectively responding to a Soviet conventional aggression on conventional terms.

Conventional defence build-ups are disliked because of their high cost in terms of human and physical resources. As was already pointed out, this fact was one of the main reasons why the Europeans preferred a dependence on American nuclear forces to strengthening their own conventional forces. Whether or not the Europeans have the economic capacity to afford a build-up and modernization of their forces is a matter of continuous and serious debate. Those on the more optimistic side can see no reason why the most rich and prosperous area in the

The Present

world should be incapable of absorbing the required 3 or 4% increase in defence budgets. The sceptics point to all sorts of limitations which they believe would seriously challenge the ability of European countries to come up with the required funds. Among the main points they raise are the following:

(1) defence budgets have been rising at a higher rate than the level of aggregate national incomes has been increasing;
(2) the volatile technology with which we are forced to live requires a constant flow of capital expenditures on research and development just to renovate the existing systems. The rise in defence budgets has therefore gone into higher expenditure absorbing all the funds that would otherwise be available for innovation and expansion;
(3) the sources of financing available to governments are limited not only in number, but more importantly, by the absorptive capacity of the economy. Financing defence budget increases through the government apparatus at a time when the economy is already overheated could reinforce stagflation through constantly increasing prices and interest rates;
(4) the welfare states of the European nations already have quite overburdened government sectors. They have to maintain the social programmes on which they depend for political support. Defence is but another sector of government expenditure, so increases in the defence budget would inevitably lead to unpleasant trade-off decisions; and
(5) the number of political difficulties that would have to be surmounted in such conditions would be very high. These barriers would not only be domestic but international as well.

There are also those, and we conditionally count ourselves among their number, who claim that an increase in conventional capabilities could be achieved without necessarily indulging in huge budgetary increases. The increase is possible, they argue, through a more rational allocation of already existing resources. In short, they argue for the 'rationalization' of NATO. In an article by Robert W. Kower,[4] the main posture of this line of thought is presented in ten suggestions to achieve rationalization. Kower argues that the more active manpower that the Warsaw Pact has been able to deploy with a roughly equivalent investment of resources as NATO, is an indication of its ability to utilize resources more efficiently. These differences in efficiency are explained in part by higher manpower costs in the West. But, even more important in justifying the differences is the fact that NATO is an alliance of sixteen sovereign states. Thus, 'parochial national considerations tend to override collective defence needs in determining national budget allocations'.[5] This results in wasteful overlaps and duplication. According to Kower, at least eleven billion US dollars are being wasted in NATO by the allies' inability to reap the benefits of common R & D, joint procurement, and common support.[6] At the same time, the situation is aggravated by the fact that there is no real NATO defence posture, but only a collection of 'heterogeneous national postures which differ far more in their equipment, organization, and procedures, than do their WTO counterparts'.[7] The solutions that Kower proposes are, in general form, the following:

(1) a change in NATO thinking from a national to a global perspective;
(2) a correction of the deficiencies in NATO's centre region ground forces posture;
(3) a rationalization of naval forces according to capacity of the countries to maintain them. The present posture of a main navy to keep sea lanes open is wasteful;
(4) a rationalization of air forces;
(5) a rationalization of communications, command, and control according to necessities;
(6) logistics rationalization on grounds of effectiveness;
(7) a more rational approach to allied weapons design and production with stress on compatibility interoperability, and eventually standardization;
(8) better trained and combat-ready forces;
(9) rationalization of the theatre nuclear forces; and
(10) revision of mobilization and alert procedures to deal with the increased dangers of a Soviet surprise attack.

A slightly more conservative approach to the problem is that which argues against this suggestion for rationalizing NATO and in favour of an increase in operational reserves. Dr Steven Canby,[8] argues that the military logic of the rationalization scheme does not bear scrutiny, for it attacks the problem by trying to solve the symptoms–NATO's conventional deficiencies. According to Canby the real reason why NATO forces are inferior to WTO (Warsaw Treaty Organization) forces is the different ways in which the two view conventional warfare. 'The U.S. fights battles to wear down opponents. The Soviet Union fights battles to avoid further battles.'[9] For this reason NATO has deployed relatively few but well supported combat forces suitable for sustained combat, while the WTO has deployed large numbers of combat units largely independent from support units. The solution therefore lies in the provision of strong reserves. They are needed for the present NATO emphasis on modern centralized airpower and for the introduction of better anti-tank weaponry. A change in strategy is also necessary. The manpower for the reserves exists, but the equipment and organization for their introduction do not. According to Canby, the solution to NATO's problems would be an integration of NATO's trained conscripts into a rapidly mobilizable cadre system. In this way, the continental nations could easily match each active division of the present force with a well trained reserve division.[10]

Canby goes on to argue that the standardization proposed by the rationalists is the 'latest mistake'. To achieve standardization, a high degree of collaboration and coordination would be required. To achieve this, the existence of a supranational authority would be required. Such an authority does not exist presently and is unlikely to appear in the near future. Moreover, the political difficulties and the implicit costs would be so high that a substantial saving would be required for such a programme to be justified. Yet, according to Canby, the eleven billion estimate presented by Kower is grossly inflated. The benefits from standardization, he insists, have not been properly quantified, and it is likely that they would be too small. The important conclusion, however, is that both Kower and Canby believe that the conventional forces can be improved and even increased from already existing forces. We agree.

Those who believe that despite the economic and political difficulties, NATO countries can cope with increases in defence budgets have also come to important conclusions. There has been a renewed sense of optimism as to the ability of NATO to meet conventional needs based on the new Deep Attack technologies. Deep Attack concentrates on 'capabilities to locate, target and destroy or delay enemy forces well forward of the lines of contact'.[11] This technology relies on the superiority of Western development and the ability of NATO's forces to adopt to their tactical and strategic advantage. It centres around the US army concept of Air–Land Battle (ALB) and the SHAPE concept of Follow-On-Force Attack (FOFA). ALB changes the way a conventional defence is conducted. It uses NATO military strengths to exploit fundamental WTO weaknesses. It aims at destroying the momentum of attacking Soviet forces by isolating the first echelon from the reinforcement echelons. FOFA aims at exploiting particularly critical enemy vulnerabilities in the reinforcement process: the rigidity of its planning for an echeloned offence, the density of forces along limited attack routes, and critical transport facilities.

Deep Attack provides the means for the linkage between conventional and nuclear strategies:

> Threatening the area 150 kms. behind the line of battle and beyond with nuclear weapons will hold strategic reinforcements from the USSR at risk and free conventional resources to concentrate on those WTO forces which are the most serious and immediate threat to NATO's defence.[12]

It therefore recognizes the importance of a strong defence triad.

Deep Attack poses a few contradictory problems in regard to strategy, particularly because ALB and FOFA are not entirely similar and could lead to conflict in terms of their requirements. However, these differences are not irreconcilable. Another problem that Deep Attack may pose is that of cooperation and coordination at the alliance level. In these two senses it is not too different from the rationalization and increased-reserves solutions. This would seem to suggest that conventional reinforcement will always come at a price, regardless of the circumstances.[13]

The solution that would be most likely to find acceptance among the critics of these strategies is that which argues for a declaration of No-First-Use of nuclear weapons by NATO. This solution is similar to the arguments for 'Conventionalization' presented above, in that it implicity assumes a heavier reliance on conventional forces. Yet, it is different in that it discounts the necessity for a strong defence triad. The implausibility of ignoring nuclear weapons is inherent in a situation in which the Soviet nuclear arsenals impose an obligation on NATO to hold nuclear weapons.[14] The debate raises interesting issues, however, as the supporters of Emerging Technologies (ET) claim that they can substitute nuclear weapons with conventional weapons of equal destructiveness.[15]

The argument for NFU policy was formulated in 1982 by a group of prominent Americans that included Robert S. McNamara, former Secretary of Defence and initiator of the actual strategy of flexible response. After stating that nuclear proliferation is useless because of the erosion of the deterrent threat, the NFU advocates conclude that NATO strategy should shift from a nuclear to a conventional mode.

The best way to diminish the dangers inherent in the present system, they argue, is to change it: rely on conventional forces for defence and renounce the first use of nuclear weapons. In so doing, the alliance would not necessarily dispose of all its nuclear arsenal but rather, it would have to worry solely about maintaining a retaliatory or 'second strike' capability. The savings derived from the disposal of the first-use weapons could be devoted to modernizing the existent forces and to help build up the new conventional forces required. Further benefits would be that by increasing conventional forces, aggression at the conventional level, which is what the Soviet power is most feared for, would be deterred; that the consensus on military issues which the willingness to declare NFU would represent would bring political cohesion to the alliance; that by declaring NFU NATO would approach East–West relations in a unilaterally pacific way, bettering the international tensions and paving the way for more successful arms negotiations; that NFU would bring hope to those countries fearful of the dangers of nuclear war.

The argument for a NFU policy is very attractive and persuasive as presented by McNamara *et al*. But, there are several issues that their analysis ignores that may undermine the relevance of the NFU position. In the first place, by stating that a dependence on conventional weapons will effectively deter Soviet conventional aggression the authors ignore the historical evidence: in the past, armies of equivalent strength have not been prevented from going to war with each other. Also nations that have been the victims of aggression have been capable of building up their armies during the war to defeat the aggressor. The nature of conventional war is such that this can be done. The Second World War revealed the truth of this, for example in the development of total war economies in Britain, America and Russia. But, with nuclear weapons, a war-time effort to build up the arsenals would be impossible, because of the lethality and rapidity of a nuclear confrontation.

In the second place, as was pointed out in a response article by a group of equally prominent West Germans,[16] NFU ignores the fact that the primary goal of strategy is to prevent aggression, all types of aggression. By declaring a NFU policy, NATO would enable the Soviet Union to calculate effectively the costs and risks of war, and therefore make the contemplation of victory a real possibility once again. As a result, the renunciation of the use of nuclear weapons makes war more likely.

Thirdly, a NFU policy would destroy the confidence of Europeans, and especially that of West Germans, in NATO. Some already believe that the NFU policy is part of an American attempt to keep an East–West confrontation limited to the European theatre. This last argument apparently implies that, unreliable as it may seem, the American deterrent may be preferable to 'standing naked' before the threat of Soviet forces. It is important to note that the argument is advanced by a group of West Germans, the same people who would presumably be the first to suffer from a Soviet aggression. In any case, what remains relevant is the fact that the nuclear deterrent is still reassuring to some people within the alliance. If this group's argument can be expanded, by convincing the populations of Western Europe that the deterrent may become reliable once again by strengthening all the legs of the defence triad, the spread of the peace movements' influence might be stopped. This is a vital consideration.

By resisting the pressure for a declaration by NATO that it will not be the first to use nuclear weapons against a full-scale conventional attack in Europe by the Soviet Union, President Reagan has reassured the West Germans that the American deterrent is still committed to the prevention of war in Europe.

The only strategy which makes sense is one which is calculated to prevent any war, conventional as well, from overwhelming central Europe.[17] The current strategy of NATO is designed to do precisely that. The deterrent is therefore a function of the full spectrum of options which NATO seeks to use to impose an incalculable risk on an agressor.

To seek to remove the risk of escalation would simply multiply the options for the Soviet Union. The deterrent would cease to exist and with it the central pillar of the alliance. Thus NATO would become an empty shell. To imagine that 'a no first use' declaration simply means a minor change in NATO's strategy is manifest nonsense. It implies an attempt by NATO to match Soviet conventional capabilities. This could involve the UK, for example, having to commit six or more additional divisions to NATO's central front together with additional airpower. America could do no less. President Reagan could not hope to win endorsement for the draft (a second Term President has much less leverage in Congress). Only the Soviet Union would welcome a 'no first use' pledge from NATO'.

It is interesting to note that a no first early use of nuclear weapons is already implicit in an adequately reinforced flexible response–deterrence posture. In other words, if the conventional forces of the Alliance were properly reinforced, a conventional attack from the Soviet Union could be matched with conventional forces and successfully be resisted. Only if NATO forces were incapable of resisting the Soviet advance would the Alliance be forced to escalate into a nuclear response. If the use of nuclear weapons became inevitable it would be as a measure of last resort. NATO must not under any circumstances deprive itself of the ability to move to this last resort. In any case, the time that this escalation would require would be precious in terms of finding an alternative solution to the problem, as for example dialogue and negotiation.

There is also a group that argues – not very convincingly – that the use of nuclear weapons could eventually be renounced completely as emerging technologies enhance the destructiveness and accuracy of conventional weapons. The emergence of improved guidance systems, more powerful munitions and submunitions, among other developments, are now enabling conventional weapons to do what only nuclear weapons were capable of doing in the recent years. At this point, one might wonder what the benefits are if nuclear weapons are substituted by weapons that are just as harmful. Is not the repugnance and fear of nuclear weapons a direct result of their awesome power for indiscriminate destruction? The advocates of ET argue that the dangers implicit in the new conventional weapons are not as great because of three particular reasons:

(1) there is a negative psychological factor attached to the use of nuclear weapons because of their effects on Nagasaki and Hiroshima which is absent with conventional weapons;
(2) conventional weapons would not have the odious side effects of radiation fall-out; and
(3) because of a greatly increased accuracy, the amount of collateral damage resulting from a conventional war would be much smaller than if the conflict was nuclear.

Despite these self-serving justifications there are still some problems with ET.[18] The main problem is that we still do not have the full benefits of the emerging technologies. Some experts believe that it will take at least five years to have the armaments that would enable NATO to declare a NFU policy.[19] There are also the problems of cost and ability to afford the programmes mentioned before. Also, there are other hidden costs as underbidding by contractors, for example, would significantly inflate the costs of ET developments. Even if the cost considerations are left aside, it is dangerous and foolish to assume that

NATO's nuclear weapons could be effectively substituted by conventional arms. This would not only require a radical change in NATO war-fighting techniques, but it would also ignore the fact that NATO's conventional and nuclear capabilities are not separate entities but synergistic components of a potentially effective defence posture. Moreover, trying to substitute strategic nuclear weapons with conventional counterparts could have a destabilizing effect, for it would accelerate the arms race between the Soviet Union and the US. It would be a simplistic assumption that the Soviets would not in due course match the development of ET with their own systems. They have done it effectively in the nuclear realm, so there is no reason why they should not catch up with Western developments. Finally, in order to spread the benefits of ET equally throughout the Alliance, a great deal of interaction and cooperation would be required. The benefits that ET can provide to the arms industry are significant and they cannot be monopolized, at least not without significant opposition, by the US. A great deal of technology transfer would be required in order to make the production of the new systems efficient. Both cooperation and technology transfer must unfortunately meet the obstacle of national interests overbearing Alliance goals.

The preceding observations would seem to indicate that the dual task of 'pacifying the pacifists' and providing NATO with an adequate posture would be best met by concentrating efforts and resources on strengthening the so-called defence triad. In other words, by making the strategy of flexible response operational. This solution must not be misunderstood as a continuation of the current dependence on nuclear weapons, but rather, as a concentration on conventional defence that contemplates nuclear escalation only as a measure of last resort. The new Emerging Technologies could be used to raise the nuclear threshold by substituting more powerful conventional weapons for their tactical nuclear counterparts. At the strategic level this practice could be destabilizing. The new technologies of Deep Attack could also be used to increase the likelihood that a conflict would be maintained at the conventional level by enhancing the effectiveness of the Allied forces.

Such a solution would obviously not eliminate nuclear weapons from the world scene. In fact, its success relies on the fact that it views conventional and nuclear weapons as complementary. As long as nuclear weapons continue to be a part of policy, the peace advocates will argue, we shall continue to live under a balance of terror. They are right of course. What is worth noticing, however, is that strengthening the conventional portion of the defence triad would restore the balance to the terror.

The prospect of a nuclear holocaust is not a pleasant one. The aim towards which both world powers should direct their efforts is that of arms reduction on the grounds of reciprocity and equality. In order for arms reduction to be effective, however, there must first be a measure of control attainable only through a stable relationship between the opposing parties. A stable relationship is one in which arms are deployed in such a way that no side is tempted to use them against the other because the consequences would be too great. The solution proposed would approximate to this stable relationship. Only then can a meaningful approach to arms reduction be undertaken.

The NATO alliance then, has succeeded in stabilizing post war Europe for nearly four decades. However, the need for change in NATO policy, which has relied on deterrence must also be recognized in order to maintain NATO's capacity to keep the peace.

Why the need for a new policy at this time? One simple reason has to do with the nature of deterrence and its inherent flaw; that is, deterrence hinges on a bluff that someday must be called to some consequence. Deterrence as a doctrine because of its impact on public opinion has no end in its need for constant reassurance through conventional and nuclear build-up.

The effectiveness of deterrence in many scenarios is also questionable. It does not counter the threat to a small area which could be politically isolated and taken over. Deterrence is also clearly ineffective with regard to 'small claims', confrontation among lesser Third World powers. Even though the United States is a superior power, nations such as Iran and Vietnam were able to embarrass and weaken her position.

The alliance itself has achieved only a partial solution in that it remains only a military organization. Europe was not absorbed into American global politics; for good reason. However, American and European global interests carry the risk of opposing each others' interests. Already, the trend has been to Europeanize NATO (as if Europe stands potentially as an entity in itself). The potentially contrary political aims of NATO members are a threat to NATO's effectiveness, unless and until this European consciousness is raised to a level consistent with the twin pillar concept of NATO.

There are two threats to NATO in the 1980s that a new policy would have to counter. The first is the potential for political blackmail of Western countries by the Soviets. The second threat is the destruction of Europe in war. The solutions to these threats are contradictory; to avert political blackmail an arms build-up is necessary. However, the second threat demands arms-control. The crux of the problem facing NATO, then, is to strike the balance between the political threat and the threat of a holocaust.

One solution, as we have noted earlier, would be a conventional build-up of European forces. This would counter the overriding threats described above, since arms would be added without nuclear risk. This would also satisfy the American demand for Europe to take greater responsibility for defence. However, is a conventional build-up feasible for Western Europe? The reintroduction of conscription would be unacceptable in Britain for example. Also, Germany would become a huge armed camp serving as a base for even bigger multinational armies. Finally, the original reason against reliance on conventional defence still prevails; nuclear weapons are cheaper.

Another suggestion which we referred to earlier – has been to give Germany a nuclear capability. This argument maintains that Germany's possession would increase credibility because it strengthens the American commitment to use nuclear weapons in defence of Europe. By making nuclear weapons at least partly a German responsibility better cooperation within the Alliance might be possible.

The policy of deterrence, then, has produced not only a one-dimensional Alliance (NATO) but also a stalemate in Europe. Although the stalemate has been productive in that Europe is no longer a place of direct confrontation, the stalemate cannot be relied upon to continue indefinitely. Deterrence offers an implicit invitation to have one's bluff called.

Options for NATO's future as we itemized earlier in this book have been widely canvassed and discussed. However, criteria for a new strategy have not been as forthcoming. A new strategy must meet the requirements of deterrence; it cannot go back on that doctrine. More importantly, it must surpass deterrence and reverse its weaknesses. Political control and strategic stability are the aim and purpose of NATO and require employment options which can be reasonably executed. The new strategy must strike a balance between the incredibility of massive retaliation and full-fledged war-fighting capability and readiness. A more precise criteria has, some suggest, been established by Carl Freidrich von Weizsacker for a positive NATO strategy.[20] The policy he advocates must account for both the political threat to Europe and the nuclear threat, without getting caught between the contrary solutions (arms build-up vs. disarmament). Unity of the

Alliance depends on the credibility of US commitment, which must be made more plausible. Therefore the new strategy cannot be offensive in any way and cannot invite an arms race with the Soviet Union.

Present strategy invites the destruction of European population centres. This weakness of deterrence is becoming less acceptable to the people of Europe and America, as the benefits and purpose seem less plausible. Therefore an old rule of strategy must be more effectively expressed: strategy must not bring, or involve jeopardy to the home population. Thus a counter-force strategy is both more moral and rational.

The new strategy must be conducted and controlled centrally. This became a requirement for the first time during the discussion of MLF proposals. Robert McNamara argued against MLF because it lacks centrality of control.[21] The problem becomes, then, the reconciliation of centralized control with the demand for greater European involvement and responsibility in the military command of NATO.

An argument favouring deterrence has been that it allows for negotiation. Professor Uwe Nerlich has correctly argued that deterrence's capacity to encourage negotiation is demonstrably overrated. Further negotiation will be difficult now that the Soviets have gained superiority. At present, NATO's re-entry into arms control negotiations takes place as a new generation of Soviet continental weapons are deployed (together with the NATO new force deployments). The negotiations have made NATO more dependent on nuclear weapons and are inhibiting innovation. Negotiation also reinforces those policies which assume that security must be based on normalization of Soviet–American relations. Nerlich believes this has led to a decline in confidence in the USA, since Europe has been encouraged to view the USSR in more accepting terms. He further outlined the conditions a new strategy must meet. Conventional forces must create optimal situations for use of theatre nuclear forces, and must be able to survive a nuclear battlefield. NATO must expand its initial use options – thus gaining greater bargaining impact.

Finally, Nerlich argues that NATO must prepare options for combined forces. He specifically cites ERW (the neutron bomb) anti-tank weapons. As a corollary, NATO must regain control over escalation.

Nerlich's ideas may be used to introduce a new model for NATO, since this model would satisfy many of his requirements. This model devised by Horst Afheldt and described by C. F. von Weizsacker calls for the use of small, mobile 'techno-commando' squads to be distributed all over West Germany. Afheldt would arm these squads with mini-nukes and implement defensive weaponry such as atomic mine fields. These commandos would have a tie-in with American strategic weapons which serve as a 'covering force'.[22] We briefly seek to evaluate the Afheldt model by the criteria established above. Not all Afheldt's suggestions are, of course, discussed in detail, instead it is the larger concept of limited nuclear options that we consider. Thus, the model is explained simply. In applying the criteria determined above, this strategy meets the requirements. It maintains deterrence because the Soviets are still threatened by strategic nuclear weapons.

The Afheldt plan does not jeopardize the Western population in the same way deterrence has. Even the population in the home country (Germany) could be saved, without the same risk deterrence invites in its implications. The plan does not target military installations which would justify enemy strikes.

An arms race, or any other defensive reaction by the Warsaw Pact is also not risked by the new model. Afheldt's plan is purely defensive, emphasizing atomic minefields and similar measures.

Centralization of command is not sacrificed either. This plan can be conducted unilaterally. It calls for German command of its own army and American dominance over strategic weapons. Thus, it fulfills the 'European requirement' and should necessarily include input from other NATO members. The question of nuclear armament of Germany is solved; Germany would be given limited nuclear means. Some of the resentment towards the American monopoly of nuclear weapons in West Germany would be countered.

With the adoption of such a plan, NATO would be free of much of the conventional burden, since armoured divisions would be greatly de-emphasized. Yet, this does not mark an end to conventional warfare, or the present nuclear-escalation. Conventional force could be kept at the same level, without involving the same numbers, NATO would lose a conventional war if one were fought today – the Soviets clearly have the advantage. However, as Ian Smart contends, the Soviet military threat is not as great as is perceived, based on conventional strength. The *raison d'etre* for superior Warsaw Pact armies is to keep the satellite nations in line. There is, in his view, no basis for the belief that the USSR would necessarily launch or fight a purely conventional war. Nuclear weaponry is a key to the Soviet military planning for war against the West. Mr Smart has plausibly shown the impracticability of bisecting a war into Stage I – conventional and Stage II – nuclear-based on the perceived strength of forces which are not necessarily intended for use outside the Soviet sphere. Furthermore, with the existence of technology and weapons that blur the conventional–nuclear distinction, there is no reason to expect an offensive to be limited to conventional weapons.[23]

The most controversial point of the Afheldt Plan is obviously its proposal to use mini-nukes – the neutron bomb.

NATO has so far refused – or simply refrained from – the deployment of this type of weapon because it blurs the nuclear threshold which is considered dangerous because advocacy of limited nuclear war seems to make nuclear war more likely.[24] In his well-argued study Guido Vigeveno, however, distinguishes the two aspects that combine to make the nuclear threshold; the material and the formal threshold. He uses this distinction to argue in favour of the development of a neutron bomb. His position may be applied to mini-nukes and the type of weapons Afheldt's plan suggests.

The material threshold, 'the considerations taken into account by the decision-makers', is first determined by the tide of the conventional battle. The threshold depends on conventional strength. The Afheldt plan would strengthen conventional forces – not by quantity – but by giving conventional forces their own nuclear deterrent. Conventional battle would invite a greater nuclear threat and would therefore be less easily undertaken. Here an argument by Bernard Brodie is helpful. All war would be horrible and devastating, but local conventional aggression is made more likely because strategic nuclear war is so incredible.

> The availability of this threat (strategic nuclear) as any kind of deterrent will be increasingly limited to only the most outrageous forms of aggression. (It was therefore necessary) to consciously limit those conflicts we may be unable to avoid.[25]

The words 'consciously limit' are the key.

One way to limit the devastation of any potential war would be through deterrence. Conventional aggression would be discouraged because it would carry a credible nuclear risk. Hence, it may be argued that not only do mini-nukes uphold the material threshold, they also raise the conventional threshold.

Another measure of the material threshold is the expected Soviet response. The argument against mini-nukes is, once again, that since such weapons cause less collateral damage they would be more easily used. Vigeveno defeats this argument stating that it is unreasonable to assume that the Soviet response to such use would differ from their reaction to an atomic strike, so that nothing is really changed. NATO has no reason to believe that limited nuclear strikes would be responded to in kind. The decision to use mini-nukes could not be made more easily or hastily than the decision to launch a massive nuclear strike.

The formal nuclear threshold, according to Vigeveno, is the system of release procedures established by NATO. The decision to use nuclear weapons is undertaken by the highest political authority in both the Western nuclear powers and in the Soviet Union. Political control of escalation is imperative. It is feared that for use against highly mobile units such as tanks, NATO's release procedure would be too time-consuming and would have to be delegated to military authority.

The scenario is not entirely, necessarily true. Although release-procedure would have to be revised, political control could still be maintained. The use of limited nuclear weapons would require a series of decisions and a hierarchy of those weapons relative to military–political priority would have to be determined. Actual first use would still be the subject of deliberation on the political level, since a conventional force would remain.

Additionally, the existence of nuclear weapons on the 'conventional' level would be a position from which NATO could negotiate effectively. Once first use became imminent, NATO could negotiate to cease hostilities.

Mr Vigeveno contends that first use is likely to have a political aim, and military effectiveness would only be required to bring about the political end.[26] Initial use does not have to be targeted to a highly mobile tank unit – by setting initial use, even of a mini-nuke, on an 'easier' target deliberation would be feasible. Once nuclear weapons are used on either side NATO's elaborate release process could go into effect.

Clearly, the mini-nukes do not threaten the nuclear threshold, and can actually raise the total 'war' threshold by making any aggression more dangerous. War of any nature is less likely.

NATO's options for strategy would be narrowed down to those that can maintain a conventional and nuclear deterrence. Instead of threat by implication and invitation to attack, the strategy should be more specific in its aims and content. Afheldt's plan has been shown, in its broader prescriptions to match the criteria of deterrence and to surpass it in credibility.

This analysis so far has focused on one of the significant problems the North Atlantic Alliance is facing, namely, that of maintaining the cohesion of the Alliance while providing a credible defence posture that will reassure the people of their security. The focus has been primarily on the latter for we have chosen to assume that a credible defence policy will restore unity to the Alliance. There are other aspects that the allies must resolve if they are to maintain a unified front against their Eastern opponent. These are, among others, adopting a common strategy, a common posture on East–West relations and a common posture towards the Third World.

What would probably help Alliance unity as well as world peace in general, would be the adoption of a more cosmopolitan frame of mind in substitution for the now so out of vogue nationalism that has dictated world politics for such a long time. This vogue has had its impact on NATO as well and raises the question of how durable the European–American relationship has become. Indeed much support for a European defence posture and effort tending towards greater independence of the US is fed by the obvious recrudescence of European nationalism which, it is contended, instead of dividing the nation-states of Western Europe would unite them against superpower hegemony. We perceive certain weaknesses in such an assumption unless the so-called European pillar of NATO is in fact developed and reinforced in a manner best calculated to keep America committed to the defence of Europe in all circumstances and on an indefinite basis.

5 European Defence: How Real is the Soviet Threat?

It is customary for those who draw attention to the Russian threat and who seek a Europeanist defence option to argue that the Soviets are aggressive and intend to rule the world and that this can be proved by looking at Soviet ideology, military strategy, military capabilities and foreign policy. They argue that the Russian attitude to war is very different from Western attitude; theirs is shaped by an ideology that stresses the role of violence as a midwife of progress. One of the precepts of Soviet Communism is that the class struggle will lead to an inevitable conflict between the exploiters and exploited which will bring about the establishment of communism.[1] At the international level, this struggle is seen through the division of the world into an imperialist camp and a socialist camp locked into a fight to the finish.

It is also pointed out that Soviet strategy is different from that of NATO. Indeed, unlike NATO strategy which is strictly defensive, Soviet strategy puts much emphasis on war-fighting and war-winning (as opposed to deterrence) and surprise attack.[2] Soviet strategists believe that nuclear war can be avoided but should such a war occur, then the Soviet Union should be prepared to fight and eventually win it. Victory can be secured through a blitzkrieg-type attack that will wipe out enemy troops and defences, and in which all weapons – conventional, nuclear and chemical – are to be used.

To ensure that victory will be theirs, successive Soviet leaders have over the years striven, successfully, to tip the military balance in their favour. Today the Russians have a 'massive conventional preponderance' and superiority in all theatre nuclear forces except in dual capacity artillery. In addition, the Soviet Navy has been transformed from a coastal defence force into an ocean-going force capable of projecting power thousands of miles away from its homeland. These

Soviet military strides and especially the acquisition of the SS-20 missiles not only have upset the balance of power but also have given a new dimension to the Soviet threat to Europe and cast doubt over the credibility of (NATO) deterrence. It is against this background, of course, that NATO countries decided to site Cruise and Pershing II missiles in Europe. Moreover, it is against this background that the European response to this challenge has been called for.

To achieve and sustain the kind of military build up they have embarked upon, the Russians, according to Western assessments, have been outspending NATO since 1960.

According to those who evaluate the Soviet threat, Soviet international behaviour provides one of the best indicators of the intended use of Russian power. They contend that the occupation of Eastern Europe after the Second World War, the shipping of Cubans to Angola and the invasion of Afghanistan are the norm of Russian international behaviour, and that they constitute irrefutable evidence of a threat which would eventually lead the Soviets to unleash their military might over Western Europe if circumstances become favourable to such recklessness. That Moscow has not yet overrun Western Europe is, according to this view, proof that the NATO deterrent is working. With their expansionist designs frustrated by NATO deterrent, the Russians have, it is argued, adopted a policy of trying to divide the NATO alliance.

This, then, is more or less the line of argument followed by those who see the Soviet threat through their ideology, military doctrine and capabilities, and international behaviour. These, starting with ideology, will be examined in turn, in attempt to discover whether charges of Soviet aggression so often asserted stand up to critical analysis.

It is certainly undeniable that the Soviet view of the world of international politics is based on the Marxian idea of a basic, inevitable conflict between the exploiters and exploited, the outcome of which would be the inevitable triumph of the exploited and the overthrow of capitalism. This conflict was originally expressed in terms of internal class struggle but later, the emphasis was shifted from the internal arena to the global level, with the belief that a war between the socialist and capitalist camps was inevitable.

In accordance with this view of world politics, the Soviets adopted a very aggressive policy which included the use of subversion and other unpalatable things against foreign governments. Today the Russians still view the world and the course of international relations through Marxist–Leninist eyes. However, within the parameters of missionary ideology and oft-proclaimed faith in the eventual victory of socialism over the forces of imperialism, the Kremlin's perceptions of the world have changed considerably. Marxism–Leninism has proved to be very flexible so far as prescriptions on policy actions are concerned, 'calculation of the correlation of forces'.[3] Soviet leaders have been able to introduce extensive alterations of national strategy without qualms as to whether they are discarding or fundamentally reconsidering their ideology.

It can be said that the post-Stalin era saw major revisions in Soviet ideological guidelines. After a careful assessment of the correlation of forces, Khrushchev concluded at the 20th congress of the CPSU (Communist Party of the Soviet Union) in February 1956 that war between the socialists and imperialists was no longer inevitable. The following year, the 21st Congress of CPSU, went a little further when it declared that the victory of socialism was 'final' in the Soviet Union even without the end of capitalism. In October 1961, the 22nd Congress of CPSU stressed that 'communism' could be built in the Soviet Union while capitalism still existed in the world; that peaceful coexistence with the capitalist nations was the new policy; and that war was not only not inevitable but also not desirable or even permissible as a means of advancing socialism. In other words, peaceful transition of capitalist countries to communism is possible if not preferable to armed revolution. The dogma that the class struggle would intensify and lead to world revolution as the final victory of communism approaches, was arguably abandoned.[4]

All this seems not only to suggest (at least superficially) a change in Soviet ideology in terms of prescriptions on policy actions but also a change in Soviet attitude to war. It is clear, then, that the Russians have a Clausewitzian view of war, i.e. war is a continuation of politics. However, what we must remember is that the Russians also argue that war cannot always serve as a weapon of politics. Colonel Ye. Rybkin for example wrote that war as 'a continuation of politics even in the nuclear age is not the same thing as to argue that nuclear war can serve as a practical instrument of policy. War is always the continuation of politics, but it cannot always serve as its weapons'.[5] The late President Brezhnev also stated on many occasions that a nuclear war cannot and must not serve as a means of solving international disputes. Yet looking at Soviet military doctrine, we are struck, in fact, by the emphasis on war-fighting and winning as opposed to deterrence. This must be understood as the apologists say against the background of Soviet historical experience of isolation, encirclement and repeated invasion which has created in the Russian people a great sense of vulnerability. But this is surely not the entire explanation because Russia has also constituted a threat itself to those countries along its own borders?

Of course, there was a time when war-fighting was not emphasized in Soviet strategy. For instance, during the period of 'asymmetrical deterrence' when the US had superiority in air and naval power as well as monopoly control of atomic weapons and the USSR had troops in superior numbers in Eastern Europe. At that time, the Soviets saw the numerical superiority of their troops as playing a deterrent role against US global superiority by holding Western Europe 'hostage' should there be a US attack.

After 1950, however, the Soviets, apart from maintaining their troops in Eastern Europe, reinforced their security with expanded naval protection and air defence systems, and developed a nuclear deterrent based on bombers and an ICBM force that could directly threaten the US heartland.

Confident of their newly-found military strength, Soviet leaders contemplated a unilateral reduction in their conventional forces in Eastern Europe, laying emphasis on their ability to directly strike America with their ICBMs. But with what they saw as the dramatic expansion of the US nuclear arsenal under President Kennedy (in response to Khrushchev's world-wide political offensive between 1957–61) the Soviets changed their strategy and embarked on a campaign to establish a deterrent based on war-fighting. The momentum of that campaign is still with us today.

While NATO's view of deterrence was (until the mid-1970s) that of threatening the USSR with unacceptable damage to its cities and industrial base, the Soviet deterrence policy was the deployment of the SS-17, 18 and 19 land-based missiles, based on denial, i.e. they sought to convince the US/NATO that it could not carry out an attack against Russia with impunity. NATO was and is supposed to be deterred by the knowledge that no military advantage can be gained by striking first. This sort of deterrence cannot or is less likely to work unless the USSR can limit any US/NATO-inflicted damage, hence the importance given to air defence and civil defence. In addition, they must also have a visible capacity to paralyse (partially at least) NATO forces; such a capacity is supposed to keep the latter at bay. This strategy of deterrence-through-denial clearly requires a war-fighting nuclear strategy, one which can both provide adequate measures of protection and the capacity to destroy the military force of the enemy.

Given that the Russians feel very vulnerable because they have provoked a counter-response, it is not surprising that they should have adopted deterrence-through-denial (and the war-fighting strategy that goes with it) and thought in terms of frustrating, negating or pre-empting enemy strikes. Seen from this standpoint, their expansion in Eastern Europe may be thought to be 'defensive'; a desire to put as much land as possible between themselves and the enemy – real or imagined.

That Soviet strategists put emphasis on war-fighting is, of course, not conclusive proof that Russia prefers war to war prevention. Soviet strategy is certainly different from NATO strategy but deterrence and war-fighting ability are not necessarily incompatible in principle. Indeed, the Russians see war-fighting ability and deterrence as complementary concepts. After all, as Simes points out, one of the tenets of nuclear doctrine is that a nuclear potential must be seen to be usable and nuclear war unthinkable for such a nuclear potential to deter.[6]

It is now clear that NATO has been considering adopting the same attitude towards war-fighting and winning as the Russians. The keynote of President Reagan's defence policy with regard to the USSR is a strategy that calls for an American nuclear build-up and which emphasizes possible conflict in 'limited' nuclear exchanges, and plans the deployment of nuclear and chemical weapons both defensively and offensively in response to a prior Soviet attack.

Some US strategists such as Dr Gray (who was appointed adviser to President Reagan in 1981) have also been arguing that US should adopt a war-winning nuclear strategy.[7] Moreover, in 1982, as we recognized earlier in this book, the US Army promulgated a combat doctrine called Airland Battle 2000 which was subsequently formally adopted with certain qualifications in December 1984 by NATO member countries as part of the rubric of the Follow-on-Force attack (FOFA) strategy.

This doctrine puts emphasis on the need to 'fight to win', using speed and mobility, and bringing in a combination of weapons from the outset. Mobility is to be used in both directions: forward, behind enemy lines, and backward to allow attacking units in, to encircle and defeat them later.

Field Manual 100/5 which propounded the doctrine explicitly applies nuclear and chemical weapons to traditional battle concepts in which the aim is to exploit advantages, isolate and destroy enemy units and strike far back behind his line from the outset. The adoption of this new doctrine certainly constitutes a NATO shift from deterrent to the deliberate search for a nuclear war-fighting capacity.[8] This attitude to war in Europe and related matters constitutes a shift in NATO's thinking but not yet a rejection of its essentially defensive posture. Indeed it can be seen as reinforcing NATO's deterrent posture.

Military analysts, however, generally have noted the residual importance of this shift in US/NATO strategy. They also noticed that on the Russian side too, things were changing. Claims of military superiority and nuclear war-winning ability are, according to Simes getting significantly less emphasis. It is relevant to note that the Russian literature quoted by analysts in connection with nuclear war-fighting and winning was largely written in the 1960s and 1970s. However, more recent Soviet literature on the subject reveals that a new generation of young Russian strategists has been challenging the (old) war-winning school of the Soviet strategy. And these writers including Arbatov and Milshtein have had a limited degree of success; leading Soviet figures have been de-emphasizing nuclear war-winning.[9] But we should not assume that the Soviets have entirely abandoned their belief that wars can be won; rather than they have begun to modify their single threshold view of nuclear war.

Indeed de-emphasizing war-winning in no way means that the Soviet Union has been reducing its defence spending. Huge sums of money are still being spent on arms. However, the assertion by Western analysts that the Soviet Union has been outspending (for the past twenty years) the West should not be accepted uncritically. Yet the evidence of increased Soviet defence expenditure cannot be seriously controverted.

The figures quoted in support of this assertion are usually based on CIA estimates. But, as Franklin D. Holzman argues, the CIA is faced with a number of methodological and data choices in assessing Soviet-military expenditure. Very often these choices lean in the direction of exaggerating Soviet spending relative to US expenditure.

It is therefore worth looking at the way such estimates are arrived at. According to the IISS, the CIA looks at the USSR military establishment and then calculates how much it would cost the USA Administration in US dollars to build the same thing in the USA, i.e. how much it could cost the US to deploy the same number of troops, planes, weapon systems and the same research and development as the USSR. This method inevitably leads to misleading conclusions, as there exist discrepancies in many areas between the two countries. Wages are an area where such discrepancies exist. A Soviet soldier is believed to earn 4 roubles a week ($8); yet the CIA estimates that each of 3 673 000

Soviet soldiers is paid $288 per week which is the amount paid a US soldier. Soviet wages calculated this way add up to $70 billion a year to Soviet defence expenditure.[10]

Another area of doubt can be seen in this: If for example the price of steel goes up in the US, the CIA estimates will automatically show an increase in Soviet military spending because the cost of tanks (similar to those built in USSR) will have gone up. This is highly misleading given that the real cost of a tank in the USSR is in no way affected by the cost of US steel. William Casey and Daniel Graham, respectively former CIA boss and Director of DIA (Defence Intelligence Agency), testifying to Congress in 1975 recognized the misleading nature of such estimates by stating that they 'were bound to give distorted results'.[11]

Repeated Western assertions that Russia is actually outspending the West run, of course, contrary to the results reached by so-called peace organizations. The much-respected Stockholm International Peace Research Institute says that although NATO outspends the Warsaw Treaty Organisation (WTO) countries, there is a rough parity between the two blocks. The US Arms Control and Disarmament which calculates that between 1970 and 1979 NATO spent $1994.6 billion against $1739.6 for the WTO seems to hold the same view in relation to that period as the Stockholm Institute.[12]

It should be noted here that about 35% of Soviet military spending goes to the deployment of about 40% of Soviet forces along the Chinese border and elsewhere whereas NATO spending is virtually all directed at the Soviet Union (though the balance of spending in this respect could change over the next decade).

Many Western analysts when looking at the military balance, reach the conclusion that the strategic arsenals of the 2 super-powers are roughly equal but that the Soviet Union has superiority in substrategic forces, i.e. theatre nuclear and conventional forces.

The conventional balance, especially, is obviously rather one-sided. Thus NATO's posture is seriously jeopardized by the rapid build-up and improvement in Soviet conventional forces which have resulted in a fundamentally new threat.[13]

It is widely accepted and documented in the West that the Warsaw Pact enjoys an enormous conventional superiority. First, the existing balance of forces provides the Warsaw Pact an advantage of approximately between 1.5 : 1 and 2 : 1 in combat power (measured in terms of armoured division equivalent – a method that attempts to equalize difference in combat power of different types of divisions).

The Pact also possesses a three to one advantage in tanks, a 2 : 1

advantage in armoured personnel carriers, at least a 3 : 1 advantage in conventional artillery, and at least a 2.4 : 1 in tactical aircraft.

The Warsaw Pact is indubitably capable of a much faster build-up of combat power (the Soviet Union possesses a huge pool of trained reserves on which to draw). Therefore it seems obvious that when viewing quantitative ratios, the maximum Pact advantage would be quickly gained within several weeks after the decision to mobilize. It must be recognized that if the United States is permitted to achieve an unimpeded reinforcement of NATO's central region the Pact's ratio advantages will no longer increase after the first several weeks of hostilities. And yet even before such reinforcement of NATO the military situation in Europe need not become desperate.

The effect of the current Warsaw Pact lead time advantage is not in itself likely to prove decisive. If the category 1 and 2 Soviet armoured divisions in the Western districts of the Soviet Union are mobilized and brought west and if the Polish category 2 divisions are mobilized, the quantitative ratios would be enhanced by about 20%. The Pact advantage would then rise to between approximately 2.2 : 1 and 2.4 : 1, the tank ratio to roughly 3.6 : 1 and the conventional artillery advantage to 3.8 : 1.

Assuming that the Soviet operational requirement for offensive operations is a minimum advantage of 3 : 1 in armour, between 5 : 1 and 8 : 1 in conventional artillery, with the same high ratios for tactical aircraft, the peak Warsaw Pact advantage does not meet operational norms. Though armour norms have been achieved Soviet analysts are palpably troubled by the effect of precision-guided anti-tank missiles on tank formations and probably with a good reason. Given the quantitative factor as the present local military balance in Europe three things seem relevant. First, the Warsaw Pact is not yet in a position to achieve a quick victory in Europe given the present risks of escalation. Second, NATO cannot be certain that it could defend successfully against a major conventional attack without resort to nuclear weapons. Third, the Warsaw Pact could acquire superior quantitative advantages if NATO does not follow through with its long term defence programme (the Pershing 2 and Cruise missile modernization included).

However, manpower comparisons are not in fact particularly valuable and that manning levels for both sides are difficult to assess.[14] But there is clear evidence of the dynamic change in Soviet conventional forces to which NATO has drawn attention. Today, for example, a Soviet motorized rifle division is equal in firepower to the strongest US modernized division. An independent tank battalion with about 42 tanks has been added to each motorized rifle division. Soviet investments in artillery, multiple rocket launcher holdings, and air defence systems are most marked. Today's 31 Soviet divisions in the groups of Soviet forces are equivalent to at least 40 '1966-equipped' divisions. It is clear that the Soviet conventional force build-up in Central Europe has been consistent with their doctrine, which dramatizes the advantages of surprise, mass concentrated firepower and shock to smash through NATO's defences and rapid movement to exploit the breakthroughs. It may be right to credit the Soviets with non-aggressive intentions, but their capabilities tell us to be sceptical. A Pentagon booklet published in 1983, for example, puts the total number of Warsaw Pact troops at 4 788 000 against 4 771 759 for NATO. This does not however tell the whole story. These NATO figures leave out the 492 850 men in the French forces. More importantly, the Soviet Union is also facing a 4 100 000 – strong Chinese army in Asia. Bringing the Chinese into this is important given the expressed US Administration's desire to have a lasting 'strategic relationship' with China. On 17 January 1983 the *New York Post* cited a document called 'Defence Guidance' which committed the US to giving China logistic support so that it would take military initiatives aimed at paralysing Soviet forces.

According to Douglas T. Stuart, prospects of a close military cooperation are not bad given that the two countries have many strategic goals in common and that they support an anti-Soviet posture.[15] Of course, if NATO and Chinese troops are put together, then the Soviet Union is outnumbered by an enormous number. If we did the same with tanks then Soviet superiority in conventional forces would entirely disappear. But this misses the point: it is the Soviet build-up in Europe which is the problem.

Even if one left the Chinese and French armies out of this rough calculus, as we really should, the claim that the Warsaw Pact enjoys huge conventional superiority would still have to be qualified. For example, the Pact may have 50 divisions or so at the theatre level against some 22–32 for NATO but Soviet divisions are smaller in numbers of military personnel. Number comparisons, as we have noted, are not an accurate measure of strength; what does matter is quality, training and experience.

Yet, it is still undeniable that the past decade has seen an extraordinary build-up and modernization of the Pact's combat capabilities. The widely mentioned Pentagon publication *Soviet Military Power* as well as other estimates made by the IISS gives the Pact a superiority of

2.5 : 1 in medium and heavy tanks; 2.4 : 1 superiority in artillery and multiple rocket launchers, and in armed personnel carriers. Even if these figures are accepted, it is still doubtful whether the situation is that hopeless or whether NATO's qualitative superiority in military has necessarily been irreversibly eroded.

The deployment of the German Leopard II tank and the US M-1 tank will almost certainly diminish Soviet superiority. We should also add to this the US XV-2 and XV-3 infantry fighting vehicles (which are comparable to Soviet equipment) to be deployed within this decade.[16]

Furthermore, NATO has qualitative and quantitative superiority in ATGMs (Anti-tank Guided Missiles Launchers) and in helicopters (though the Soviet do lead in number of armed attack helicopters).

There is also the comparison of weapons systems performance, Soviet doctrine, and the organization and use of firepower assets, which reveal serious flaws in the contention that the Pact has unchallenged conventional superiority. Some Soviet weapons may have greater range and firepower than NATO but NATO's systems are qualitatively superior. Certainly blanket statements about Soviet firepower superiority seldom account for how they are to be used. The Pact's firepower assets would be used in such a way that NATO would not face the full brunt of it all at once.[17]

In so far as the number of aircraft is concerned the Pact had a commanding lead by 1983 with 7240 against NATO's 2975 planes. However, 60% of the Pact's aviation was only suitable for air defence and not for ground attack (most of them being short-range interceptor aircraft). This leaves NATO with a slight edge in fighter-bombers and ground attack aircraft. Hence the importance for NATO in exploiting this lead through the concept of the air-land battle strategy.[18]

Even more worrying for the Pact, is the suggestion made by Epstein that the Warsaw Pact pilots are not as proficient as NATO's in the air. He argues that the Pact with its highly centralized command structures and rigid training, lacks the flexibility, initiative, and the ability to adapt to changing battlefield conditions.[19]

There are other problems; for instance maintenance problems which keep Pact's aircraft on the ground for long periods; the air-force's reliance on ground-based controlled air operations. Indeed, targeting and other important combat orders to pilots are transmitted from stations on the ground. It may well be that this has resulted in a situation whereby Soviet pilots gain little experience in autonomous operation and could consequently suffer severe disorientation should their link with the ground-based authorities be cut off.[20]

The Soviet navy is also undeniably a growing threat. This was revealed in the recent Soviet naval exercises; it was perceived that Soviet naval forces were assembled with a speed which surprised NATO policy makers and caught Western intelligence agencies unawares, although this was denied by General Rodgers (Commander of NATO forces in Europe).

The Soviet navy has certainly come a long way since 1945 when the USSR had virtually no navy at sea. Soviet naval forces which now include 1297 surface warships, 377 submarines, 755 auxiliary ships, and a naval aviation arm numbering 1440 airplanes, no doubt constitute a serious challenge to US superiority at sea.

Yet formidable as this navy may appear in numerical terms, it has many problems, including logistical ones. The United States has more marines than the USSR (185 000 against 16 000). Soviet submarines may be more modern than they were 10 years ago but compared to US ships they are old-fashioned. For instance, many of USSR attack submarines are still old-fashioned diesel vessels which today are of little significance when compared to the nuclear attack submarines. Furthermore, while the US has 44 naval bases around the world, the USSR has none outside its borders. It has 6 major bases inside its territory, four of which freeze up in winter.

At the level of theatre nuclear weapons the SS-20s are seen as the greatest threat; they have upset the delicate balance in the European theatre.

The SS-20 is a medium-range nuclear missile capable of hitting any target in Europe. As we noted earlier SS-20s were deployed in replacement of missiles deployed in the early 1960s. Each missile carries 3 warheads which are smaller than the SS-4 and SS-5 but their increased precision gives them about the same destructive power. Western claims that SS-20s upset the balance because they can hit any target in Europe must be taken seriously. The vulnerability, however, of targets in Europe is nothing new given that the SS-4 and SS-5 have been able to hit such targets for 20 years.

The record of NATO leaders' tardy and over-complacent response to the deployment of SS-20s in Europe, chronicled by Nino Pasti,[21] makes an interesting reading even though his account lacks judgement and balance. NATO military analysts and high command had known about SS-20s for years. The threat of the SS-20s did not really loom large until the West German Government grew alarmed. By this time, fortunately for NATO, contracts were signed between the Boeing Aerospace Corporation and the US defence department, signalling that Cruise missiles were shortly to be manufactured and could therefore become available for deployment in a bid to restore the military balance in Europe. For two years, all NATO meetings including the Atlantic Council of 6 December 1976, 9 December 1977, 11 May 1977; the NATO Defence Planning Committee of 6 December 1976; NATO Ministerial Guidance of May 1977, quite inexplicably expressed no concern about the SS-20s in their final communiques. NATO's line then, was that only the Pact's conventional forces constituted a threat to NATO. It was only on 6 December 1978 that the Defence Planning Committee realized the danger that NATO was facing, and then not against the SS-20s as such but about the possibility that they might be transformed into intercontinental missiles of the SS-16 variety. In the communique of the NATO Planning Group of May 1979, ministers at long last took note of the SS-20 missiles and stated that their examination of a modernization of the long-range capability of NATO would have to be carried out 'without increasing dependence on the nuclear weapons and prejudicing long-term defence improvements in conventional forces'.[22] It was also emphasized that consideration of a modernization effort would need to take full account of arms control possibilities. Here, three points stand out: first the low-profile response to the SS-20 and hence the slow perception and sluggish NATO response; second the concern about not increasing or over-emphasizing the role of nuclear forces; third the patent concern and anxieties about arms control.

However, a more mature and reasoned response occurred with NATO's decision to agree to the deployment of Cruise and Pershing II missiles in Europe on 12 December 1979. This was evidently a painful decision but a totally inevitable one.

The initial official rationale for wanting these new missiles emphasized the SS-20s' threat. This one soon rightly developed into an increasingly strong indictment against the Soviets for not having proposed arms control negotiations before building the SS-20 missile. To have a moratorium on weapons, it was plausibly argued, would lock a Soviet advantage in place. Thus, the Cruise missiles were needed both to keep parity and to establish the linkage between European defence and America's involved in any war with the Soviets.

By June 1981, the official rationale hardened the connection between deployment and the course of the arms control negotiations. European governments started emphasizing the arms control potential of the Cruise and Pershing II missiles. Arguments about the threat of SS-20s and about the Soviet failure to seek negotiations were emphasized. The new line of argument stressed that the NATO decision to adopt Cruise and Pershing II missiles offered the only way to convince Moscow to reduce the number of SS-20s.

This shift of emphasis, however, brought about a major divergence of view between the European leaders and the Reagan Administration. The US fearing what it saw as the European temptation to pursue arms control uncritically, warned that over-emphasis on arms control would make NATO's military policy too dependent on negotiations with Russia. The logic of the US warning proved in the event fully justified. European optimism was groundless.

It was around this time that German Chancellor Schmidt unveiled his 'zero-option' proposal calling for NATO not to deploy Cruise and Pershing II missiles if the Soviets would not deploy their SS-20s. US strategists thought that such a proposal was remote and even undesirable. Secretary of State, Haig found the idea 'preposterous'.[23]

In Europe a substantial minority of public opinion was alarmed that US strategy was evolving a nuclear war-fighting capability based on the notion of first strike in a 'limited' war. It was erroneously assumed that by deploying Cruise and Pershing II missiles, NATO was planning to unleash a first strike in that particular 'theatre', with the intention of keeping the conflict 'limited' to Europe. These fears appear to be vindicated when President Reagan foolishly stated that 'you could have the exchange of tactical nuclear weapons. . . . without bringing either of the major powers to pushing the button'.[24] This was a terrifying idea but it was also not part of US strategic doctrine either in Europe or elsewhere. Mr Reagan was simply mistaken: he revealed a poor grasp of the risks of nuclear escalation.

Mr Brezhnev lost no time to capitalize on Reagan's gaffe, denouncing the US notion of limited war as 'insidious'. The Americans were on the defensive and had to come up quickly with a proposal; a proposal that would probably fail even though it would not disrupt deployment of the Cruise and Pershing II. The West did not have to wait for long.

On 25 November 1981, live broadcast world-wide, President Reagan offered to the Russians a 'four-point agenda for peace'. First the US would willingly cancel the deployment of the 108 Pershings II and 464 ground-launched Cruise missiles if the Russians would dismantle the 600 or so SS-20, SS-4 and SS-5 intermediate range missiles it had in place. This was Schmidt's 'zero-option' proposal, rejected by the US only a few months before (June 1981). Secondly, Reagan called for a new round of talks on strategic nuclear weapons, aiming not only at setting a limit to both superpowers' arsenals but at actually reducing them. The acronym for these talks would be START *The Strategic Arms Reduction Talks*. Thirdly, Reagan asked for the shrinking of conventional forces in Europe – 'equality at lower levels' for both NATO and the Warsaw Pact. Finally the Soviets were urged to accept a European plan for advance notification of military manoeuvres anywhere between the Atlantic Ocean and the Ural Mountains in Russia, traditionally the Eastern boundary of Europe.

The proposal was brilliantly timed, completely upstaging Brezhnev on the eve of his visit to West Germany. Its net effect was to put the Russians on the defensive. Predictably enough, they dismissed the proposal as 'propaganda' while the European peace movement reacted with scepticism. Mgr Bruce Kent, the controversial General Secretary of the British CND, fairly predictably, saw the whole thing as 'a rather obvious piece of political gamesmanship, designed to confuse well-meaning people in Europe and make them think that Reagan is doing the right thing'.[25]

The Russian rejection of Reagan's proposal meant that NATO could now reveal Russian 'intransigence' and then go reluctantly ahead with the deployment of Cruise and Pershing II missiles.

But it should not be assumed from all this that SS-20s were not as threatening as they were made out to be because for two years NATO raised no concern about their existince and deployment. Indeed what the SS-20s could do, the SS-4 and SS-5 had been only able to do on a smaller scale and without the enhanced range and multiple payload of the new systems. NATO's fear was justified.

Most European governments began to perceive the truth of the belief that the SS-20 was a threat of such magnitude as to justify the deployment of Cruise and Pershing II missiles. Some even feared that the development by the Soviet Union of weapons systems that were specifically deployed against Europe pointed to the Russian hegemonic aspiration towards the continent. Indeed, the fear grew amongst the less sanguine that given the collapse of NATO, the Russians would indeed invade West Europe and that this was more likely now that they had achieved nuclear parity with the US. But paradoxically it was even more widely recognized to be the case that NATO was still strong and viable enough to be a major impediment to untoward Soviet ambition.

After all, the existence of parity between the USSR and USA did not mean that a Soviet attack on Western Europe was imminent. The International Institute of Strategic Studies, in its authoritative review of the military balance in Europe in 1982 estimated that 'the overall balance continues to be such as to make military aggression a highly risky undertaking'.[26] Quite so.

Mr Alan Ned Sabroski, writing in *Orbis* in summer 1981 went even further, stating that there was little reason to expect a Soviet attack in virtually any circumstances given that Europe intact is much more valuable to the Russians than Europe devastated by a war that is bound to go nuclear. Mr Jonathan Steele argued that the Soviets had enough problems with controlling Eastern Europe and Afghanistan. They would certainly not want another load of problems that the occupation and control of Western Europe would entail.[27] He argued that the impression that the Russians have only had successes in the international arena was somewhat exaggerated.

In the years after the Second World War, the Soviets adopted a very militant policy designed to put political pressure on Western Europe. The main aspects of this policy included the withdrawal of West European communist parties from so-called bourgeois governments, the coup in Czechoslovakia, the attempt to intimidate Tito into the Soviet orbit and the creation of the Cominform. This policy, however, failed. If rightly the Soviets wanted to keep Europe weak and divided, then their policy produced the contrary result: it promoted European solidarity and sparked a heightened sense of the Soviet menace in the US, which resulted in responses like the Marshall Plan and the creation of NATO. The European–American relationship was the result.

The Russians quickly realized that their dynamic foreign policy was circumvented by events they could not control. They also took note of the fact that they were operating in an international environment which was suspicious of, and hostile to their intentions. This, then, injected an element of extreme caution in Soviet foreign policy.

Indeed, with the important exception of the Cuban missile crisis in 1962, when Khruschev tried to pull a nuclear bluff on Kennedy, Soviet leaders have by and large acted cautiously and have pulled back when seriously challenged. Khrushchev was apparently the only Soviet leader to use the threat of nuclear weapons in a particular situation – during the Suez Crisis and the Cuban missile crisis.[28]

In Berlin and Cuba, Khrushchev's attempts to gain political advantage through nuclear threats demonstrably failed. He was soon deposed by Brezhnev and Kosygin. Under Brezhnev, Russian policy assumed a dual aspect. Bragging about the USSR military capabilities was one aspect. Brezhnev, in the short-term, however reduced military spending in favour of consumer goods and adopted a policy of 'peaceful coexistence', in an attempt to woo some of the newly independent Third World Countries into the Soviet orbit. He also tried to find some form of compromise between cooperation with and challenge to the US. *Détente* can be said to have been born out of this policy of peaceful coexistence.

Cautious as the Soviets may have been, the history of Soviet international diplomacy has, then, been one littered with more setbacks than with successes. They have certainly managed to establish their presence in South Yemen, Angola, Afghanistan, Cuba and Mozambique. But these are – with the exception of Cuba – relatively unimportant countries. They have been kicked out or cast aside by numerous countries including China, Indonesia, Egypt and Somalia where they had the only naval base outside of the Soviet Union. Furthermore, they are palpably bogged down in Afghanistan, and do not know how to get out. They are also proving inept at maintaining their grip over Eastern Europe, as shown by events in Poland.

In evaluating the reality of the Soviet threat, firm conclusions prove to be positive. Proof of the Soviet threat can be said to reside in Soviet ideology, foreign policy, military doctrine and capabilities. Yet a careful examination of each of these reveals that such threats can be deterred or indeed contained. Communism remains the official Soviet ideology, but because of the West's positive response it has undergone such major changes that Russia can no longer be regarded as a revolutionary force in world politics. Indeed, if anything, Russia has learnt that power is inherently inhibiting, with the result that it has turned into an imperial power suspicious of any challenge to its authority.

Soviet foreign policy has also significantly changed. Thus, any assessment of Soviet military doctrine and intentions must be complex and uncertain and because of this, emphasis must be put on measurable capabilities, and intentions inferred from such capabilities. But we must never confuse intentions with capabilities, because the Soviet threat lies in its ideological character which takes systemic conflict for granted.

Russia does certainly possess greater military power than it needs to protect its territory and allies around it from any likely enemy. There is, however, no clear evidence to suggest that they actually expect to rule the world and we have to agree with Brodie that the Soviets 'have given us little cause for discomfort in the use of military power, though we clearly dislike the continuing growth of it'.[29]

But although the Soviet threat should not be exaggerated, given their military preparedness, the West should not allow any real military imbalance to arise. Such caution might be said to be politically and militarily justified. This caution relates to the Soviet perception that the international class power (the systemic struggle) is determined by the correlation of forces.

The 'correlation of forces' is the term used by Soviet strategic thinkers to describe the power relationship between capitalism and socialism. It is a much broader concept than the West's nuts and bolts balance of power as it embraces moral, ideological and political elements. Professor Lawrence Freedman relates this idea by characterizing the growth of Soviet military might as a sum of economic, political, moral and military forces behind the contending parties in the international arena.[30]

While the West's balance of power is a static concept with its focus on the status quo, the 'correlation of forces' is a dynamic concept. In fact, the Soviets view it as a way of changing the status quo. The Soviet writer Sanakoyev promotes this interpretation:

> A change in the balance of power was steadily developing. ... Experience has demonstrated that the process of change in the relationship of forces between the two systems is an objective process which arises out of the advantages of the new social system. This process can rightly be called irreversible because it has been dictated by the objective laws determining the contest between the systems.[31]

Indeed an easily discernible undercurrent of intellectual arrogance pervades the Soviet view. This theme can be seen as a result of the fact that Soviet thinking about the uses of military power is deeply rooted in the official Marxist–Leninist ideology of the state. This deterministic ideology asserts that the world is moving from capitalism to socialism, and that this transition began with the 1917 October Revolution. Moreover, the Soviet victory over Germany, which set the foundation for the socialist state, and the emergence of client states like Angola and Ethiopia have convinced many Soviet thinkers that the 'correlation' is inevitably moving in their favour.[32] However, we shall see that any movement in the 'correlation' towards the USSR would be difficult to support empirically unless major weight were attached to the military factor. The implications of this conclusion are undoubtedly of great significance to any attempt to reorganize European defence with reference to the European powers themselves.

Before elaborating upon the Soviet Union's security or lack of security *vis-à-vis* the 'correlation of forces', some discussion of the

USSR's overall strategy is necessary. One pivotal idea is that when Soviet political and military leaders assert that Soviet Military doctrine is defensive in nature, they are referring to the political goal associated with the defence and furthering of communism. That is, any political or military action taken in the name of communism is defensive, wars of 'national liberation' for example. Soviet military strategy, however, is clearly offensive in character, and no Soviet military leader has ever argued otherwise. Therefore one concludes that a defensive doctrine depends upon an offensive strategy for its implementation.[33]

In this context we can appreciate the Soviet statement that:

> in modern conditions the external function of the socialist army is naturally becoming broader and deeper. This is explained by huge socio-political changes in the international arena.[34]

In fact, the functions of Soviet military power, as presented in the context of the 'correlation of forces', are three-fold. The main function is to prevent a world war by deterring a nuclear attack through the threat of certain retaliation. The second is the goal of defending the socialist community and its individual member states. Finally it serves the function of aiding national liberation movements and helping newly independent states to resist the 'forces of imperialism'. The growth of Soviet military power is seen to contribute to all these purposes by weakening the ability of the imperialist states to use their military power to stop the movement of the correlation of forces towards socialism.[35]

In a 1978 speech before a German audience, Brezhnev stated that 'The Soviet Union believes that rough equality and parity are sufficient for defence needs'. (*Pravda*, 4 May 1978). Yet he also implicitly declared that the approaching change in the correlation of forces in favour of the Soviet Union would be most welcome. Given the West's predominantly military view of the balance of power, Brezhnev's conclusions would seem contradictory.

In fact, this apparent contradiction in Soviet thinking does not represent outright falsehood. Rather, it may be regarded as a sort of 'cognitive deception'. The state of military balance is a critical component in the correlation of forces and the two concepts are obviously interrelated. Nonetheless, it is important to understand that it is possible to achieve superiority in the correlation of forces without simultaneously enjoying military superiority. Professor Vernon Aspaturian suggests that while the military element in the correlation is the most, reliable, visible, and measurable, the more amorphous, intangible elements are not ignored – and may, in fact, be over-emphasized by Soviet thinkers.[36]

A look at Soviet history helps to explain how this view of the correlation of forces as a blend of many elements evolved. The Soviet Union has had to survive and develop its power for many decades when it was militarily weak. Thus it came to rely upon other factors to compensate for this military deficiency. Through this process, the Soviet leadership gained tremendous prowess in the manipulation and mobilization of various 'exotic' non-military elements in constituting the correlation of forces. A. Sergiyev relates this theme in the following excerpt from a 1975 issue of *Foreign Affairs*:

> The foreign policy potential of a state depends not only upon its own forces and internal resources but, to a considerable extent, on such external factors as the existence of reliable socio-political allies among other states, national contingents of congenial classes, mass international movements and other political forces in the world scene.[37]

We might share Aspaturian's conclusion that the Soviet leadership has long realized that social conflicts, tension, frustrations, and resentments, particularly those between classes, represent huge reservoirs of pent-up social power. These reservoirs can be detected through Marxist–Leninist dialectical analysis and, ideally be tapped and mobilized as a foundation of Soviet political power. In short, these internal factors, and the direction of their movements – for or against the status quo – can be viewed as formidable components in the power equation.[38]

The concept of the correlation of forces, while germane to the analytical process of Soviet leaders in the assessment and building of strength, is less appropriate or relevant for Western leaders. There are two principal reasons for this. First of all, Aspaturian cites the diverse and amorphous nature of Western ideologies as a major hindrance. More important, however, is the fact that Western leaders are not as versed as the Soviets in the assimilation and manipulation of the various social, political, and revolutionary elements belonging to the correlation of forces equation. Therefore, Western analysis is more apt to reveal emphasis upon the traditional 'elements of national power', i.e. military force, in its calculus.[39]

In sum, the Soviet concept of correlation of forces, diverges most profoundly from the West's notion of balance of power. While the balance is seen as the product of deliberate policy decisions on the part of the state, the correlation of forces is a 'balance' arrived at through historical and social forces in which the policy of the state is only one component. In fact, to the Soviets, the correlation of forces is the basic substructure upon which the interstate system rests. Moreover, the correlation of forces can be affected only marginally by state policy while, in general, state policies are shaped by the ever-changing correlation of forces.

Given this notion, that is, of an historically determined substructure, it can be concluded that equilibrium is *not* invariably a good thing and efforts shouldn't necessarily be made to correct imbalances between the superpowers. The object of Soviet power is to further the movement of the correlations of forces towards socialism, not to maintain a balance of power between capitalism and socialism.

In fact, the Soviets view any states' attempt to sidestep the correlation of forces as an endeavour doomed to failure. History, of course, dictates this. Adjustments of the military power of individual states can have only limited and temporary effects. That is, states may be able to slow down, speed up, or slightly modify the correlation but they cannot significantly shape it. In other words the spheres of the correlation of forces and interstate relations cannot be mixed or interchanged.[40]

In April of 1971, Soviet Foreign Minister Andrei Gromyko asserted Soviet 'equality' with the United States in an address before the 24th Congress of the Communist Party. He stated that:

> Today, there is no question of any significance which can be decided without the Soviet Union or in opposition to it. (*Pravda*, 14 April 1971)[41]

Whether or not the proclamation represented reality, anticipation, or mere pretension, it was clear that the USSR was determined to assert its legitimacy and right to be afforded equal superpower status with the United States.

Within one year of Gromyko's message the United States seemed ready to accept the Soviet Union's status. During the SALT I ceremonies at Moscow, the US voluntarily recognized the Soviet Union as an 'equal strategic power', for couched in the May 1972 document *Basic Principles of Relations Between the United States of America and the*

Union of Soviet Socialist Republics was a statement involving 'Recognition of the security interests of the Parties based on the principle of equality.'[42]

By 1974, the USSR's newly assumed global stature was exhibited in the wake of American paralysis over Vietnam and Watergate. Taking advantage of the vacuum created by America's timidity, the Soviet Union cautiously embarked on its first global expedition by orchestrating from Moscow an ingeniously conceived series of military interventions by its Caribbean client state Cuba in the remote reaches of Southern Africa.

In response to this challenging activity, President Nixon and Kissinger contested their earlier SALT I acquiescence to the USSR. Washington had perceived the SALT I agreements as instruments designed to domesticate and contain Soviet power rather than unleash it.[43]

However, by this time, Soviet assertiveness had been firmly and irrevocably established and Moscow's foreign policy as an expression of the correlation of forces took on ever greater significance.

In October of 1977, just after the events in Southern Africa, a new Soviet constitution was adopted which, indeed, expressed foreign policy in comprehensive global terms. In article 28 of this constitution is the statement:

> The Foreign policy of the USSR is aimed at ensuring international conditions favourable to building communism in the USSR, safeguarding the state interests of the Soviet Union, consolidating the positions of world socialism supporting the struggle of peoples for national liberation and social progress ...[44]

The question remains whether or not the Soviet Union was and is, in fact, capable of consolidating its new acquisitions and achieving 'global power' status commensurate with its 'super-power' status. Both the USSR and the United States had, by the 1970s achieved recognition as 'super-powers'. As such, they shared a number of important common characteristics which set them apart from the other states in the international community. Each had a large, diversifed, and highly skilled population; each boasted a powerful industrial-technological capacity; each occupied a large, strategically located territory; each had a leadership position in an ideological-military system; and each assembled an entourage of client states from various parts of the world. Nevertheless, the most salient characteristic was the shared ability to unilaterally and almost instantaneously incinerate the globe.[45] Yet neither saw this option as attractive.

At this point, however, there comes a divergence between the terms 'super-power' and 'global power'. The last of the aforementioned characteristics is the one that denotes a super-power – that is, the magnitude of military power that a state possesses. Nevertheless, while the capability to destroy the entire planet is an indispensable prerequisite for super-power status, it is by no means sufficient for a state to qualify as a global power. Global power implies not only the magnitude of military power that a state possesses, but also the range and reach of that power. In other words, the consolidation and effective maintenance of power and influence are as important as the military power itself.

The Soviet Union is a super-power but has not achieved the status of a global power. That is, the USSR is manifestly unequipped to provide sustained leadership in the event that it should succeed in unseating the US as the predominant world power. The Soviet Union could not provide global financial leadership. Its economy could not act as a locomotive for global development and technological innovation. In 1950, the Soviet GNP accounted for about 11% of the global product: three decades later it is still only 11%. Manifestly, the Soviet Union is not yet a global power.

Furthermore, the Soviet Union's leaden mass culture has no great appeal. Any American displacement could not be followed by an effective Soviet replacement. Only a vacuum would then exist where once American power stood supreme though not uncontested.

All of this can lead to only one conclusion: The Soviet Union conducts its relationship with the West from a position of military parity but economic and social backwardness. Professor Zbigniew Brzezinski has gone so far as to call the Soviet Union a 'one-dimensional power' for which the conduct of foreign affairs relies primarily upon military force.[46] Moreover, the Soviets now have military global reach but they lack political global grasp, they feel themselves both too strong internationally to accommodate the status quo and too weak domestically not to fear it. Therefore, their outlook on the world is one of possessive defensiveness and disruptive offensiveness. In short, they have become a menace because their real power is not great enough.

Soviet writers implicitly recognize that the equality which they so strongly yearn for remains essentially an ascriptive one. Although they express confidence that the impersonal but objective forces of history present in the 'correlation of forces' will render it permanent and therefore free Soviet equality from its dependence upon American recognition, they are aware that for the time being that is not the case.[47] In sum, the Soviet Union is desperately insecure in its super-power–global power relationship with the United States.

In spite of the 'impersonal forces of history', Soviet leaders must realize that any true global power status must be self-achieved, self-asserted, and self-sustained. Furthermore, they must be aware that Soviet military power, the principal factor supporting that nation's super-power status in the absence of any viable economic or social leadership, has been realized only at tremendous cost. The USSR has had to stretch its resources to their limits while the enormous material and human potential of the West has barely been tapped. And, even with this tremendous expenditure the Soviet Union has achieved a favourable correlation of forces largely through default in the post-Vietnam era.

Several important conclusions can be drawn from this assessment. First of all, the correlation of forces is favourable only in respect to blitzkrieg operations and the preservation of the Soviet version of the status quo. Hence the tremendous importance attached to the peace movement as two of the most significant foreign policy concepts, peaceful coexistence and detente, are directly linked in Soviet eyes, to the growth influence.[48]

Also, the Soviets' insecurity *vis-à-vis* their correlation of forces relationship has led them to overstate the various moral, social and political elements in the correlation, in efforts to compensate for an artificially heightened reliance upon the military which contradicts the idealistic Leninist vision of history. Furthermore, this insecurity factor has most certainly magnified the traditional Soviet suspicions regarding the Western world.[49]

Some serious questions are raised as well: For example, how will the NATO countries be able to discern what weight is being given to the various elements in the correlation of forces calculus and how will this growing uncertainty affect Western strategic planning. Will the military factor become more and more important as the Soviet Union becomes more and more interventionist in its attempts to supersede the United States? Or finally, will a new 'correlation of forces' emerge as the present theory's ever-decreasing viability is finally acknowledged by the

Soviet leadership?[50] Moreover, how would the correlation of forces be affected by the growth of a European centre of deterrence developed either within the framework of NATO or outside it, say, as part of the defence dimension of the EEC? And how would the Soviets respond to this?

6 The Transformation of the Soviet Navy: the Threat to Europe and NATO's Response

In late March 1984 NATO aircraft spotted five 3000-ton Krivak-class frigates west of the Lofoten Islands. The next day, four more Krivaks, a 4400-ton guided missile cruiser of the Kynda class, and three submarines emerged from the Baltic. Then a 22 000-ton nuclear powered cruiser was seen rounding the North Cape. These manoeuvres were part of a Soviet naval exercise which included more than 250 Soviet combat and support ships accompanied by supersonic Backfire bombers in the Norwegian Sea. This naval exercise clearly demonstrates Moscow has decided it must devote major forces in any European conflict to the northern flank. But there is greater significance to the display of maritime power. It represents the emergence of the Soviet navy from relative obscurity to a position where it can pose a credible challenge to the Western navies for mastery of the seas.[1] This is one of the most remarkable military developments of the post-war period.

The architect of Soviet naval development is, of course, Admiral Gorshkov, Commander-in-Chief of the Soviet Navy and Deputy Minister of Defence. These spring manoeuvres were also a tribute to his triumphant career spanning some thirty years. When he took on the job of Commander-in-Chief in 1956, the Soviet Navy was little more than a coastal defence force. At the time, the Kremlin was anxious to counter the American nuclear threat of land based missiles. Moreover, international confrontation such as the Korean War, Suez Crisis, and the 1958 US landing in Lebanon demonstrated the importance of Western naval power.[2] The future development and effectiveness of Soviet naval power would increase Soviet political influence and strategic reach throughout the world. Moreover the Soviet capacity to influence events in Europe was given an added boost.

The naval build-up received further impetus arising from the Soviet humiliation in the Cuban Missile Crisis of October 1962. This crisis increased Soviet determination to become a global maritime power. As a result, Gorshkov enhanced the naval construction programme and inaugurated the forward deployment of Soviet naval units. This would enable the Soviets to respond to an increasing US threat from carrier-based aircraft and nuclear-firing submarines (SSBN).[3] In addition, the shift to forward deployment in the 1960s produced numerous opportunities for coercive diplomacy in the Third World. Proximity of Soviet naval forces capable of projecting direct power ashore creates an impressive forcible potential.[4]

By the mid-1960s, Gorshkov was winning a larger share of the defence budget. He was a convincing advocate of the benefits of a huge ocean-going navy, arguing it was the best means of projecting power. The expansion of Soviet naval defence included the need to maintain surveillance of potentially hostile forces. In 1972–73, Gorshkov wrote a series of eleven articles entitled *Navies in War and Peace* which appeared in *Morskoi Sbornik* (Naval Review). He discussed the role of navies in the post-war world. In 1976, these articles were expanded into a book which incorporated a good deal of new material on the development and use of modern navies.[5] It is interesting to note the notoriety Gorshkov received stemmed from when the Soviet Union was directly challenging American influence in the Third World. A strong Soviet Navy would greatly aid in exerting political and military influence in this volatile region of the world.[6]

Clearly the Soviet Navy has been the key element for a more assertive global role in non-contiguous areas to the Soviet Union over the past three decades. Throughout history, the greatest nations and empires have maintained strong navies to defend and promote their interests abroad. The European members of NATO were now conscious of their former neglect of naval power. The British naval staffs predictions were seen to be justified. In a Bookings Institution study of 41 incidents showing use of force between 1957–79, two-thirds have involved naval forces.[7] Thus, the transformation of the Soviet Navy was crucial in elevating the Soviet Union to a position of overall strategic parity with the United States.

The pressure for change in Soviet defence policy came mainly from developments in military technology. The Soviets became concerned about the apparent invulnerability of American submarine-based missiles. In response to this threat, remarkable progress has been achieved in military equipment. The Soviet Navy benefited from a substantial share of this programme. There is no reason to believe this share will diminish as long as the leadership remains convinced of the significance of the sea in Soviet foreign policy.

It is often complicated to deduce the ramifications of this Soviet Naval build-up. There is considerable dispute in European defence circles about what it all means. Defence staffs are divided about what it is for, about its roles and priorities and how effective it is. Thus, there are several different recommendations about how the West and NATO in particular should react. It must be understood for the sake of the general security of Europe, it nevertheless remains a puzzle. There is a tradition of furtiveness by the Soviet Navy in addition to evidence which is intrinsically ambiguous. Therefore, it is necessary to explain the differences between the naval strategies of NATO and the Warsaw Pact. These differences constitute something of a crisis for NATO because the debate about naval or maritime strategy within the alliance obviously divides opinion between the continental strategists – the proponents of land and air campaigns as promulgated in the FOFA and air–land battle proposals – and the maritime strategists who argue that NATO's naval capabilities must be expanded and improved.

Since the early 1950s, the Soviets started equipping submarines with conventional and nuclear anti-ship Cruise missiles. The Soviet response to Western superiority in major surface combatants and shipboard aircraft is the Cruise missile. Presently, the Soviets have approximately seventy submarines specially designed to carry Cruise missiles, as well as numerous sorts of surface ships. In 1981, the Oscar Class, a new class of Cruise missile submarine was introduced. It carries 24 SS-N-19 Cruise missiles with a range of 450 km.[8]

In addition to the development of the Cruise missile, the Soviet Union has built a powerful land-based naval air force comprised of strike bombers – 270 Badgers, 40 Blinders, and 80 Backfires. These bombers are equipped with conventional or nuclear Cruise missiles which can hit a warship at a distance of 700 km.

Despite the extensive defence encompassing US aircraft carriers, such as sophisticated interceptor aircraft and escort ships, NATO chiefs wondered over what duration they could repel coordinated saturation attacks by SLCM followed by ALCM once the ships were within range of Backfire bombers. It is uncertain whether carriers could launch air strikes on land targets because long before continental Europe would be within reach of their own aircraft, the carriers would be bombarded by Soviet and land based bombers. These gigantic American carriers could probably survive several conventional hits, but a nuclear strike would be fatal.

Yet Soviet Naval strategy places considerable emphasis on nuclear strikes to overwhelm enemy naval forces. The Soviets believe, probably correctly, that opting to use nuclear weapons at sea would be less escalatory and therefore less dangerous. Such a decision could present a possibility of winning the sea battle despite the relative inferiority of their naval forces. The nuclear capabilities of US naval forces do not play as prominent a role as in Soviet strategy. It is generally accepted by NATO's naval strategists that the Warsaw Pact is less likely to gain the upper hand at sea without resorting to nuclear weapons.[9]

Generally speaking European naval opinion believes that the Soviet navy lacks the capabilities to sustain a lengthy naval engagement on the high seas. But with its vast number of Cruise missiles, it could probably inflict serious damage on Western navies if it were to initiate a first-strike attack. If executed with nuclear weapons, such an attack could be decisive since a great deal of NATO's naval power is concentrated in its carrier battle groups.

One of the greatest successes in the Soviet naval build-up, it was noted in Europe, is the evolution of the amphibious force. It consists of five regiments of 12 000 infantry troops, an amphibious sealift fleet of 86 ships, 26 suitable for extended operations and open-ocean transit. This force is dispersed among four fleets – two in the Pacific and one each in the Baltic and Black Sea. However, any large scale amphibious assault must include regular ground force units restricting the range of operation. Despite current limited capabilities, two deployments have particularly aided this facet of naval operations. First, the Ivan Rogov-class amphibious ship, a 13 000 ton vessel, is nearly three times the size of previous Soviet amphibious ships. This deployment was recently observed in the Indian Ocean. Second, the construction of a 40 000 ton replenishment oiler has improved sea-borne logistical support for sustained open-ocean operations.

In peacetime, the presence of naval infantry troops on amphibious ships, part of small naval task groups, enhances the diplomatic value of a naval show in the Third World and on the northern and southern flanks of NATO. NATO noted the various amphibious ships in operation in the Mediterranean, Indian Ocean, and as part of the patrol off West Africa. Soviet naval ships visits to Third World countries often build up their prestige and influence in the region. If this naval presence occurs with regularity, NATO chiefs fear that local governments may be persuaded to become de facto Soviet bases. The British naval staff perceived that the Soviet Union was determined to produce an ocean-going balanced navy appropriate as a coercive diplomatic instrument in peacetime.

During wartime, naval forces are expected to contribute to the defence of the Soviet Union and its allies against maritime strategic nuclear strikes (SSBN). Moreover, the navy is supposed to provide offensive retaliatory SSBN strikes. It is also essential to all forms of attack from sea and providing support for ground forces when necessary. It is quite evident the Soviets are prepared to conduct ocean warfare on a conventional and nuclear basis.[10]

Today, the Soviet Union is engaged in a period of change from a sea-denial navy to one that will look much like the US Navy. The construction of large deck aircraft carriers, which are probably nuclear propelled, is well under way. Until recently, the Soviets had only three small carriers never trying to match the US carrier force. These new ships are not intended to fight the US fleet but provide control of the air and sea support for direct and indirect intervention in the Third World. The development of the Oscar-class submarine and the Backfire B strike aircraft will help to defeat US surface naval forces that may attempt to counter Soviet actions in the Third World as well as to deny US forces access to the sea approaches of the Soviet Union. There is also considerable development of the command, control, reconnaissance, and communication systems for directing worldwide naval operations. From the perspective of NATO it was clear that the Soviet capacity to disrupt the reinforcement of Europe from across the Atlantic meant that any notion that NATO would fight a protracted war in Europe was a non-starter.[11]

In the mid-1980s, the Soviet Union has the world's largest fleet in number of warships. In terms of displacement, the fleet is second only to the US. The US tonnage advantage is due primarily to the relatively few large aircraft carriers and amphibious helicopters. Current trends in Soviet naval construction could lead to equality in tonnage by about the year 2000. This will almost certainly be true if the current long-range shipbuilding programme developed by US Secretary of the Navy, John Lehman is curtailed.[12]

Direct comparisons of US and Soviet fleets are useful but it is recognized by the Europeanists in NATO that they cannot be considered absolute indicators of relative strength. The two super-powers construct different kinds of ships for different missions that require different tactics. The Soviet procurement philosophy is based upon the belief of producing adequate equipment rather than the best. Despite the enormous progress of this naval transformation over the last three decades, the Soviet Navy is confronted with a few serious problems. It suffers from several labour and quality control difficulties. In addition, there have been some significant accidents and losses in the fleet. A November-Class nuclear submarine sank off the coast of Spain in 1970 and a few Kashin-Class destroyers caught fire and blew up in the Black Sea in 1974. Often, the attention of the West is centred on recent commission of combatant classes in the Soviet Navy. Yet, little attention is given to the most critical weak link in Soviet naval power – at-sea logistical capability. Soviet at-sea logistics resemble the methods and procedures developed thirty years ago when the navy was a coastal defence force. When looking at the Soviet Navy, it is just as important to analyse its weaknesses as its strengths.

The Soviet manoeuvres in the Norwegian Sea in the spring of 1984 provided the West with additional information for evaluating its navy. New ships like the Udaloy and Sovremenny Class guided missile destroyers were displayed along with the 820 foot 22 000 ton nuclear powered cruiser, Kirov.[13] More importantly, it indicated how seriously the Soviet Union regards the latest shift in NATO naval strategy of maintaining control of Norway and its sea in event of a Soviet attack on Western Europe. This change in NATO naval strategy moves what was long thought to be the primary defence line from the Greenland–Iceland–UK gap to a position close to the Soviet Union. NATO's goal is to bottle up Soviet fleets before they can reach the open Atlantic and hinder US reinforcement of its European allies. Many of NATO's naval defence planners were impressed by the Soviet sea-readiness particularly by their shadowing of NATO's Teamwork exercise in March 1984. Control over the Norwegian Sea is a principal tenet of Warsaw Pact naval strategy which aims to interdict Western sea lines of communication and prevent US aircraft carriers from interfering with the land battle. NATO fears that the naval balance on its northern flanks has moved in favour of the aggressor.

The Soviet Union, then, has undergone spectacular growth within a relatively short period of time. There are important lessons to be learned about the Soviet regeneration rate and their ability to maintain a high state of combat readiness.

NATO strategists seem primarily concerned with the potential Soviet threat in Central Europe. But, NATO is now beginning to grapple with the implications of the Soviet naval challenge. There is no doubt the West still retains an overall advantage in naval forces. However, the

West must not underestimate Soviet abilities to build an even stronger navy to further project its political and military influence throughout the world. The Reagan administration's determination to build up its naval resources and virtually rediscover a naval strategy is likely to promote alliance cohesion within NATO over the years that lie ahead. The real problem for NATO will be to relate these developments to the new thinking about NATO's forward offensive strategy to which the alliance is committed. So far NATO's military thinking has been too concerned with the air–land battles on the central front as Admiral Wesley McDonald, Supreme Allied Commander Atlantic, has repeatedly made clear.[14]

One clear prerequisite of any attempt to Europeanize NATO would be the need for a proper maritime strategy. Currently despite extensive consultations between NATO military and national representatives and agreement by political leaders, NATO's maritime goals are simply going by default. Britain, France and West Germany must press hard to provide NATO's maritime commanders with the resources of ships, aircraft, submarines and back-up they need in the face of the Soviet maritime challenge. NATO's manifest weaknesses at sea lie in the Atlantic area and this capability deficiency weakens the overall goal of deterrence.

But beyond the need for enhanced naval capabilities, there is the need for NATO to achieve early agreement on a design for a standard naval frigate for the 1990s. This ambitious project should go ahead even if the United States goes back on the current memorandum of understanding to set up a joint feasibility study between the eight members involved – Britain, Canada, France, West Germany, Holland, Italy, Spain and the US. It is clear that the NFR 90 (NATO frigate replacement for the 1990s) project must produce a compromise between the different requirements of the North Atlantic, the Baltic and the Mediterranean. Should the European members of NATO resolve their technical differences and suppress their industrial rivalries, then the joint development of a NATO frigate would mark an important step towards genuine defence integration and the growth of a latent European defence consciousness at the maritime level. But, of course, NATO is an alliance of self-evidently sovereign states, and as such, is condemned to deal with the constant conflict between national interests and alliance objectives.

Throughout the early years of the alliance this conflict was resolved easily, for it was virtually non-existent. The United States, having the strongest economy in the world and a unique nuclear arsenal, became not only the benefactor of the weaker Europe but its guide as well. The European nations were only too happy to rely on the American nuclear arsenal for their defence, and on American aid for their recovery. Everyone was too busy overcoming the effects of the Second World War, and all were immersed in the effort to reach a common goal: to rebuild in strength and counter the perceived Soviet threat.

Indeed, the Soviet challenge to Western ideals was the catalyst that promoted North Atlantic unification. The prospect of liberal–democratic states losing their rights and liberties they associated with national independence were enough to encourage the US to treat European problems as its own; and, this in turn, to force Europeans to concentrate on the requirements of economic recovery. By pledging to respond to a Soviet act of aggression on Western Europe with a massive nuclear blow, the US not only deterred the Soviets from acting belligerently but also reassured the Europeans that they could safely concentrate on economic and social programmes for development.

As the European countries recovered they gradually lessened their economic dependence on the US. But, the welfare economies that had been the product of their efforts required too much from their governments for them to equally lessen the dependence on American nuclear weapons for their defence. The high levels of expenditure that conventional forces required meant too many sacrifices in terms of social programmes. As long as the Europeans had the American commitment for their protection they could count on getting 'defence on the cheap'.

The dependence on the American nuclear weapons led West Europeans to discount the importance of their own defence. At the same time as economic recovery restored to them their sovereignty, the grounds for conflict and contradiction were laid: sovereign states must have a say in matters of their own defence for they believe no one can judge the circumstances better than they can from their position. In nuclear terms this could mean that each member of the alliance should have its own nuclear force. Such proliferation, however, would be senseless and extremely dangerous. The likelihood of starting a nuclear war by accident would be increased dramatically, and the international community would be greatly tense and uneasy. Nuclear power control should be in the hands of the strongest ally. Yet, this is in direct conflict with national sovereignty interests, for it denies individual countries the right to change or determine strategic or political views at will.[15]

The absence of an external authoritative power within the alliance to settle disputes, implicitly led the US to such a position. Consequently, the once-again-sovereign nations were alienated by the authority that they had themselves delegated: they now painfully manifested their often strident opposition. This opposition had actually materialized in the British and French initiative to build their own independent nuclear forces. It has been recurring since then in different forms: disagreements in strategy and policy, different conceptions of what constitutes the Soviet threat, and quarrels as to the position of the alliance towards the Third World.

At the core of NATO's problems is therefore a conflict between national interests and community goals, coupled with resentment and opposition to American leadership. In the light of these considerations we will focus, once again, on one of the main forces of change within the alliance, the debate on the 'conventionalization' of defence and the development of a genuinely European twin pillar within NATO.[16]

With the significant development in recent years of Soviet strategic and tactical nuclear forces to a critical position of parity, and even overt advantage, the former value of the American deterrent has greatly eroded. A nuclear confrontation would be most likely to escalate into dreadful all-out nuclear war in which the destruction of both sides, and possibly the whole world, would be most likely. The painful realization that the deterrent on which defence depended was one of such unreliability led, as we noted earlier, to the adoption of a more flexible approach to deterrence in the late 1960s, the strategy of flexible response. This strategy attempts to increase the incalculability of the risks and perils of engaging in aggression against the West by presenting the prospect of controlled escalation to the aggressor. A response would be proportional to the strength of the aggressive blow, and increased aggression would be met by resort to more powerful means of destruction. But, even this option seems to be unreliable and conducive to a nuclear holocaust: NATO lacks the required strength and flexibility at the lower rungs of the escalation ladder. As a result, a sustained Soviet aggression on Western Europe would result in an incredibly terrifying and rapid escalation to tactical nuclear weapons. This would be certain to unleash a hectic Soviet response, which in turn would have to be desperately matched by the West, and the vicious circle would probably continue until all strategic missiles were fired. The result would be an appalling disaster.

Such a dire prospect is responsible for the melancholy fact that the American nuclear arsenal no longer indubitably reassures the populations in the alliance. This is particularly the case with the European populations who feel the danger more imminently, for a nuclear war would affect them before any other part of the world. This has led, as we later evaluate, to politically active peace movements that are exerting significant pressures on their governments, and are voicing bitter and irrational anti-American complaints. This is a clear example of an instance where Europeans resent the leadership role that the Americans have undertaken. But, it can also be seen as a consequence of the dependence on the American nuclear arsenals which the Europeans chose to extend.[17]

The deployment of American intermediate range nuclear missiles in Western Europe created a significant impact upon the peace movements. The fact that a consensus was reached for their deployment became a reason for congratulation over alliance unity and was considered a triumph over Soviet propaganda instigations. However, there was and is also considerable opposition to their arrival. This opposition is significant because it may grow in size as the political influence of the peace movements grow in magnitude. It is indeed possible that a future Labour Government in Britain would opt for total nuclear pacifism and perhaps even a policy of neutralism (this is discussed in Chapter 10). If this comes to happen, a serious division will emerge within the alliance. Americans, who see the Europeans as less than delighted with what they consider efforts to promote European security, might feel tempted to withdraw into an isolationism similar to that which characterized their policy in the periods prior to both world wars. A withdrawal of the US from NATO would sharply increase the dangers of Soviet adventurism in Western Europe, and contribute to the uncertainty of European security in general. It would work to the melancholy detriment of Western interests and to the clear advantage of Soviet interests.[18]

Another incipient danger that the peace movements pose is that their policies could lead to a demand for strategic unilateral disarmament by NATO. This would be particularly significant since Soviet forces are armed with a superior conventional capability and strong nuclear strategic and tactical arsenals. It would leave the West open to political intimidation and nuclear blackmail from the East. It would, in fact, be an open invitation for the Soviet Union to engage in blatant aggression and overt expansion (or at the very least in open subversion).

The fact that the Soviets are now in possession of nuclear weapons of equivalent quality and destructive capacity to NATO, compels the conclusion that it must maintain its arsenals also, even if only for defensive reasons. As Professor Henry Kissinger has put it, we 'cannot "unlearn" the secret of the atom. We are doomed to some kind of deterrence equilibrium, or balance, at some level and in some form'.[19] The West must therefore find a way to 'pacify the pacifists' and at the same time provide NATO with an adequate defence strategy.

Much, then, of the current anti-American sentiment in Europe can be attributed to the feeling that the US as an external power is dictating Europe's defence policies without adequate consultation.[20] Europeans fear that the US is likely to involve them in a war in which they have no interest but which serves American interests. This has led to the frenetic notion that the US is insidiously plotting a limited nuclear war cynically confined to Europe to settle super-power differences without exposing America to the brutal effects of nuclear war. Such notions as these, however unfounded, foster resentment against the US and the belief that the US military is the major cause of international tension rather than a deterrent to possible unbridled Soviet ambition.

7 National Perspectives within the Alliance: Impediments to Defence Integration

The US's relationship with Britain is very different from its relationship with West Germany, despite the supposed equality of all NATO members. The US has a 'special relationship' with Britain which had its roots in pre-war politics and the crisis following the fall of France in 1940 and the Second World War cooperation. The 'special relationship' was always more than a mere cultural affinity. The US and Britain perceived that cooperation with the other was of deep mutual interest. The US and Britain collaborated during the Second World War on the Manhattan Project to develop the nuclear bomb. British scientists and German scientists living in Britain made major and brilliant contributions to the development of the A-bomb. Although the US Congress claimed exclusive rights to nuclear technology in 1946, the special relationship may explain why Britain painfully acceded to this action with little protest. Britain was secure enough in her relationship with the US to relinquish a large portion of her security to the US. Britain trusted the US and had confidence in the promise of extended deterrence made implicit in NATO. Although the US wielded a good deal of influence over Britain with Marshall Aid, Britain dealt with the US as an independent nation from a position of victor in the Second World War. Although Britain was no longer a real world power, she maintained her dignity and her autonomy. More than any other European member of NATO, Britain was a partner of the US which was consulted and worked closely with the US. Much of the military integration and cooperation established between the two countries during the Second World War was maintained. The US and Britain also shared common interests outside of Europe; they both favoured the promotion of international stability.

It is in the context of this special relationship that NATO was formed. The respective positions of Britain, West Germany and France were each different in terms of dependence and influence.[1] France and Germany were both defeated nations in the Second World War. The US and Britain were victors and the major military contributors to the allied effort in the West. The distinction between Britain and the continent was far greater in the early years of NATO than it has been during the past two decades. France tended towards a policy of a united European community, while Britain enjoyed her autonomy and privileged position in NATO as well as her role as a colonial power with commitments in the Middle East and beyond. West Germany was not offered membership in NATO until 1954 and had to endure in effect the status of defeated nation for nine years. It can be said that Britain had something like a superiority complex towards the rest of Europe, something which caused no small degree of resentment on the part of France, even though Britain remained committed to the security of Europe and considered European security vital to the security of Britain.

The US did not initially want to commit itself to a nuclear deterrent policy in Europe. Rather it hoped that Europe could provide an adequate conventional defence. The projected force goals of each NATO country were specified in the Lisbon agreement in 1952. It quickly became apparent that these goals were not going to be met. Europeans were unwilling to contribute such large resources to defence at the expense of recovering economies. Domestic concerns took priority over international affairs. Moreover, the Russian threat was not perceived as imminent, nor indeed as inevitable. It was much easier and cheaper to rely on a US nuclear deterrent for the security of Western Europe.

The policy of massive nuclear retaliation on which NATO's security depended for almost a decade was never explicitly declared or made official by the alliance, although both Britain and America adopted the doctrine of massive retaliation in officially promulgated documents in 1952 and 1955 respectively. It was implicitly understood by NATO that Russian aggression against Western Europe would be met with strategic nuclear strikes on the Soviet Union. This policy was contingent on a clear American nuclear superiority. At the end of the Second World War the US possessed less than ten nuclear devices. Russia possessed none. In 1949 Russia exploded her first atomic bomb. This came as a shock to the West; Russia was not expected to develop a nuclear capability for at least another five years. Although by 1962 the Russians still only had few operational ICBMs, the 1949 explosion created apprehension and dread among Europeans and cast profound doubt on the credibility of massive retaliation. Dr Henry Kissinger wrote a widely read book on this subject. The improvements in air defence made it less likely that alliance bombers would reach their targets. Sputnik raised deep apprehensions about Soviet technological superiority. These factors combined to create the first crisis in NATO – one that has never been completely resolved. The current crisis is in a sense a recrudescence of the 1962 crisis which centred on the actual meaning of flexible response.

The rethinking of deterrent strategy in the early sixties as we have already noted in various contexts resulted in the policy of flexible response as advocated by Robert McNamara. This policy offered a variety of responses short of nuclear suicide. Britain, like the US was reassured by this policy. These countries wanted to avoid the use of nuclear weapons, especially in small conflicts. West Germany, on the other hand, interpreted this as an American attempt to get out of its European commitment.

NATO is and will throughout the eighties experience recurring crises. This threatens to destabilize the alliance and destroy its unity. As NATO becomes less unified politically, deterrence weakens. Political unity is possibly the most important element of deterrence. Russia is poised to exploit dangerous divisions in NATO. Isolationism and neutralism are two alternatives to a unified Western stance which threaten to gain more support if the current continuing NATO crisis is not remedied.

This crisis was partly deepened by the different perspectives inherent in British and German defence policies and how they related to NATO.[2] This can be demonstrated by their respective reactions to various alternatives to the strategy of the flexible response. The differences between the two countries are geographical, historical, strategic and political. Their common bond is an ideological commitment to democracy and vulnerability, in varying degrees, to Soviet aggression.[3]

Britain's sizeable colonial commitments greatly determined her postwar defence allocations. Britain held important strategic assets in the Middle East and was reluctant to relinquish them. Britain was still regarded until the end of the 1960s as a great power and was determined to remain one. Special attention was given to the Royal

Navy, the pride of the British nation and arguably still the best in the world. The navy would be instrumental in potential conflicts in the Mediterranean and Persian Gulf. It provided the best means of assuring a mobile force free to defend interests in such places as the Falklands and Suez. Britain also maintained her air force which had held its own US – British air exercises. Also the Royal Navy's tactical aviation was brilliantly displayed in the Falklands War. But by and large Britain over-extended herself by pursuing a foreign policy which was too ambitious for the desperately weakened British economy. Britain placed highest priority on a strong independent defence and an over-long retention of her post-colonial commitments. In many respects it was this obligation to the Commonwealth which determined British defence policy during the 1940s and 1950s. The British commitment to the British Army on the Rhine (BAOR) was not always perceived as a high priority. Britain's contribution to forces on the continent was adequate but certainly not as substantial as it could have been had Britain not been preoccupied with her role East of Suez. Britain demonstrably refused to meet Lisbon force goals at the same time she was maintaining forces East of Suez. Britain was already overextended: her capabilities were not commensurate with her vast commitments.

The US was content with the British policy because British footholds in such places as Hong Kong and the Persian Gulf allowed them to do things for the alliance which the US couldn't. The US favoured the maintenance of a strong British Navy because it freed the US from having to completely provide for maritime defence. The US viewed British colonies both before and after independence as strongholds against communism and rampant nationalism, which were valuable to maintain. The British could best provide insurance against the spread of global communism through political guidance and, if need be, military intervention. Again, this freed the US from having to station troops in the Middle East and get involved in new and hazardous ventures.

Britain derived another benefit from her colonial obligations. Britain's imperial role brought her influence over the US and also ensured US commitment to Britain's security. Britain was, from a US and British viewpoint, more useful to NATO in an extra-European naval capacity. Britain's relatively modest commitment of troops to the continent was thus justified, to the US if not to the rest of NATO. France especially resented Britain's special status in NATO and her preferential treatment by the US. France initially pushed for Europeanization of NATO and formation of a united European community. Britain rejected this proposition and did not regard herself as part of Europe. It was only in the late 1960s, when Britain felt she was losing influence in NATO and not being consulted by the US, that she began to identify her interests more closely with Europe than with the United States. The seeds of the current crisis were sown.

During the first two decades of NATO, and to some extent even today, Britain was a miniaturized version of a larger power. Britain maintained a balance between the three services – navy, air force, army – that is characteristic of a powerful nation, instead of specializing, which would have been more in line with a Europeanist or continental strategy. Britain sought to maintain her independence, international prestige and special relationship with the US at the expense of integration with Europe. The Nassau Agreement of December 1962, which authorized the release of US nuclear technology to Britain with the stipulation that Britain's deterrent was committed to NATO, was a slap in the face to France. This agreement may have cost Britain membership in the EEC in 1962 and certainly worsened relations with France. Britain still preferred the Atlanticist option.

It should not be inferred, of course, that the defence of Europe is not a vital British priority. The fact that Britain has not contributed as much as she could have to continental ground forces lies in a different perception of foreign threats. Britain has always been aware of the possibility of a conflict with the Warsaw Pact originating on the periphery of Europe. A strong naval force would be necessary to transport troops to the scene quickly, protect supply ships and keep waterways open. Britain has not limited consideration of an East–West confrontation to the invasion of West Germany.

It would be unfair to say that national pride was the sole reason for Britain's rejection of Europe and less than generous contribution to continental forces. Britain believed that France, and Germany after she was granted membership in NATO, could provide ample ground troops for European defence. One reason Britain refused to join the European Defence Community (EDC) is because it would have meant giving up some component of her military capacity and integrating her forces with those of France and other European countries. Although Britain made her forces available in the event of a conflict in Europe, she reserved the right to use her forces when and where she saw fit. Integration in EDC would have curtailed or even destroyed this prerogative.

More recently the British success in the Falkland Islands War underlined the utility of having a modern well-equipped navy and air force. The Falklands victory solidified public support for the maintenance of a competent and sophisticated naval force. It is precisely because of the Falklands victory that the British Government decided not to proceed in the short term with the extensive planned cutbacks of the navy. As long as Britain's armed forces accrue political benefits for the country, in a Clausewitzian sense, it is unlikely they will be allowed to deteriorate beyond an irreducible level.

Another element of British defence policy is her independent nuclear deterrent. Britain's nuclear deterrent is consistent with her conventional priorities. Her Polaris submarine force gave Britain an additional degree of independence from the US as well as France. The reason for Britain having an independent nuclear deterrent was not always obvious. The US strategic deterrent provided a nuclear umbrella for Britain. A nuclear exchange between Britain and Russia would undoubtedly involve all of NATO. There were three reasons why Britain saw the need for an independent nuclear force.

Firstly, there was a great deal of scepticism following the adoption of flexible response. Europeans questioned the willingness of the US to risk her own annihilation in Europe's defence. The Soviet Union might also have doubts about the US's commitment. Britain could find herself vulnerable to nuclear blackmail. If Britain possessed her own nuclear weapons, however, there could be no doubt about their use in the event of an attack on British sovereignty. The Polaris missiles are targeted on cities and population centres; they are strategic, not tactical. This is why NATO rejects inclusion of British and French independent nuclear weapons in tallies of NATO tactical weapons. This attitude was restated at the INF talks when the Soviet Union attempted to include them in a European trade-off *vis-à-vis* the SS-20s.

Secondly, the possession of independent nuclear weapons gave Britain influence in NATO and a place at nuclear bargaining tables. Britain has participated in the nuclear test ban and non-proliferation talks with the Soviets. The need to have influence became all the more pressing once France developed her own nuclear arsenal. Britain needed to stay credible as a powerful second-class power. There is an element of national pride involved in desiring an independent nuclear force. This is bolstered by the tangible benefits of upgrading one's status to a significant independent nuclear power as implied in the Trident procurement programme. Britain's motivation differed from France's. De Gaulle wished to establish independence from the US and NATO. Gaullist policies culminated in a French withdrawal from

NATO in 1966. Britain was not antagonistic towards NATO but sought to achieve more influence in it and make it more credible. The creation of the Nuclear Planning Group (NPG) was largely a British achievement.

A third reason for Polaris is the uncertainty about NATO's future and a US withdrawal. The US and Europe have different security requirements. A non-nuclear Britain without US protection would be vulnerable to Soviet and even conceivably prospective Third World nuclear blackmail. An American shift towards isolationism could lead to French neutrality in the Swedish mode and the possibility of Germany going nuclear. Britain's nuclear force is an ultimate security guarantee against unwelcome changes in international alignments. This aspect of the nuclear issue could assume greater importance in the years that lie ahead. Moreover, this justification for an updated British deterrent is no less applicable today even though the US has stationed Cruise missiles in Britain. Any attack on Britain would involve the US because of the existence of both the indigenous deterrent and the US controlled Cruise missiles. For Britain, on the other hand, it may be a question of survival. An over-extended America may be insensitive to British priorities. Today this is rendered less likely since the respective fate of Britain and the US are inextricably linked by the advanced weapons-connection. American Cruise missiles in England also make this coupling. This coupling is the life-blood of an interdependent relationship.

Britain's nuclear weapons have had until recently bipartisan support, even though the Labour Party has periodically advocated unilateral disarmament. When the Labour Party has held a majority in Parliament it has failed to follow through on its promises. Yet when the Labour Party has been in the opposition it has always made unilateral disarmament an issue (in order to exploit pacifist sentiment and fear of nuclear war to its electoral advantage). This has in the past been chiefly a political ploy, not a serious goal. Today, given Labour's new radical posture this anti-nuclear commitment is more than just a declaratory commitment. (See Chapter 9.) This phenomenon is also evident in West Germany. The SPD now opposes the Pershing and Cruise missiles but when Helmut Schmidt was Chancellor he favoured them. Of course, when a party comes to power it feels a responsibility for the security of the nation whereas in opposition it enjoys the freedom to criticize the government without any consequences.

The utility of unilateral disarmament is dubious. A non-nuclear Britain would not make nuclear war less likely. Indeed Britain, because of her geographical location, would sustain extensive devastation from nuclear fallout in the event of a nuclear exchange between the superpowers. Britain is going to be affected by any nuclear war, whether she is struck directly or not. It would be unwise to give up the degree of influence over nuclear policies of NATO and the US which possession of nuclear weapons affords.

It has been suggested periodically that one function of the independent nuclear force is to 'trigger' the use of American weapons. This notion is not credible and is unfair to Britain. Britain would only use nuclear weapons if her security were threatened in a last resort to avoid total defeat. British nuclear weapons serve only as a deterrent. It is irrational to think Britain would use them in response to anything less than a threat to her survival. Any use of British nuclear weapons would certainly involve Soviet retaliation against Britain. Britain could ill-afford any nuclear attack, however limited. The entire country could be destroyed with less than six warheads. Britain cannot afford a national policy of controlled nuclear escalation. Any use of the British nuclear arsenal is paramount to mutual suicide for the countries involved.

In Britain the defence debate has revolved around economic costs. Britain does not base defence spending entirely on estimates of the Soviet threat but on the spending of NATO allies. Britain has been reluctant to commit forces to the continent and has increasingly linked her defence contribution to that of France and other NATO members. This is consistent with Britain's perception of foreign threats. England has always been threatened in places away from her shores. In the past she has been challenged by France, Spain and Italy on the high seas. Britain believes that reductions in BAOR do not harm NATO's defensive position but cast doubt on Britain's commitment to NATO. BAOR is a political rather than a strategic commitment. This therefore makes BAOR susceptible to defence cuts in the years that lie ahead and reveals that Britain regards the defence of German territory as subject to redefinition.

But for West Germany, Central European security is synonymous with Western German security.[4] Germany has never been a great naval or air power even though Hitler's airforce played a decisive part in the early stages of the Second World War. She has based her military on ground forces. Historically Germany has been a nation surrounded by hostile forces. Many wars have been fought on her soil. Germany has had no colonial holdings since the First World War. West Germany's fate lies entirely in Central Europe.

West Germany's exposed position as the NATO nation closest to the

Warsaw Pact accounts for much of her defence preferences. In the event of a super-power confrontation in Europe, West Germany will be the battle ground. This is acknowledged in both NATO and Warsaw Pact strategies. West Germany's population is densely concentrated in a relatively small area; she is only 80 miles wide at her narrowest part.[5] Even a conventional war would inflict unacceptable damage on Germany and cost millions of German lives. It has been estimated that a conventional war would be almost as destructive as a nuclear war from Germany's point of view. West Germany's defence policy emphasizes deterrence rather than defence. Germany wants to prevent any war, not just nuclear war. Neither of the two divided German states can gain from a war of any kind in the nuclear-missile age.

West Germany has always rejected a conventional defence of Europe. She wants to keep the nuclear threshold relatively low. The Germans want there to be no doubt that any war in Europe will escalate into a nuclear war. Any heightening of the nuclear threshold may tempt the Russians into adventurism if they believe a war in Europe would remain conventional. Conventional forces should serve as a device to trigger a nuclear response, according to Western German strategic thought. These conventional forces should be positioned as far forward as possible, to avoid invasion and occupation of West Germany by enemy troops. This has been the rationale behind NATO's forward defence strategy because once Warsaw Pact forces break through the forward line nuclear weapons will be used. There is no alternative other than surrender. It would take six weeks to get reserves to Europe from the US. Western Germany wants to keep the front line forces elaborate enough to delay a massive Soviet attack in order to make it obvious to Moscow that any war must go nuclear. A withdrawal of American troops from Germany would be consistent with such a strategy, as Henry Kissinger pointed out in his 1984 article in *Time* magazine. The presence of American troops in Germany is a symbolic coupling of US and German defence. As far as the Germans are concerned these troops are not supposed to provide absolute defence.

West Germany did not, of course, become a member of NATO until 1954. The Paris Agreements allowed Western Germany to rearm and contribute to European defence. She was not permitted to use her forces outside of Germany or a NATO context. She was also solemnly forbidden to manufacture nuclear weapons on her soil or to possess her own nuclear weapons. All nuclear weapons – with exception of some dual-key systems – in Western Germany are under US control. West

Germany has neither positive nor negative control (veto power) over long-range theatre systems, only consultative privileges. Since joining NATO, West Germany has been one of the most cooperative members of the alliance in terms of defence contributions. Germany had to adapt from an attempted conventional defence to massive retaliation and back to flexible response, with increased emphasis on conventional forces, within a decade. The policy of flexible response raised many concerns and nagging anxieties in Germany because it called into question the US's commitment to Germany. Some Germans perceived that the US was not willing to risk its own destruction in defence of Germany and was looking for a way out of its nuclear commitment. Germany did not protest too loudly, however. She did not possess the influence in NATO that Britain and France did, until that is, Western Germany began to contribute a large number of conventional forces to NATO. Influence is a function of military strength, potential for independent action and the possession of nuclear weapons. West Germany is now only deficient in an independent nuclear capability.

West Germany's relationship with the US was unique. Never before had a major country depended so substantially on another for her security. Germany, as a defeated nation and latecomer to NATO, had to accept an inferior position. She did not at first have the degree of influence Britain and France did but she had more at stake in the cohesion and effectiveness of NATO than any other country.

West Germany is prohibited from possessing nuclear weapons or manufacturing them on German soil. The reasons for this were not entirely articulated at the time of the Paris Agreements and have become less relevant over the years. Certainly French apprehensions about a rearmed Germany so soon after the Second World War were a major factor in the restriction. West Germany was not considered to have any revanchiste ambitions. The Western German economy had recovered remarkably; she was politically stable. Despite these assets, allowing Germany to rearm conventionally nine years after the Second World War was a large concession for the French to make. To allow Germany to have nuclear weapons in the mid-1950s would have been too unsettling for France, to say nothing of the likely Russian reaction. Russia's fear of Germany indeed persists to this day, a result of being overrun twice in this century by German armies and coming within a few weeks of being defeated.

One result of German dependency was an alternative solution to her security dilemma – Ostpolitik. Ostpolitik was a version of *détente* between West Germany and Eastern Europe. It involved trade, cultural exchange and a move towards normalization of relations to defuse tensions. Ostpolitik was engineered by the then Chancellor Willy Brandt in the late 1960s. Brandt's loyalty to NATO and the West was beyond question. Through Ostpolitik Brandt had two objectives – to increase West German security and work towards a semi-political reunification of East and West Germany. The concept of two states within one nation was born.

Ostpolitik created some concern in the US where some Americans accused Germany of shifting towards the Warsaw Pact and appeasing Russia. The Germans did not consider Ostpolitik incompatible with NATO's goals. They considered themselves as possible mediators between East and West, while remaining firmly entrenched within a NATO framework. Germany considered herself more responsive to Eastern Europe and better able to understand their problems than other Western nations. The US at times thought Germany was too lenient and generous in assessing Soviet actions and intentions. The Russian invasion of Afghanistan and the Soviet pipeline were issues on which US and German opinions diverged. Germany has had some difficulty justifying the juxtaposition of Ostpolitik and NATO commitment. To Germany the two are not contradictory but complementary; they minimize the threat from the East while ensuring national security in the event a threat arises. Only in the context of NATO, with US backing, is Western Germany in a position to initiate and sustain Ostpolitik.

The difference between German and US policies lies in the fact that Germany has a higher ideological threshold in relation to the East. A policy of peaceful coexistence is vital to Germany's survival, especially in the eventuality of a break-up of NATO. The US can afford to wage an ideological war with the Soviet Union. Germany lacks the resources and is too close to the enemy to afford such a policy. The NATO alliance is a defensive alliance intended to deter aggression. This aspect of NATO is basic to German security. NATO was built on the cornerstone of US strategic nuclear forces. However, Germany regards many of the US's policies towards the Soviet Union as aggressive and antagonistic. US and Germany also disagree on many extra-European issues such as the Third World and Central America. This dissent is sometimes believed to be divisive and destructive to NATO's political unity. What are sometimes termed crises are often nothing more than normal differences of opinion to be expected in an alliance of independent nations. Germany has never questioned the need to maintain a credible deterrent, although she has disagreed over the best deterrent strategy. West Germany does not under-estimate the Soviet threat, rather she is probably more vulnerable to and aware of it than any Western country.

Ostpolitik is a result of the crisis in defence which flexible response created. Ostpolitik was Germany's only means of increasing security. Improving relations with the potential enemy seemed the best way to ensure peaceful settlement of disputes and avoid misunderstanding. Also, making points with Eastern Europe is not the same thing as extending a hand to Moscow. Russia is still apparently fearful of West Germany. Of all the NATO countries Germany has the greatest responsibility to improve relations with Russia, since Germany in a fundamental sense is one of the causes of the present situation.

West Germany, of course, according to conventional wisdom, hopes for an eventual reunification of Germany. Reunification will not occur in the near future but it remains a long-term goal. West Germany refused to grant East Germany *de jure* diplomatic recognition because that would make the partition of Germany appear permanent. Germany opposes arms control concepts for disengagement and nuclear free zones because they tend to perpetuate the partition of Germany. The only way to reunification lies in improving relations with Eastern Europe, perhaps by circumventing political structures. There has been a great deal of cultural exchange and contact between East and West Germany at a sub-political level. Functional reunification may be achieved even if Germany remains divided politically. A withdrawal of American and Russian forces from the two Germanys would sanction the partition. Western Germany wants American troops there and does not condemn a Russian presence in Eastern Germany.

Berlin is the symbol of eventual reunification for Germans. Its survival is of the utmost priority. Any modification of its status is unacceptable to Germany. The defence of Western Germany starts at the Berlin wall. An invasion of Berlin could elicit a controlled nuclear response from the West. West Berlin is difficult to defend with conventional weapons. The significance conferred on West Berlin by NATO derives from the value Germans place on it. Russia is also aware of the importance attached to the city and has respected agreements on it.

A Franco-German alliance is emerging which could upset the balance of NATO. It is a bit ironic that the country most apprehensive about Germany should become her chief ally. France and Germany, as continental nations, share a common heritage and predicament. France and Germany have been members of the EEC longer than Britain has and they have developed a cooperative economic relationship. Britain has tended to alienate herself from the continent. Britain and France are constantly bickering in the EEC. West Germany, on the other hand, has done quite well in the EEC. Her economy is not fraught with the economic woes which plague Britain. Germany and France share a common geographical situation and share an historic border. The two countries have become integrated to an unprecedented degree. The hostilities of a woeful past have been all but forgotten. France, like Germany, sees the main threat to her security in Central Europe. A coherent Europeanist perspective has evolved over the past decade.

A polarization of the Western alliance with West Germany and France in one camp and the US and Britain in another is a future possibility. This is a situation which Britain must prevent happening, hence the growing British interest in a European pillar of NATO based on a European self-reliance in defence. France has achieved substantial autonomy from the US. She could in certain circumstances provide nuclear security for Germany, which would result in increased German independence. At present, however, Germany bridges the gap between the American and French approaches. President Mitterand revealed himself to be staunchly anti-Soviet like the Reagan American administration but France is not pursuing an ideological and imperial struggle. This appeals to Germany and is more consistent with her own foreign policy than the American ideologically motivated approach. Germany is fearful that the US will drag her fortuitously into a war through adventurism somewhere else in the world. The US with its global interests may not be a suitable or an ideal ally of Germany, especially now that Germany and Europe are more prosperous than in the past but, perhaps, less prosperous than they are likely to become once the global recession passes from view.

Great Britain would not be happy to see a Franco-German alliance. That would put Britain in a minority position in NATO and erode her influence. Britain has always tried to prevent close ties between the US and Germany, preferring to preserve her 'special relationship'. As Britain's colonial commitments withered away she became less cardinal to the US. The loss of her role East of Suez strained relations between US and Britain. Central Europe became a greater concern. In recent years Britain has become less of a partner and more a dependent ally. The US did not consult Britain before invading Granada, as it had during the Cuban Missile Crisis and at other times. A British withdrawal from NATO or neutrality would hurt the alliance less than

German neutrality would. Germany has become the central focus of NATO as Britain's status in the alliance has been downgraded. Yet the greatest possible threat to Britain still remains its poor economic performance despite her mild recovery in 1984–85.

West German defence policy is a balancing of two conflicting concerns. One, to ensure US commitment, especially of strategic nuclear forces, to the defence of Europe. Two, to ensure that the US will not drag Germany into an essentially American war which will destroy Europe and leave the US untouched. The stationing of Cruise missiles in West Germany actually reinforces the first objective. Although the official justification of the Cruise and Pershing missiles was to balance Soviet SS-20s, they actually do nothing to substantially counter the Russian missiles. They are as we argued in earlier chapters – a new system intended to link the US strategic nuclear force to the defence of Germany. They serve a political rather than a strategic role. The new weapons lower, not raise, the possibility of a theatre nuclear war limited to Europe. Soviet strategic thinking considers any use of American missiles against Soviet installations, cities or troops as a strategic attack by the US. It is unthinkable that Cruise missiles could be launched against the Soviet Union while the US remains untouched.

The growing peace groups in Germany who oppose deployment of Cruise missiles are against all forms of war rather than one weapon.[6] They make nuclear weapons the focus of their protest but they also oppose conscription and conventional weapons. These are contradictory aims considering that any alternative to the present nuclear deterrent would necessitate a conventional build-up and compulsory military service in Europe and the US. The length of compulsory military service in West Germany would have to be extended past two years. Germany would turn into an armed camp; she would have to tolerate the presence of large numbers of foreign troops on her soil. This would be unacceptable to German peace groups and the more radical right wing, nationalist elements of German society.

Both the right and left in Germany traditionally share an anti-American sentiment. Those on the left, including pacifists, neutralists and communists, think the US is leading Germany into war, perhaps limited to Europe. The anti-American sentiments of the right go a bit further; they resent the US as an occupying imperialist power which usurps Germany's right to independence and self-determination. They oppose all foreign presence in Germany including the US. The anti-nuclear campaign has temporarily fused both groups over a common issue but they perceive it from entirely different perspectives. The left desires peace and possibly neutralism; the right emphasizes national pride, resurgence, resentment against foreigners and frustration about German humiliation after the Second World War. The heirs to the Nazi party have a minor but squalid role to play on the extreme fringe of the right in German politics. They have little influence amongst the rising generation of Germans. The left are the greater threat.

Moderates in Germany are worried about the consequences of a no-first use policy which would involve a withdrawal of US Cruise missiles. Those in power were pleased that the Russian campaign to fuel the peace movement and prevent deployment failed. They fear that if radical elements succeed in removing the Cruise missiles, their next target will be conventional weapons in an attempt to completely disarm Germany. This would undeniably create a volatile situation in West German society, resembling the late twenties. The circumstances would be ripe for a radical solution. The West German government is sensitive to US actions and statements which indicate a weakening of US resolve to defend Germany.[7] Such indications could fuel radical groups which portray the US as a self-interested power which considers Germany expendable. West Germany has been suing for more consultative privileges with regard to the use of nuclear weapons in Germany. This would give Germany a feeling of greater independence and defuse perceptions of the US as an occupying force.

Britain's peace movement is different in character from Germany's. British peace movement initiatives have so far been directed against the independent nuclear force, not ostensibly American forces. The British peace movement is not as motivated quite so strongly by a distrust of America as the German one. British and German peace movements have different long-term goals beyond nuclear disarmament. The British movement is supported by a wide range of political persuasions. These people are predominantly peace-loving and pacifist. They oppose war on moral grounds and see nuclear armament as redundant and a waste of resources. While these sentiments are certainly shared by some Germans, they constitute only a fraction of the larger German peace movement which includes violent and revolutionary groups. These groups have ulterior motives for opposing nuclear weapons. They consider these weapons barriers to destabilizing German society. The British peace movement is made up of worthy citizens led until recently by an unworldly priest whose only but overweening fault may be a foolish under-estimation of the Soviet threat. Some participants of the German peace movement have no interest in maintaining the existing political system. They seek to alter the status quo in order to pave the way for something more radical. The German movement may also be prepared to use violent means to achieve its goals. The British peace movement is a dignified affair with only fringe groups favouring prolonged violence (even the Greenham women restrict their activities to climbing fences and shouting slogans at British soldiers).

Yet nuclear disarmament has advocates within the mainstream political structure in Britain and Germany. The Green Party is an environmentalist, anti-nuclear party which represents the views of the German peace movement (and which increased its representation in the European Parliament in the Election of Summer 1984).[8] They constitute less than 10% of the Bundestag, however, they could desperately destabilize a coalition between the FDP and SPD. They have been quite disruptive of politics-as-normal in Germany. There is, fortunately perhaps, no equivalent of the Green Party in Britain. The Liberal Party platform is officially but not unanimously committed to a policy of no first-use and abolition of the British nuclear force. The Labour Party bases its opposition to nuclear arms on the contention that it is impossible to control escalation or win a nuclear war. It advocates never using nuclear weapons but recognizes – or some of its more responsible leaders do – that they do introduce uncertainty and in that sense deter. The Campaign for Nuclear Disarmament is the oldest anti-nuclear organization in the world and has among its members Labour and Liberal members of Parliament. CND is a mainstream organization with a popular base of support, a result of its long almost Fabian-like tradition. It draws its members from a broad left-wing spectrum of society. The Green Party and German peace movement are more obviously vocal minorities on the fringes of the political arena. This curiously enough makes them less of a threat to traditional defence policies than their British counterparts: Labour is likely to win the next election in 1988.

A number of alternative NATO strategies intended to strengthen credibility and reassurance have been proposed in recent years. The proposals can be divided into two groups – those which involve a transition from nuclear to conventional weapons and all the others. The majority fall under the former category. Conventional defence raises a number of difficulties which have thus far prevented an implementation of alternative policies. A conventional build-up requires a reinstatement of conscription in Britain and the US. A draft would be politically unpopular and few politicians are willing to advocate it; a conventional build-up is also increasingly expensive and would mean a hoist of more than 3% in the NATO defence budget. It requires more popular support and participation than a nuclear defence. Defence structures can absorb nuclear weapons relatively easily; they require little manpower to maintain and operate. Nuclear weapons can be deployed against the known political will of the population. A conventional defence is dependent on political will. Britain doesn't want conscription and is reluctant to contribute additional conventional forces to the continent. An increase in conventional spending would not be well received in Britain and a Labour Government would diminish it still further. Germany opposes any distinction between conventional and nuclear weapons because it weakens international laws against all war. The West German government emphasizes that 'special emphasis on the renunciation of one form of force – the first use of nuclear weapons – decreases the importance of the general prohibition against the use of force laid down in article 2 of the UN Charter, resulting for all practical purposes in a diminution of the prohibition against the use of conventional force'. A large conventional force stationed in Germany would turn the country into a military camp, another reason why the Germans are not disposed towards favouring all-out conventional defence.[9]

Another alternative which deserves consideration, as we suggested earlier in this book, is the creation of a German nuclear force. This would remove any doubt about nuclear weapons being used in an attack on Germany. It would also allow the Germans to confront their own security problems and make strategy decisions on their own, freeing the US from responsibility and criticism. Germany is a stable representative democracy and has the most prosperous economy in Europe. Surely she can be trusted with nuclear weapons? Still, conventional wisdom believes that a nuclear Germany would be unsettling to Britain and especially France. It would require a modification of the 1954 Paris Agreements. If Germany, the richest nation in Europe, had nuclear weapons she would be the most powerful nation in Europe as well, with the potential to become a third super-power. No country, including Germany, desires this destabilizing situation. Germany is happy to be free of the responsibility of nuclear weapons. Britain and France persistently oppose it because it would erode their influence in European affairs. Finally, it would be most troubling to Russia which is apprehensive of a revanchiste Germany. Russian memories of both world wars are still salient and cause the Soviets to fear a dominant Germany, for understandable, if no longer justifiable reasons. A nuclear Germany could create a crisis in East–West relations. Yet we believe that this crisis must one day be faced

Europe could become more self-reliant for defence as the US becomes less willing to pay more for it and then find her allies deserting her in times of political crisis, i.e. economic sanctions and condemnation of the USSR for actions in Poland and Afghanistan. European self-reliance would require greater cooperation between Britain and France. British and French nuclear forces could be combined into a European nuclear deterrent. Britain is not anxious to shoulder a greater share of the conventional defence burden. She is happy with the US providing most of Europe's defence. Britain fears being without American protection and losing the special relationship. British reliance on America is older than the alliance itself. The US has consulted Britain on military and political matters more often than any other nation. If NATO disbands Britain will surely lose influence in world affairs.

Great Britain and West Germany are members of an alliance intended to deter Soviet aggression and, if need arises, defend Western Europe. They share a common interest in ensuring the security of Western Europe. There has been no wavering in either country's commitment to NATO. Different geographical locations, relationships with the US and military traditions colour the way each country views the Soviet threat and the best way to deter it.[10] Germany has had less autonomy in the alliance and therefore more reason to feel victimized by it. Britain has less at stake in the success of deterrence, at least in preventing all aggression, than does Germany. As Germany becomes more important in NATO because of her central location, military contribution and competitive economy, Britain's influence will undoubtedly erode. Britains' economic conflicts with France in the EEC have distanced her from the continent. Meanwhile Germany and France are on the best terms since the war as they are coming closer to forging a Europeanist view on foreign policy. Britain will try to oppose or rather modify this trend but it is unlikely she will be successful. Britain is not anxious under Mrs Thatcher's Government to form a European Defence Community. She would rather continue under the present arrangements with marginal modifications. West Germany would be willing to contribute more coventional forces to European defence, especially in the event America withdraws. She would oppose a withdrawal of America's strategic nuclear commitment or a heightening of the nuclear threshold. An American troop withdrawal, however sensible in a strategic context, could be misinterpreted as a loss of American interest in Europe. It is highly probable – and we think desirable – that West Germany should acquire nuclear weapons within the next twenty years. Some dramatic American action such as a troop withdrawal will probably be necessary to prompt any fundamental change at all in NATO. And it is clear that such American troop withdrawals related to American exasperation with the apparent failure of the European members of NATO to increase their share of the defence burden became a distinct possibility in the mid-1980s.

8 Differing Priorities: the Lesson of the Siberian Pipeline Drama

United States policy regarding the building of the Siberian pipeline in 1981–82 was indubitably dominated by East–West defence considerations. However, the situation was primarily an economic one for the two major participants: the Soviet Union and parts of Western Europe. In this discussion we briefly review the facts concerning the three main actors in the Siberian pipeline crisis; the Soviet Union, Western Europe and the United States, examine what perceived defence needs dictated the United States policy reaction, and evaluate the effectiveness of these policies. Some concluding remarks will generalize and consider the broader implications raised for the Western alliance, and, for the European powers in particular, by this particular drama in view of its importance *vis-à-vis* the security interests of Western Europe.

Towards the end of 1981, a mutual set of agreements were signed by the Soviet Union and several West European nations concerning specifically priced supplies of natural gas to the West for a guaranteed 25 years in return for capital, equipment and technology to be transferred to the Soviet Union in the construction of a massive natural gas pipeline.[1] The project was an ambitious one, including seven different pipelines, one of which was planned to reach from Urengoi in Northwest Siberia to Uzhgorod on the Soviet–Czechoslovakian border.[2] Equipment considerations such as high quality compressors and pipeline tubing were a major test for the Soviet industrial sector. Soviet capability in this area was largely dependent on imports from the West. Despite these problems there persisted a strong Soviet economic motivation to complete this project. The Soviet Union hoped to take advantage of her vast natural resources in Siberia, particularly in the reserve-rich Urengoi field, by establishing the capability to supply pipeline natural gas to the West.

The West European economic situation was complementary to that of the Soviet Union. While strong in technology and manufacturing, the Western European economy was dependent on energy and raw materials. Stan Woods describes the contrast to the United States:

> Although the United States imports nearly half of its oil needs, this only represents one-fifth of the total American consumption. The situation is very different in Western Europe where France and West Germany, for example, are heavily dependent on energy imports to satisfy domestic demand, importing 95 per cent of their petroleum requirements from abroad.[3]

The West European decision to enter into pipeline agreements with the East was merely a logical collective policy initiative based on a realistic assessment of their own economic situation. The American perspective, however, was very different: the strategic dimension was for them the compelling factor.

The United States expressed strong disapproval of the entire project from its very inception. Concrete economic counter-measures were not pursued, however, until the 13 December announcement by General Wohciech Jaruzelski of martial law in Poland. In 10 days the United States initiated economic sanctions against Poland and the Soviet Union. Within a week after this, the measures were broadened to include a complete ban on all technology and equipment being transferred to the Soviet Union and involved with '... the export of oil and gas exploration and production ... [and the] "refinement and transmission" of oil and natural gas'.[4] The West European response was neither as immediate (the first coming only on 23 February 1982), nor as deliberate. It consisted of a ban on luxury goods, '... a mere 8 per cent of Moscow's trade with the ten ... and even these minor controls were subsequently relaxed'.[5] The severity of the United States reaction escalated further as more demanding sanctions were imposed on 19 June involving all equipment and technology, be it foreign or domestic based, requiring an American licence. This extensive and draconian policy proved difficult to sustain and under strong European pressure and barely concealed outrage, the sections of the policy directly affecting Western Europe were lifted by President Reagan on 13 November 1982.

There were three principal strategic considerations which played a major role in the formation of United States policy concerning the building of the Siberian pipeline. They were: the deepening crisis in

Poland, the growing of West European dependence on the Soviet Union, and the potential enhancement and widening of the Soviet defence capacity.

The fact that the United States imposed concrete economic sanctions concerning the pipeline immediately after the Soviet involvement in Poland illuminates one of the principal goals of the policy: to convey a message to the Soviet Union that the United States was vehemently opposed to the repressive developments in Poland, and that she was prepared to impose specific economic sanctions in protest. Furthermore, there was implied in the policy a goal of deterrence against a possible Soviet invasion of Poland. This illuminates the general fact that alliance policy decisions are rarely made in a time vacuum. In fact, effective policy decision-making in NATO cannot ignore relevant contemporary international developments; often, as in this case, an international development was actually the catalyst for the formation of a particular policy. It is often in this way that defence considerations enter into an economic or otherwise seemingly unrelated situation.

Another major American consideration centred on the fact that energy was in question. Without underscoring the obvious significance of energy in decades prior to that of the 1970s, it is important to point out that because of the 1973–74 OPEC oil price-hike, the nations of the alliance very quickly became acutely aware of the conspicuous significance of energy resources. This has led to a wide-spread realization that with any type of dependence upon an energy source, there are associated a wide range of political, economic, strategic dangers and vulnerabilities. It was the fear that Western Europe could become too dependent on Soviet natural gas which became incorporated into the American policy.

A final defence consideration to be considered here concerned the American calculation that the completion and effective use of the proposed Siberian pipeline could enhance the war-making capacity of the Soviet Union. This fear rested on two projected scenarios.

Firstly, to enhance the production efficiency of the project, certain economic and civilian technologies were being transferred from the West to the Soviet Union. Based on the correct observation that in the previous years what had initially been exclusively civilian or economic technology was being increasingly converted to military purposes, the United States policy-makers feared that the pipeline technology would suffer a similar fate going into the Soviet Union. In this way Western technology would indirectly end up aiding the Soviet defence effort.

Secondly, it was widely agreed that once this pipeline was in place, the Soviet economy would receive a healthy boost. The American fear here was that this would provide incentive and capability for the leaders to devote a greater share of Soviet resources to defence. To the extent that the two scenarios were viewed as realistic by US policymakers, and they were readily believed, the consequent policy clearly reflected the fears. Although these were not the only considerations taken into account by American leaders, the resulting policy revealed that these were certainly among the most significant. It is to a critique of these assumptions and of the effectiveness of the policy that we now turn. The episode is indeed loaded with implications for future policy clashes between the Europeanists and the Atlanticists over the issues of trading links with Eastern Europe.

The considerations set forth above were flawed to the significant degree that the resulting policy proved virtually ineffective. The first consideration concerning the relationship to the Polish crisis is complex. Only a detailed study of the political overtones surrounding the complicated Polish crisis could result in a legitimate conclusion regarding the effectiveness of the United States policy with respect to the Soviet Union and Poland. The second two considerations, on the other hand, are relevant and lie within the realm of this study.

Turning first to the matter of possible energy-related dependence upon the Soviet Union, however easy and instinctive it may be to understand the American fears, closer study reveals that the foundation of three underlying assumptions creating the fear was very weak indeed. First, it was assumed that once the Soviet Union exporting capacity was being fully utilized, the threat of a Soviet embargo would become a formidable strategic weapon. Jonathan Stern summed up the conclusion he and other scholars have reached on this vexed point:

> A decline in Soviet oil capacity to the West with no commensurate increase in gas exports would have serious repercussions for the Soviet hard currency earnings and it is likely to be in this sphere that natural gas exports to the West are important for the USSR, rather than any political or strategic advantages to be gained as a result of control over Western ... energy supplies.[6]

It must be added here that the Soviet Union is acutely aware of her dependence upon the West (particularly Western Europe) for technology and manufacturing, the imports of which would be placed in serious jeopardy with any threat of an energy embargo to Western Europe.[7]

A second doubtful assumption underlying the United States policy was that Western Europe could rapidly become too dependent upon the Soviet Union for energy supplies. This argument was always less than soundly based. In fact, studies show that due to the decreasing levels of Soviet oil exports, overall West European dependence will be falling despite increasing volumes of imported natural gas. As Woods describes it '... gas sales will merely replace, rather than augment, West European energy purchases'.[8] Woods went on to conclude that no West European nation, at present projected estimates, would be more than 11% reliant on Soviet energy, and that this estimate was probably too high.[9] Thus Western Europe was not exposed to an unacceptably high energy dependence on the Soviet Union.

Finally, President Reagan provided what he considered to be an alternative package of supply to fill the void which would be left by the avoidance of Soviet energy supplies. The sources suggested were Norwegian, British and Dutch gas reserves, Algerian liquified natural gas, and United States coal and nuclear power. There are serious problems with each of these sources. President Reagan was more optimistic about Norwegian, British and Dutch reserves than the countries were themselves. The sentiment in each country was not very sympathetic to the idea of becoming '... the "gas tank" for Europe'.[10] The expense and unreliability of Algerian gas, the inadequate amounts of US coal available, and the political unpopularity of any nuclear fuel were all mentioned by Woods in his critique of the feasibility of Reagan's proposed alternative package.[11]

Turning to the two scenarios mentioned earlier concerning possible use of civilian technology by the Soviet Union in the military arena, and possible enhancement of Soviet defence capabilities through successful energy agreements, there are several considerations which considerably weaken the case for either scenario. The development of military weapons systems takes a very long time and usually does not develop from only one source of technology.[12] Furthermore, the ability of the Soviet Union to develop its own technology must not be underestimated '... the Soviets have an impressive capacity to overcome their own technological shortcomings and produce "indigenous hightech" systems which do not depend on Western technology'.[13]

The overall Soviet investment in Western technology has not tended to help Soviet growth by any significant margin, only 1%, for example, from 1968–73.[14] The reason for this probably lies in the poor Soviet capacity to assimilate foreign technology due to its '... primitive social, economic and transport infrastructure, a generally low standard of civilian research and development, brittle industrial planning procedures, and a scarcity of technically literate workers'.[15] It seems clear, then, that the withholding of Western technology is probably hurting the economy without having significant detrimental effects on its intended target, the military. This leads us to the second scenario which is implying that any possible economic benefit might be converted to a military asset by the Soviet Union. Here the United States is opening itself up to restricting any possible trade agreements, be they in energy or something else, which could possibly aid the country in general and therefore their military effort indirectly. This would be too antagonistic and unrealistic as well as being unenforceable to be the basis for a sound policy. Besides, the Western European countries have legitimate trading interests in Eastern Europe.

Finally, the economic effectiveness of United States sanctions on technology for the pipeline project was seriously over-estimated and over-stressed. Despite the imposition of the sanctions, the pipeline production continued with almost complete West European defiance and denial that such measures were ever in place. The dissent within the Atlantic Alliance on this issue emerged clearly as a formidable display of weakness. The crisis it engendered was potentially and actually most divisive and damaging to alliance unity and revealed a deep sense of European malaise.

Most fundamentally, despite President Reagan's overtures that the renouncement of the American sanctions was a '... victory of the allies ...'[16] there remained an underlying split between two perspectives of East–West trade. The Europeans saw the situation from an economic viewpoint, while the American viewpoint was almost exclusively strategic. Perhaps the fatal flaw of the American policy, then, was its overestimation of the defence considerations involved. American policy was based on the perception of a global struggle with the Soviet Union. The European policy stance, however, revealed distinct regional interests and commitment to regional understandings.

Any attempt to draw broad conclusions concerning United States foreign policy or alliance relations in general from only one case study would be hopelessly inaccurate and poorly founded. That is not to say, however, that the Siberian pipeline case is not without relevance as a pointer to the need for a more coherent alliance consensus on such issues. Clearly, the United States undertook a policy which over-estimated the significance of the strategic dangers the policy was aimed at controlling or averting, and under-estimated the economic and commercial motivations making up the momentum of the pipeline project which the policy was aimed at hindering.

It is clearly the case that when defence considerations become merged with economic and political factors, alliance agreement becomes rather complex. The Siberian case is of such a nature. In fact, in a world with escalating emphasis on defence and increasing economic and political interdependence, agreements or contracts between and among nations of pure economic or political motivation are becoming rare indeed. It is this compelling situation which leads to such tension and confusion among military allies. Obviously, then, from an alliance perspective if policy is to be successful today, the process of decision-making leading up to the policy must be one of careful balance between defence, economics, and political interests. The balance will naturally vary in each case, therefore, this process must be followed on a case by case basis with no illusions that some type of formula will alleviate some of the inevitable clash of national interests. What could motivate hard and high-minded policy agreements between America and her European allies would be the realization that a policy based too much on strategic issues, for example, may be unfeasible, inefficient, and ineffective. A policy founded too strongly in economic considerations, however, could be disastrous for the security of the allies. Finally, without political considerations, the effectiveness of a policy is undermined as it stands a very low chance of being accepted by other involved and necessary participants.

Applying this general framework to the case at hand, not only did defence considerations play too large and economic considerations too small a role in the development of American policy, but the policy was lacking in the political area as well because there existed a fundamental disagreement between Western Europe and America concerning the role of East–West trade. As mentioned before, the former held an economic viewpoint and the latter was looking from an almost exclusively strategic perspective. Harmony in the form of a compromise and an understanding here between Western Europe and America would provide the political basis for greater harmony in the formation of an international security policy. The economic interests which the European members of NATO have in Eastern Europe are not necessarily in conflict with their long-term defence interests.[17] The American failure to perceive this on this particular occasion greatly damaged relations between the NATO allies and produced no tangible gain for America as the dominant alliance partner. The Siberian pipeline controversy however revealed the growing dichotomy between the economic and security interests of the European members of NATO and the United States which need to be reconciled within the framework of a more comprehensive alliance policy based on the promise that national economic interests must not heedlessly be sacrificed for indefinable and unrealizable strategic gains. American policy with regard to the Siberian pipeline issue was mistaken in principle and appallingly divisive in execution. The West Europeans were right to oppose President Reagan on this issue and America was wise to give way once European dissent was made apparent. The whole episode reinforced the Europeanist tendencies in Western Europe and laid the basis for a desire to shape policies which were free of an American veto.

9 The British Nuclear Defence Option

In the contemporary debate about European defence policy the case for a non-nuclear defence option has been powerfully argued by a number of left-wing inclined analysts as well as by those who could be regarded as being to the right of the political spectrum. Thus a kind of coalition is being formed at the level of the intellectual exchange on the place and role of nuclear weapons in modern warfare in which a number of options have been developed in favour of an essentially conventional response to a possible Soviet attack. This coalition of diverse opinion embraces a spectrum from Lord Carver through the late Lord Mountbatten to the spokesman of the School of Peace Studies in the University of Bradford.

Indeed within NATO itself General Rogers now favours some expansion of the non-nuclear option. Such a capability, he argues, would render less likely an early resort to battlefield nuclear weapons in the event of a Warsaw Pact conventional attack. General Rogers quite properly though eschews the current debate about NATO's modernization plans with respect to long-range battlefield weapons. He accepts the need to support the deployment of Cruise and Pershing II missiles both as a response to the SS-20, in order to restore a balance in the local defence of Europe and as a bargaining counter in the current INF negotiations with the Soviets.

NATO's opposition to the adoption of a no-first-use of nuclear weapons policy is sensible because such a posture would render a limited war in Europe more likely. Moreover, General Rogers supports the contention that NATO's forward strategy would be more effective and, therefore, more credible as a deterrent to aggression if the deployment of 'area munitions' were given an extra boost by having possibly some Cruise and Pershing missiles fitted with these weapons.

The deployment of 'area munitions', some of these mounted on precision-guided missiles, would be used to strike the opponent's airfields and troop reinforcements deep behind the battlefront. This enhanced capacity would be derived from the area-impact munitions themselves and since they comprise clusters of bombs within a single warhead would constitute a non-nuclear pillar of deterrence on the central front of NATO.

The magnitude of the resulting destruction would be comparable in scale to that achieved by low-level battlefield weapons. This would therefore prove an effective deterrent as well as being a practical war-fighting capability for use against aggressive forces mobilized in depth and in strength.

This brief excursion into current NATO thinking reveals the interest in strengthening a conventional response to a Soviet attack as part and parcel of the flexible response strategy to which NATO has been committed since the late 1960s. However, the main thrust of this chapter lies in showing the basic inadequacy of the exclusively non-nuclear defence option when applied to the United Kingdom itself. Of course the logic of what follows could be said, with certain reservations, to apply to France, as well, with regard to the retention of an independent nuclear capability.

The well-established arguments in favour of a British nuclear capability are also fully understood by British public opinion which does indeed reveal some opposition to the deployment of Cruise but overwhelming support for an independent deterrent. Incidentally, let us dispose of one argument in advance, the existence of an independent deterrent is in no way weakened by its being procured, as far as the means of delivery are concerned, from abroad, namely, in the British case, from the USA. Britain could still use the weapon as she thinks fit.

The case against the abandonment of a British nuclear capability lies in a careful examination of the historical circumstances which led in the first place to its creation. It will become clear that the strategic justification for a British nuclear capacity still remains valid even though the strategic arguments need constant renewal and redefinition in the light of changing circumstances. The case for the nuclear equipped 'V' bombers, the Polaris missile submarine and the Trident system envisaged for the 1990s, remains fundamentally the same as was the case at the outset when Britain decided to acquire nuclear weapons.

The development and composition of the Strategic Nuclear Force, together with Britain's external role, constituted, for the last three decades or more, the real source of British influence over the USA, as well as the source of independent military power upon which Britain's independence itself relied. In the strategic nuclear relationship between

Britain and America lies the real motive force of the Atlanticist solution to security and, too, a striking indication of the metapolitical relationship between the two English-speaking nations whose interests, over basic issues, have more often than not converged.

The Manhattan Project, under which, from 1942 to 1946, the atomic bomb was successfully produced, was based upon the two wartime agreements of August 1943, signed at Quebec, and the Hyde Park Agreement of September 1944. This Anglo-American collaboration was breached by the McMahon Act of 1946 which contradicted the solemn agreements of 1943 and 1944. But by January 1946, the independent nuclear programme was initiated and the decision to proceed with the actual making of weapons was announced in May 1948. Meanwhile under the Blair House Agreement, negotiated in January 1948, and which sought to establish nine areas of research (none having any relation to weapons), some degree of Anglo-American collaboration was restored. All the same, the brilliant research programme initiated by the Attlee Government resulted in the first British atomic bomb being built in 1952, the appearance of which gave greater substance to the reality of the American committment to defend Europe. The often expressed British fear that the USA might be less than reliable was one important though not decisive, reason for acquiring atomic weaponry. When the decision was taken to acquire atomic weapons, the weapons base of the UK was still that of a great power. Since the British armed forces built their own equipment, a capacity equalled only by that of the USSR and the USA, the decision not to proceed with nuclear weapons would have been surprising in the post-war period.

The Defence White Paper of 1955 disclosed the decision to acquire thermo-nuclear weapons and these were first tested in May 1957 when the programme was announced, the justification advanced by the Prime Minister of the day, Sir Winston Churchill, was based upon a counter-force strategy: counter-force in the sense that the main justification was military as well as political. 'The independent nuclear programme', said Churchill in the defence debate in the House of Commons in March 1955, 'enabled there to be a British scheme of priorities, as opposed to an American scheme of priorities, if war should come.'[1]

Churchill argued that relative priorities in targeting had been, and would remain, a vitally important subject, especially in the light of past actual experience. For example, in the closing stages of the Second World War the Royal Air Force had attacked the V-1 and V-2 missile sites, which in the alliance scheme of priorities might not have been removed at all. Indeed, the old war-time leader referred to his 1940 decision to withhold fighter aircraft for the defence of Britain, the outcome of which determined the Battle of Britain and the course of the war itself. Decisions of that kind depended upon military capability together with the will to commit it to use in the supreme interests of national security.

Interest in a strategic nuclear force was inherent in several earlier policies, as Churchill made plain, and in particular to the war-time effort to effect strategic air bombardment. The interest in the efficacy of strategic bombardment had been a much earlier preoccupation which had been propounded by Lord Trenchard, the Chief of the Air Staff from 1919 to 1929. He had articulated the doctrine that aerial bombardment could be decisive. Even so, the actual contribution of strategic bombing in the Second World War has been subjected to analysis which suggests that aerial bombardment did not decisively harm the civilian–industrial base of Germany. Only in the last year of the war did strategic bombing really hurt the German economy. None the less, the development, in 1945, of atomic weapons seemed to herald a technological breakthrough which, in the fullness of time, would vindicate the devotees of Trenchard who supposed aerial bombardment to have cataclysmic qualities capable of decisive result. This development coincided with the development in 1947, by the RAF, of long-range bomber aircraft which included the Vulcan and Victor subsonic bombers that were due for service in 1956. These were later augmented, as 'further insurance', by the Valiant, procured in 1953 for the creation of a 'Strategic Air Command' model for the RAF. And interim aircraft, the Canberra tactical strike reconnaissance aircraft (the 'TSR-1', as it were), was brought into service in 1950. By the end of 1958 the 'V' bombers were reaching their peak of effectiveness as the strategic means to deliver nuclear weapons, based upon either a counterforce or a counter-city strategy. In fact, in terms of capability the Victors and Vulcans possessed better heights and speeds than the American B-52, the chief delivery vehicle of the time.[2]

With the announcement in the 1957 White Paper that the intercontinental ballistic missile (ICBM), Blue Streak, would be in service by 1960, the scene was set for the next leap forward, to the requirements of complex retaliatory deterrent systems. Then came the great payoff – joint strategic planning with America's Strategic Air Command. This least considered aspect of joint planning enabled Britain to help determine the targets actually to be attacked and, in political terms, could be considered Atlanticist, rather than Europeanist, in orientation. The real significance, however, is that this joint planning was the prelude to the restoration of the pre-McMahon Act situation permitting the exchange of nuclear information, confirmed in the agreement of October 1957, which restored to good health the Anglo-American connection on advanced weaponry.

From 1957 onwards a speedy build-up of nuclear stocks took place and, given the excellent means of delivery, the British deterrent was then both credible and independent. The 'V' bombers gave a brilliant showing when, in 1955, the RAF flew them in the US Strategic Air Command bombing competition, gaining ninth and twelfth places respectively out of 164 crews. The US Administration had every reason to consider that Britain was a strong and dependable ally. Her Suez aberration was soon forgotten.

At the first post-Suez encounter, when President Dwight Eisenhower and Mr Macmillan sought to defuse overcharged diplomatic relations, it was agreed to install in Britain 60 Thor liquid-fuelled intermediate range rockets, each with a two megaton warhead. This move was actually to increase the influence of the British Government over its super-power ally and was further evidence of the Anglo-Saxon preference for Atlanticist solutions to their joint security. An earlier antecedent had been the stationing of US B-29s in East Anglia in 1948 at the request of Attlee. And, indeed, the decision to help the USA develop the ballistic missile early warning system (BMEWS) was confirmation of this fact.

The critical issue was, nevertheless, the future of Blue Streak, which was to supersede the 'V' bombers as the major means of delivery (the 'V' bombers themselves having had their performance enhanced by the development of the Blue Steel 'standoff' weapon enabling the attacking aircraft to launch its attack 100 miles from the target out of range of a local air defence). Cost escalation, the realization that the liquid-fuelled rockets had been rendered obsolescent by the solid-fuelled variety and the search for credible second strike retaliatory systems, made cancellation of the project inevitable. Skybolt, an airborne and air-launched missile system, was the logical replacement. The cancellation of Blue Steak, however, raised the whole issue of the future of the deterrent system itself, and it signalled an end to Britain's technical capability to construct a long-range ballistic missile system at an acceptable cost.

Britain's deterrent force was considered to be essentially 'second-strike', even though it would have been more effective as a first-strike force and its joint role with US Strategic Air Command, in the context of alliance policy, made it a powerful addition to the West's retaliatory system.

The credibility of the British force would none the less be enhanced, it was decided, by the attachment of Skybolt, a two-stage air-to-ground rocket. The US Administration was prepared to sell the rocket and the British Government wanted to buy it to extend the life of the manned bomber over the late 1960s and 1970s. President Eisenhower raised no objections to the prospect, if it was technologically possible, of supplying the RAF with a weapon the US Air Force was going to take into service anyway. But it was not technologically possible at an acceptable economic cost. Two years later this fact was faced.

Following the liquidation of the Cuban missile crisis in 1962 the Kennedy Administration decided to forgo the Skybolt project. The decision was related, in the American context, to the so-called McNamara thesis on nuclear strategy propounded by the US Defence Secretary at Ann Arbor, in the University of Michigan, earlier that year. This analysis of Mr McNamara's was the pristine version of Atlanticist strategy. It is worth recalling its central features:

(1) the construction of an invulnerable second-strike capacity;
(2) the implementation of 'graduated deterrence' in which 'controlled escalation' would limit the chances of an outright nuclear exchange;
(3) the concept of 'centralized control' in which the notion of the flexible response was geared to a process of rational decision-making largely in the hands of the USA within the context of alliance policy; and
(4) a counter-force strategy directed towards disarming the enemy and sparing his cities as a hostage to fortune.

The thesis was a sophisticated concept of a self-denying ordinance in which great restraint would be the order of the day. One disturbing corollary, from the British point of view, was that the idea of a 'centralized control' meant, in effect, an end to 'secondary deterrent systems'.[3] But Britain took the view that the need to strengthen conventional forces should not be an excuse to ignore nuclear force requirements.[4]

British defence policy, in so far as it had to cope with competing commitments, both within and beyond Europe, relied very heavily on a strategic capacity that was supplied by the Strategic Nuclear Force and the Strategic Reserve.[5] This accordingly meant an overt reliance on sophisticated weapons-systems which were, because of their inherent complexity, largely dependent on American technological expertise.[6] Nuclear deterrence came to rest increasingly on a credible means of delivery, which Skybolt might have made possible. Beyond Europe, in situations east of Suez, a British capability required a high performance tactical strike reconnaisance aircraft, such as the projected TSR-2.[7] The demise of both these projects, therefore, made an enormous impact on British defence policy.

The crisis over the Skybolt project was an important episode in the history of Anglo-American relations. Yet it, too, was further evidence of the Atlanticist solution to security. A brief description of the crisis is necessary. For the cancellation of Skybolt raised an acute problem for the Macmillan Government; namely, how to keep Britain in the nuclear business. One obvious solution would have been to find an alternative weapons-system. And one did exist. On the other hand, perhaps, the US Administration might be persuaded, it was thought, to develop Skybolt with a heavier British share of the research and development programme. This suggestion was eventually made. In the end President Kennedy offered Polaris, the nuclear submarine, on acceptable terms, but not before a crisis in relations between the two respective governments.

What the Nassau Agreement provided was a weapons-system actually superior to that originally sought by Britain. It made explicit the Atlanticist option and this the communique confirmed, as spelt out in articles 6, 7 and 8. Article 6 sought to place the British Polaris echelon under a multi-national force (MNF). Article 7 carried a commitment to place (later) the British force in a multi-lateral force (MLF). Article 8 envisaged a commitment to either force. Now it is perfectly clear that, although, in a situation of extreme national peril (the escape clause) the British had the right to withdraw the force from either commitment (that is, either to the MNF or the MLF, as the case may be), the Nassau Agreement was an expression of Atlanticist policy.

Indeed, President de Gaulle was widely understood to have vetoed the British application to join the EEC, in the winter of 1963, largely because of the above agreement (although there may have been other important reasons as well). But the agreement itself was largely advantageous to Britain. The cost of the Polaris centre-sections, to be emplaced in five British-built submarines, was £350 million which, spread over five years, worked out at £70 million a year. This was a very modest investment for the most durable and sophisticated of second-strike retaliatory systems currently available. The cost to Britain of the Skybolt project had been expected, on the other hand, to be in the region of £500 million and since, in any event, that weapon would have had to be replaced later by the Polaris system, or something like it, the total cost of both systems would have been close to £1000 million. The Nassau Agreement was a triumph for Mr Macmillan and a striking indication of the American regard to the importance of the Anglo-American alliance. The concept of interdependence had been dramatically endorsed.

The substitution of Polaris for Skybolt led to the British deterrent becoming an integral part of the US system.

Mr Wilson's first Labour Government, elected in October 1964, took office committed to phase-out the British deterrent. In the event it opted for the retention of the British Nuclear Force (though reduced in scale with the curious decision to reduce the number of Polaris submarines from five to four). The question of what to do about the British Nuclear Force was not raised again in British politics until the arrival of the Callaghan government. Then it was decided to delay a decision to embark on a replacement system for Polaris until well into the 1990s, thus avoiding the need for any decision on replacement until the mid-1980s.

In March 1978, the Secretary of State for Defence made this clear:

> In our view the existing Polaris fleet will be effective for many years and, that being the case, there is no need to take a decision on whether any other arrangements would have to be made.[8]

Meanwhile Government policy was stated as maintaining the effectiveness of the deterrent while not moving to a new generation of nuclear weapons. This policy did not prelude a replacement for Polaris which did not go beyond existing capabilities; the original Labour Party pledge on not moving to a new generation of weapons was made in the context of discussion of the US Poseidon with independently targeted re-entry vehicles (MIRVs) which would constitute a step forward in capabilities. The Government had felt able to develop and deploy new warheads for Polaris and though no plans to replace the whole force existed some effort appears to have been made to keep options open for the future.

There was, then, a major reversal of policy by the Labour Government when returned to power in February 1974. The nature of previous party utterances on the subject were not regarded as binding.

The Labour Party Manifesto for the October 1974 election had declared that:

> Starting from the basis of the multi-lateral disarmament negotiations we will seek the removal of American Polaris bases from Britain. We have renounced any intention of moving towards a new generation of strategic nuclear weapons.[9]

This major proviso was extended to cover the replacement of the Polaris force by Secretary of State for Defence Roy Mason (as well as American bases). When asked in January 1975 when the Polaris force was to be phased out, Mr Mason replied:

> This will be subject to multi-lateral negotiations. We would like to get the Conference on Security and Co-operation in Europe and MBFR negotiations out of the way first before we start talking about Polaris and its withdrawal.[10]

This statement neatly encapsulated the British contention that the possession of nuclear weapons also implied a positive attitude towards arms control negotiations. That the existence of her arsenal of nuclear weapons has 'provided Britain with a seat at the top table is not to be doubted. She was involved at every stage of the Partial Test Ban Treaty in 1963 and the Non-Proliferation Treaty of 1968; she sat alone with the Soviet Union and the United States in the negotiations on a Comprehensive Test Ban Treaty (France and China have excluded themselves), participated actively in the talks on mutual force reduction on Europe (MFR)' and though not involved in the Strategic Arms Limitation Talks (SALT) took part in NATO consultations; and in relation to the new strategic arms reduction conference (START) played a part in shaping America's negotiating stance for the current round of talks.[11]

Throughout the post-war period British Governments have assumed an active role in arms control negotiations.[12] The principle of seeking diplomatic means whenever possible to deal with pressing security problems has been generally accepted as has the need to reduce the risk of the outbreak of nuclear war.[13] The development and deployment of Britain's own nuclear forces has not been considered inconsistent with this positive approach to arms control. These forces have been presented as an unfortunate necessity in the absence of effective arms control and disarmament treaties and thus liable to substantial adjustment and even scrapping in the event of the successful conclusion of such treaties.[14] The Thatcher Government has indicated that it is not inclined to take radical steps in its nuclear weapons policy until major steps have been taken in the direction of international disarmament.

But the Thatcher Government's decision to opt for a new generation of strategic nuclear weapons does not exclusively rest on the purchase of diplomatic influence at the top table.[15]

Whether Britain exercises much influence while sitting at the top table is, of course, debatable. Unless key decisions on Britain's nuclear forces are in some way subject to the outcome of arms control deliberations her negotiating position is weak.[16] The fact is that Britain's forces represent only a limited feature on the strategic scene; the big issues involve the forces of the Soviet Union and the United States. Nevertheless, future agreements may well focus more directly on Britain's forces.

This may now be the case since the Soviet Union has attempted to place the position of the Anglo-French separate deterrents on the negotiating table in the context of the Intermediate Nuclear Force Negotiations (INF).

But the case for a renewal of a British deterrent lies in strategic analysis rather than in the likely impact its existence has on the arms control dialogue. It would be incautious to expect too much from arms control. History suggests that it is a limited process, related more to management of arms competition, imposing some stability in certain areas, than to radical disarmament. The achievements of arms control, such as they are, 'have tended to define the rules of the arms competition (prohibiting deployment of nuclear weapons in Outer Space, Antarctica and Latin America and on the sea-bed, prohibiting atmosphere testing of nuclear weapons and keeping the number of nuclear weapons states at five)' rather than dealing with the causes of the competition.[17] Yet, despite the lack of spectacular achievements, those agreements that have been reached have come only after long and complex negotiations. SALT II – which was never ratified by the United States – took six years of negotiations. MBFR has been pursued since 1973 without a breakthrough. Both these negotiations reveal how complex the questions are at the level of the technical difficulties as well as at the level of building up enough political trust to carry forward the agreements reached.

Merely to replace Polaris helps to shape British defence and foreign policy. This is evident in 'such for a as *Task Force 10 on Theatre Nuclear Modernisation of NATO's Long Term Defence Programme*. It is even more the case in the variety of arms control negotiations in which Britain participates or takes a keen interest. The provisions of arms control agreements likely to be signed over the next few years will help to determine the possible lines of development for Britain's nuclear forces'.[18] To anticipate developments, then it is likely that the Polaris forces – and Trident in the fullness of time – could be involved in an arms control trade-off either in the context of the Strategic Arms Reductions Talks (START) or the Intermediate Nuclear Force talks (INF) in Geneva, but not necessarily as a concession in the situation of a possible compromise over the deployment of Cruise missiles by NATO vis-à-vis the SS-20 deployments.

It is clear that the Soviet bid to gain popular support within Western Europe was the motive behind Mr Andropov's offer to cut its SS-20 missiles targeted on Western Europe to 162, equalling the number of British and French medium range nuclear weapons. In return NATO would have to cancel its decision to deploy 108 Pershing II missiles in West Germany and 464 Cruise missiles in Britain, Belgium, Holland, Italy and West Germany. This would be a one-sided arrangement which would confer on the Soviet Union virtual hegemony over Western Europe. The British and French deterrent systems are not the problem – the Soviet SS-20s are the real menace.

Moreover, it should be recognized that the British and French systems are essentially strategic retaliatory systems ill-suited to the arms control requirements of intermediate forces. They are aimed at strategic targets, and principally population targets (the old British counterforce target plans have since been abandoned) and at present lack the accuracy that would direct them against specific counterforce or point targets. Also French nuclear systems are not committed to the alliance as such and, therefore, predictably enough the French government has reacted strongly to any idea that they could be counted in any East–West balance. Even given multiple warheads the British and French nuclear forces remain insignificant beside the superpower nuclear armouries, with little spare capacity. All in all, the Soviet proposal is irrelevant. If the Soviets persist in including the British and French systems – not least because it appeals to the British peace movement and their European equivalents – then they should be told that the proper forum is to be found in the Strategic Arms Reduction Talks (START) and not in the intermediate nuclear force negotiations.

Leaving aside, then, the place of the British deterrent in the arms control process, there still remains the issue of the global proliferation of nuclear weapons. It is alleged that the British bomb does much to stimulate the secondary arms race; though why this should be said is not all that clear.[19] But the drive to limit the proliferation of nuclear weapons around the globe is relevant to Britain's own nuclear programme in two ways. Firstly, aside from an understandable desire to minimize the risk of nuclear war, new nuclear weapons states might raise direct security problems for Britain. Secondly, commitments undertaken to secure the support of non-nuclear weapons states for the objectives of non-proliferation palpably restrict the development of Britain's own programme.

There are a number of issues involved in the proliferation argument which relate to the position of the British deterrent because of the Non-Proliferation Treaty signed in 1968 (and ratified by over a hundred states) which circumscribes the number of nuclear weapons states to five. Without entering into a prolonged discussion of the proliferation problem, we can perceive that the menace is often exaggerated.[20] India exploded a nuclear device in 1974 but is still a long way from developing a weapons capability. There still remain only five nuclear weapons states. The most likely proliferators are vulnerable states, Israel, South Africa, Taiwan and South Korea, and others who feel 'that a threatening regional power might 'go nuclear' which focuses attention on the Middle East, the Indian Sub-Continent and Latin America (where regional rivalries may get the better of cooperative endeavours)'.[21] Argentina is a case in point because since the Falklands War she is even more determined to become a nuclear power. But even then she could not deliver the bombs on Britain's cities; Britain could destroy hers on any day before breakfast. In reality both countries would deter each other from nuclear war. It is better though for all concerned if Argentina were not to develop a bomb – she could well become more bellicose towards the UK. In all of these cases proliferation could complicate conflicts that are already extremely difficult to resolve and a nuclear war, however much contained in some far-off region, could not but have major implications for all international activity. Nevertheless it is worth noting that 'it is extremely unlikely that any of these proliferators would have the means or the inclination to develop delivery vehicles that could attack targets in Britain (though a number of dependencies would be at risk). For example, the People's Republic of China, which exploded its first nuclear bomb in 1964, has yet to deploy an ICBM capable of reaching Western Europe or the United States. Thus while an energetic nuclear non-proliferation policy makes sense for all sorts of foreign policy objectives, it is not essential for the purpose of preventing new nuclear threats of the United

Kingdom. The major qualification to this point is that, in the event of a break-up of NATO, most of Britain's current allies could 'go nuclear' without much difficulty.'[22]

The non-proliferation measure relevant to Britain's nuclear weapons programme is Article VI of the Non-Proliferation Treaty:

> Each of the Parties to the Treaty undertakes to pursue negotiations in good faith on effective measures relating to cessation of the nuclear arms race at an early date and to nuclear disarmament, and on a treaty on general and complete disarmament under strict and effective international control.[23]

At a ceremony marking the entry into force of the Treaty, in March 1970, the then Prime Minister Harold Wilson, said that:

> We know that there are two forms of proliferation, vertical as well as horizontal. The countries which do not possess nuclear weapons and which are now undertaking an obligation never to possess them, have the right to expect that the nuclear weapons states will fulfil their part of the bargain.[24]

Yet current non-proliferation efforts do not have a direct impact on Britain's nuclear weapons programme. The most direct pressure is felt by Britain's civil nuclear programme. Not only are there limits to British suppliers' freedom of manoeuvre with regard to exporting, but Britain's domestic programme, particularly the development of the reprocessing facility of Windscale, has been criticized by the United States as contributing to the erosion of controls over sensitive nuclear technologies. There is a possibility that under the US Non-Proliferation Act a refusal by Europeans to allow their civilian nuclear programmes to be constrained by US norms, could result in a refusal to provide nuclear fuels in the future.

Article VI embodies a promise to negotiate, 'yet as a commitment it is extremely weak. The obligation is attached to all parties and not just nuclear weapons states. The obligation is to pursue negotiations, not to make them succeed (which is why the non-nuclear powers insisted on adding a clause which at least requires that the negotiations be pursued "in good faith"). The immediate objectives are modest, requiring neither complete disarmament nor even a cessation of the arms race, but only "effective measures relating to cessation of the nuclear arms race". There is, therefore, no binding obligation to do anything more than enter into arms control negotiations with some serious intent'.[25]

However, the signatories to the treaty wish in principle to see a termination of the arms race. The present nuclear powers are caught up in the arms race and are unlikely to be susceptible to moral pressure alone.

It is doubtful that there is any real expectation that Britain will abandon her nuclear status in the absence of a more general agreement covering all nuclear weapons states, nor is there any evidence that 'unilateral action by Britain, however drastic, will have anything other than a marginal effect on the attitudes and behaviour of non-nuclear states. The move to increase, in a significant manner, Britain's nuclear capabilities rather than simply maintain them at existing levels, generated some criticism and served to underline the value that the nuclear weapons states continue to attach to their possession of these weapons'.[26] And this is perfectly understandable since the possession of nuclear weapons does bring a form of ultimate security from attack when confronted by a nuclear power even of superior rank.

Britain could not expect to be regarded so morally meritorious that if she were to renounce nuclear weapons, as the CND would like, other actual or potential members of the nuclear club would follow suit. India, for example, is unlikely to renounce its nuclear potentiality because Britain renounces hers. India, should she proceed to acquire a military nuclear capacity, will do so because it serves her national interests. Pakistan not Britain, therefore, becomes the determinant of what India accomplishes. Likewise, Israel, would acquire nuclear status – or admit to having acquired one – once Libya or indeed Egypt acquired a similar status. That decision would be totally unaffected by whatever Britain decided to do in respect to nuclear weapons – whether to renounce them or to retain them.

Britain, then, made her decision in the light of her perceived national interests. The case for a nuclear deterrent or its renewal lies in powerful strategic calculations which have an enduring quality. What are they and why is a non-nuclear option inadequate as a basis for British defence policy in the 1990s and beyond? We must examine the rationale of the Thatcher Government's decision to acquire the Trident missile system because the case for it is also, by the same token, a repudiation of the argument for a totally conventional capacity.

The heart of the argument lies in the uncertain situation in Europe over the long term in which America's role in Europe could change.

With France remaining a considerable nuclear power in its own right, a non-nuclear Britain, or a Britain with a semi-obsolescent nuclear force, could be in danger of being over-shadowed by Soviet power; together with the prospect that the strongest military power in NATO at the non-nuclear level, namely, Western Germany, could be forced into a neutral posture or be squeezed into becoming a nuclear power in circumstances where America was perceived to be a broken power.

Given the above scenario Britain decided to re-invest in its nuclear deterrent with the latest system – the Trident being the obvious candidate because of its range and power. A not inconsiderable idea in this has been the attempt by the British to ensure that its nuclear deterrent is seen as 'strategic', even though under the Nassau agreement of 1962 it is committed to NATO's regional defence with the escape clause that it could be used in defence of the UK as an ultimate weapon.

The need to retain and enhance a strategic capability is greatly complicated by the emergence of so-called 'grey area' weapons. These are now covered by the INF Talks but are not covered by the START process nor indeed in the Mutual Force Reduction Talks. Yet they could be merged into a future negotiation involving all three levels of negotiation as implied in the resumption of East–West talks early in 1985.

Certainly there are voices calling for the merging of the INF and START process which could, therefore, include in the negotiation the British and French deterrents. The 'grey area' refers to Europe-based weapons which are discussed by the Intermediate Nuclear Force negotiations, excluding those Soviet systems targeted against the United States and US submarine-based systems not assigned to SACEUR.

There is a distinction between systems designed for use against large, fixed targets to the enemy's rear, which might normally be described as 'strategic' systems, and those for front line use against enemy forces– 'tactical' systems. But whereas the differences between a 105 mm 1t Field Gun and an F111K bomber are evident, many strike aircraft are capable of performing a variety of missions. Moreover, many of these strike aircraft are of dual-capability and certainly large numbers of them in the European forces would not be used with nuclear weapons. However, large numbers of longer-range super-power strategic systems could be used within the European theatre. The 66 US FB-111s would normally 'be considered "grey areas" systems, as would the contents of the 10 US Polaris submarines allocated to SACEUR's strike plan, but other systems could also be used against Warsaw Pact targets. On the

Soviet side there are a number of SS11 ICBMs deployed in medium and intermediate range missile fields'.[27]

The British Government, therefore, recognizes that the 'grey area' problem is somewhat artificial and that particular anxieties, from NATO's stand-point, centre on traditional British concerns about the risks which America's allies run when so obviously separated from their super-power protector sited an ocean away.

Clearly there was a need to bridge the oceanic gap by linking US strategic forces as closely as possible with the defence arrangements in NATO. Because of this concern the US made a determined effort throughout SALT I to avoid bringing Forward (i.e. European) Based Systems into the negotiations. These were very much part of NATO and it was felt that they could not be proper subjects for super-power arrangements. Such arrangements might exacerbate European fears that their fate was being decided in a super-power condominium. There was strong pressure from the Soviet Union to include the 66 US FB-111s medium-range bombers based in Europe, which are directed against the Soviet Union. These systems were kept out of SALT II, but European-orientated systems have become implicated because of the US attempts to include the Backfire bomber and the Cruise missile, which though designated by the United States as a strategic weapon, is attractive when considered as a theatre weapon. Britain perceived that a long-term agreement to restrict the SS-20 deployment by the Soviet Union could be achieved by a trade-off against the ground launched Cruise missile. In the event that such a link failed to materialize, then the British deterrent would be there to ensure that America still remained coupled to the defence of Europe, through the possible catalytic use of the British warheads.

The need for a trade-off with the Soviet Union became critical to the West as the Soviet Union pressed ahead to modernize its generally obsolescent (though still lethal) intermediate/medium range forces with the Backfire and the SS-20. Hence the INF dialogue which may or not end in failure. The Soviets appear unwilling to compromise or accept an interim agreement. Of course this focus on the 'grey areas' proved vexatious and complex for Europe and for Britain in particular. The need for the British deterrent in these circumstances appeared that much more compelling given the perceived indivisibility of deterrence and the urgent coupling of US strategic forces to the defence of Europe.

The question of Britain following a non-nuclear policy was, then, a non-starter. The Thatcher Government, in the summer of 1981, inevitably decided that Britain should continue to be a nuclear power, provided that a credible force could be financed without weakening other parts of the defence effort. The issue was that of credibility: how credible does the British Nuclear Force have to be? It has to be capable of penetrating Soviet defences. It was already clear that the Polaris force would become less able over time to perform that task. The case for Trident seemed incontrovertible as the best system available in the world.

The alternative investment in Cruise missiles, though much cheaper, appeared less compelling because they would require frequent programmes of re-equipment. Trident on the other hand has an expected life of 30 years or so. Nothing else, pound for pound, could give the same punch as Trident. The decision to procure Trident, then, became a question of how to reconcile it with Britain's defence programme as a whole.

Britain's maritime force of hunter-killer submarines and surface vessels has to be retained in order to keep up the Royal Navy's role as Europe's most powerful navy. They must be able to play their role in European waters and beyond. The latter capacity was demonstrated in the Falklands War. Also the defence budget – inflated by the cost of the Falkland's Garrison – needed to be stretched to pay for the Rhine Army.

Though the budgetary constraints were real enough the government took the view that the Trident missile was above question even though over the next 10 years roughly a £1000 million a year would have to be removed from the defence budget (this costing has since been revised – – see below). The Trident missile system and its four submarines were expected to cost about £6000 million – a less than prudent estimate – – most of which would be spent during the 10 years for which the costings have since been revised. Britain in 1983 was allocating some £16.4 billion to its armed forces – less the £230 million taken away by the Chancellor.

Defence costs had risen sharply with a three per cent boost, after inflation, on the 1982–83 figure, plus £624 million for the extra cost of looking after the Falklands. This made Britain the largest defence spender outside the United States, the biggest spenders in NATO – absolutely, per head of the population and in proportion to our national income.

Such a financial outlay covers the nuclear deterrent, the protection of the United Kingdom, the air and sea guard in the eastern Atlantic, a substantial ground and air contribution in continental Europe and various other low-level, but potentially escalatory responsibilities from the Falklands to Belize.

The pressures to save costs are now mounting with the Treasury likely to press for a review of the defence budget. However, the Trident Nuclear Missile System is so fundamental to the Government's whole notion of deterrence – for the reasons we have discussed – that it seems an unlikely candidate for financial sacrifice.

But something must give. As *The Times* argued in its editorial of 16 August 1983, 'the time for a fundamental reform of NATO's strategy is now long overdue'. This could yet enable Britain to meet its defence obligations within a substantially reduced defence budget. Trident will stay. But a new strategy could help Rhine Army's role to be reassessed which would enable the UK to save money. Its present deployment makes little sense. BAOR could become a tactical reserve for the whole of Northern Army Group. This would relieve Britain of a huge responsibility.

To renounce Britain's Nuclear Force which has existed for 25 years would mean making a best-case calculation about the strategic environment of the future, say, about the world of AD 2020. This no prudent government would wish to risk given the very considerable uncertainties about the future military balance in Europe. There are obvious divergences between Europe and America over their respective security requirements. No one can say whether Britain may yet have to play its part with France in providing NATO-Europe with a second centre of deterrence of a truly European dimension should American power become over extended in meeting her global responsibilities.

In the meantime, the deterrent provides reassurance to Britain that the Soviet Union would pay an awful price for any nuclear strike against this island. As Churchill once remarked 'peace may yet be the sturdy child of terror'.

It is clear that a non-nuclear Britain would be but a short step away from becoming a neutral Britain particularly if the power balance in Europe collapsed. Britain therefore, should ensure that European balance is restored and held against the Soviet Union. Also the UK's deterrent force must be modernized to the fullest extent possible. As the late John Strachey wrote some 20 years ago in a Fabian Tract (he attacked the unilateralists of his day for assuming that a non-nuclear Britain was a step towards averting nuclear war) that the

> scrapping of our alliances and a consequent British surrender,

whatever its consequences for Britain might prove to be, could do little or nothing even by way of example to prevent the outbreak of nuclear war. They would leave Russia and America still facing each other in 'the balance of terror'. In certain circumstances – if, for example, America were ahead at the time – the elimination of Britain from the balance might, it is true, tend to stabilise it. If, on the other hand, Russia were ahead at the time, the elimination of Britain would tend to de-stabilise the balance and might actually cause the outbreak of nuclear war. Nor would there be any guarantee that a disarmed Britain would be spared in such a war. She might well simply be fought over instead of fighting, occupied by one side and devastated by the other.[28]

There can be no escape from a world in which risk and danger abound and in which the search for absolute security is an illusion. But Britain has achieved relative security in NATO and could expect in the last resort to deter a direct attack on its integrity through the continued deployment of a nuclear retaliatory system. The non-nuclear defence option, in so far as it implies a heightening of the nuclear threshold is sensible, but seen as an alternative to nuclear weapons it would be a reckless gamble.

But can Britain afford not to have nuclear weapons? Most unilateralists base their case on the horrors of nuclear war and are inclined to leave the matter there. They suggest that the way to prevent catastrophe is the immediate, unilateral, nuclear disarmament either of Britain alone or the Western Alliance as a whole. Those unilateralists who are primarily concerned to save Britain from devastation in the course of a nuclear war, which they regard as the inevitable outcome of belonging to a nuclear alliance or from the mere possession of nuclear bombs, usually wish to advocate a naturalist policy for Britain. They believe on balance that Britain would be safer without nuclear weapons and without allies. But the issue is simple: could Britain avoid a nuclear war in this way? It is extremely doubtful but even if we suppose this to be possible the Soviet Union need not actually invade Britain at all. All they need to do is to threaten not indiscriminate nuclear attack but a threatened selective attack on one British city. They would then deliver a note to the British government – whose conventional forces would be powerless to act – that they (the Soviets) must reluctantly destroy one British city a day until the British government agrees to surrender. No British resistance would be possible. Vulnerability in respect of Russia, or any other nuclear power, would be only the beginning of Britain's nightmare in these circumstances. No. There is no alternative to continued membership of the Western Alliance whose forces must be equipped with, at least, the same type and number of nuclear weapon systems available to the Soviet Union and the Warsaw Pact must also retain its nuclear forces as a loyal member of NATO and as a means of ultimate deterrence should the collective defence of the West collapse. Also the existence of the British deterrent could serve the wider aims of British foreign policy. In the years that lie ahead the strength and cohesion of European defence could come to rest on the residual nuclear capacities of Britain and France whose retaliatory systems might, before the turn of the century, merge into a Europeanist instrument within the Western alliance as a whole. Such a European instrument could confer on Europe an effective ultimate deterrent within the framework of a more equal relationship with the United States. To destroy the opportunity of being able to bring about a more balanced and equal security community in Europe by divesting ourselves of our nuclear capacity now would be a betrayal of Britain's diplomatic traditions and heritage. Because of the transparent need to face up to the realities of the nuclear age, in Part III of this study we examine the sombre proposition that the peace campaigners have become the unlikely merchants of death because they advocate a course of action more likely to end in disaster than that which is inherent in the maintenance of a second-strike retaliatory system.

Part III
The Future

10 The Unilateralist Threat to Peace: the Rise of the Peace Movement

Contrary to the opinion which is currently held by many political elites, much academic opinion throughout Europe and the Peace Movements alike, the Soviet threat to the Western liberal tradition of freedom and democracy is a real one. In 1980 alone, the Soviet Union built up its ICBM force by more than 200 and added to its stockpile of multi-targeted SS-20s. Soviet defence spending has increased by a steady 4% per year for the past ten years. Twelve to fourteen per cent of its gross national product is currently devoted to defence spending. In terms of conventional forces, the Soviet Union has three times as many divisions stationed in Western Europe as does the NATO alliance. And finally, behind all of this weaponry lies the conflict-ridden Marxist–Leninist ideology fired by a quest for security.

This position is indeed frightening in itself, but, the international situation is being made even more potentially destabilizing by the growth in size and strength of the peace movements. The growth in power of the peace movements in Europe over the past three decades has been considerably enhanced by new devastating technological development; the campaigners for unilateral disarmament have extended their power into all elements of the public sector, e.g. government, business and education.

Unfortunately, however, the campaigners for unilateral disarmament by Britain and presumably by a medium-size nuclear power like France, for example, fail to see the dangers to international security and stability associated with one-sided disarmament. We intend in this chapter to outline the arguments put forth by the peace movements for unilateral disarmament and to systematically criticize them in an effort to illustrate the grave dangers posed by the efforts of a medium-size nuclear power to unilaterally disarm. The general case against unilateral disarmament by a medium-size nuclear country will be put forth while examining additional and specific arguments against the unilateral disarmament of Great Britain. This analysis will not address in any great detail the problem of what type of deterrent force would be the most viable and stabilizing for a medium nuclear power because this problem was addressed in an earlier chapter. It is only argued that in the contemporary world, a nuclear force once attained and used properly can offer a credible and safe deterrent to overt aggression by a medium nuclear power. Thus the logic of what follows applies equally to both Britain and France but by refuting the unilateralist case we seek to establish the rationale of a European deterrent system.

The first and foremost argument put forth by campaigners for unilateral disarmament comes from the heart. It is the following: the possession and/or use of nuclear weapons is morally and ethically wrong. It is also maintained by the peace movements that if medium nuclear countries such as Great Britain disarm, other countries will follow her example and will lay down their arms as well. The campaigners argue that this will promote peace and stability.[1] This argument is stated time and time again in unilateralist publications. One need only pick up any edition of the British CND magazine, *Sanity*, to find that this is so.

The first part of this line of thought is difficult, if not impossible to challenge. Those who are pacifists in the absolute sense of the word and who truly believe that nuclear weapons are morally wrong, will never be convinced otherwise. This brings us to the second part of the argument. Clearly, there exists no evidence whatsoever that if a country like Britain were to lay down its nuclear arms, other countries would follow its example.[2] The proliferation of nuclear weapons has gone on for some thirty years. Why would any country stop developing a nuclear armament because of the unilateral disarmament of Britain? Middle size countries on every continent are developing or have the potential to develop their own nuclear weapons.[3] The ability of currently non-nuclear states to reach the capacity to develop nuclear weapons is increasing rapidly due to the growth of civilian technology. While there are still only five countries who have obtained the military capacity to build nuclear weapons directly (i.e. United States, Soviet Union, Great Britain, France and China), it is predicted that by the end of the 1980s, at least forty countries will be using plutonium fuel in their reactors. This will enable them to make their own nuclear weapons.

We must also consider the fact that when the Non-Proliferation Treaty was signed in 1986, many states recognized the importance of and need for nuclear weapons as a part of their defence policy and refused to sign the treaty.[4] Among these countries were France, Brazil, India, Israel and Pakistan. Of course, they are all candidate members of the nuclear club. In light of this, it would be foolish for unilateralists to propose that their decision will have any impact at all on other medium-size nuclear powers. It would also seem apparent that in a world in which the prospect of the birth of forty nuclear powers in two decades exists, it would be infinitely more prudent to retain nuclear weapons than to surrender them.[5]

The second most popular criticism agains a nuclear deterrent force for a medium-size nuclear power is that the possession of nuclear weapons heightens the possibility of the occurrence of accidental war.[6] This argument has been put forth by unilateralists since the very beginnings of nuclear proliferation. They claim that medium-size nuclear powers will not have the will nor the capacity to wait out a warning of an attack in order to determine whether or not it is an actual cause for alarm.[7] It is argued that they will have an incentive to over react and will be inclined to launch on the warning of an attack. There is little evidence to support this lurid fear and there is strong reason to suppose that a medium-size nuclear power would only use nuclear weapons in response to a direct attack on its integrity by a power already committed to their use.[8]

A country with second strike capabilities can afford to wait out warnings of possible attack because they are secure in the fact that they can punish the offending country.[9] The fact that a country can inflict an unacceptable level of damage on an aggressor even after a first strike deters an aggressor from launching an attack.

Herein lies the essence of deterrence: dissuasion through fear of punishment. An effective deterrent force is of course, composed of three parts: the possession of a strong second strike force; the ability to wait out a warning; the retention of a nuclear weapons-system not susceptible to accidental or unauthorized use.[10] McGeorge Bundy elegantly stated the case for successful deterrence through second strike punishment capabilities very forcibly in his 1969 article in *Foreign Affairs*:

> Think-tank analysts can set levels of 'acceptable' damage well up in the tens of millions of lives. They can assume that the loss of dozens of great cities is somehow a real choice for sane men. They are in an unreal world. In the real world of real political thinkers – whether here or in the Soviet Union – a decision that would bring even one

hydrogen bomb on one city of one's own country would be recognised in advance as a catastrophic blunder: ten bombs on ten cities would be a disaster beyond history: and a hundred bombs on a hundred cities are unthinkable.[11]

It is clear that it is within the economic reach of a medium nuclear power such as Great Britain to be able to maintain this kind of second strike capability. Indeed the acquisition of the Trident system in the 1990s will confer on Britain an impressive and sophisticated second-strike system. This type of capability induces caution on all sides through the fear of punishment and thereby reduces, not increases, the possibility of the event of accidental war.

The third argument for unilateral disarmament is that it is better to be alive in a Soviet dominated world than to be blown up in a nuclear holocaust. Or, in other words, 'Better Red Than Dead'. It is maintained that it is better to give up nuclear weapons and face the possibility of being taken over by the Soviet Union than to face nuclear war.

Unfortunately, however, the choice between accepting Soviet expansionism and nuclear war does not necessarily exist. The fact that a medium nuclear power no longer possesses nuclear weapons will not eliminate the possibility of a breakout of nuclear war. A nuclear war may still occur between the United States and the Soviet Union in which case the country such as Great Britain would suffer great damage even if just from the nuclear fall-out and radiation alone.

In the argument, we see again the lack of understanding held by the unilateralist groups and peace movements as to the importance of nuclear weapons as enforcers of international peace and stability. It is important for these groups to come to grips with the fact that weapons do not cause wars, they are merely the symptoms of conflict. Were a medium nuclear power to disarm the Kremlin would most likely interpret it as a sign of weakness and the defenceless country would no doubt be subject to Soviet pressure in a crisis situation. Peace movements claim that this would be a better alternative than nuclear war. What they fail to understand is that it is not an 'either/or' situation. This would not decrease the chances of war. Since the knowledge of how to build nuclear weapons will always exist, the way to guarantee peace is not through giving up weapons but through learning how to procure and store arms in such a way as to provide a credible, but not threatening deterrent force.

The Future

The fourth, and final argument put forth by the unilateralists which must be scrutinized is one that has much support within the Labour Party. The argument is based on the promise that Great Britain's role in NATO has been reduced to that of a minor power, especially in terms of nuclear weapons, and that it would better serve its own best interests if it stopped building nuclear weapons and concentrated on the domestic affairs of government. It will be shown that this argument demonstrates not only a lack of understanding of international politics and deterrence theory, it also displays a simple-minded notion of what the NATO alliance is all about. This argument as put forth by members of the Labour Party and other supporters of unilateral disarmament fails on several important counts.

The first is that this policy of unilateral disarmament could undermine Anglo-American relations and thereby dangerously weaken the NATO alliance. The peace movements have already in our view gone a long way in terms of weakening the stability of NATO. As the NATO countries become more and more introspective and insular in order to solve their internal economic problems, they become less concerned with the collective well-being of the NATO alliance. In reaction to this, the United States has been developing strong isolationist feelings which have revealed themselves in repeated congressional attempts to persuade the US President to reduce the size of the American army in Europe. The feeling of many Americans is that it is defeatist to insist on providing a system of extended deterrence to countries who resent nuclear arms (and who also resist the build-up of conventional forces) and their ties to collective security through NATO. Yet the prospect of a weakened NATO alliance could indeed invoke a response from West European countries; the collapse of NATO could lead to the emergence of a great power Europe which in turn, would be regarded by the CND as likely to frighten the Soviet Union into increasing its nuclear armaments. Thus, according to this view the arms race would be intensified by the weakening of NATO due to an Anglo-American split over the question of unilateral disarmament.

The second reason why the plea for unilateral disarmament based on the changing role of Great Britain in NATO presents problems is that it is based on hypocritical and contradictory ideas. While the unilateralists denounce the use and possession of nuclear weapons for their own country, they simultaneously continue to rely on the balance of terror provided by the nuclear weapons of the United States and the Soviet Union to ensure world peace and stability. This appears to be the least consistent of all the views held by the unilateralists. Indeed, as Hugh Gaitskill, the former leader of the Labour Party, remarked over twenty years ago, 'this argument for unilateralism reeks of hypocrisy'.

Finally, the third criticism of this argument for unilateral disarmament based on Britain's changing role in NATO is that it depends on the current situation of the balance of power remaining unchanged for an indefinite period of time. It fails to consider the possible future weakening of the NATO alliance or the further disintegration of US–Soviet relations and the balance of power. Great Britain and other medium-size nuclear powers, like France and China, cannot rely solely on the balance of terror to provide security and stability. The future military position of the NATO alliance and the security of Western Europe is questionable at best. If Great Britain does decide to pursue a policy of unilateral disarmament where will that leave it in, say, thirty years? There are many who would answer that question with the words, 'East of the Iron Curtain'. Thus, we see how on three separate counts, the arguments of those in favour of disarmament from the standpoint of Britain's current position in NATO fall apart when examined closely. Labour's policy on defence is therefore the most contradictory since the 1930s: an uneasy compromise between pacifism and fellow-travelling. This constitutes the rejection of the Bevin–Healey realism which hitherto had dominated the Labour Party's thinking on defence. Today Labour's thinking on defence contains much that would please the Soviets and much that would dismay NATO. Indeed Labour virtually rejects the latter and seeks to make life for the Warsaw Pact a good deal easier.

According to its declaratory stance Labour would immediately cancel the Trident programme, phase out Polaris, and order the removal of all those American bases from Britain which have any kind of nuclear deterrent role. Thus the Cruise missiles would be removed from British soil without any attempt being made to force concessions out of the Soviet Union by way of recompense in arms control negotiations. The policy is intended to foreshadow the virtual rejection of NATO by Britain.

This is to be achieved through the pursuit of two goals: the removal of *all* nuclear weapons from British forces in central Europe *unconditionally*; the rejection of current NATO strategy based on any implied threat to use nuclear weapons, even if this is in the retaliatory role. Both these goals, if they were realized, would render NATO's deterrence strategy totally incredible. Labour would create a situation in central

Europe that would leave NATO deprived of its capacity to counter an invasion from Warsaw Pact forces.

The Warsaw Pact would then possess undisputed hegemony in Europe. It would leave the Soviet Union in sole possession of nuclear weapons in Europe. This would confer on the Soviets the capacity for outright victory in any war and therefore they could threaten a nuclear war certain in the knowledge that Western Europe would have to surrender before a single shot had been fired in self-defence.

Labour's defence policy would guarantee the success of any offensive strategy implemented by the Warsaw Pact. Moreover, it is advocating a policy which best suits the existing war plans of the Warsaw Pact. Soviet defence planning is based on the immediate use of both tactical and strategic nuclear weapons in any war in Europe. They are committed to a quick forward move in overwhelming strength in which nuclear and chemical weapons would be used to overcome NATO's static defences. This attack could be neither deterred nor contained by essentially non-nuclear forces however well-equipped or well-trained.

Labour's policy is therefore both inadequate and irresponsible in purely military terms. In political terms it is based on the proposition that there are no *real* enemies on the Left. Labour appears to be saying that fundamentally the Soviet Union is peace-loving and essentially unaggressive. This indicates a shallow grasp of what the Soviets have done and are capable of doing in international politics.

However the real thrust behind Labour's re-think on defence is based on an even more dubious proposition. It is the belief that there is nothing to choose between totalitarian communism on the one side and the United States on the other when it comes to power politics. Hence Labour's call for the abolition of the blocks in Europe. Behind such thinking lies the concept of neutralism and non-alignment. Britain under Labour appears ready to join the Third World (if not the Warsaw Pact if the hard-left get their way!) with a defence policy nothing like as credible as Sweden's which is ultimately based on NATO's maintenance of the balance of power. Of course, it is true that Labour says that it still wishes to belong to NATO; but what would be left of NATO once Labour has carried out its half-armed defence strategy?

Surely the logic of Labour's stance is clear enough: that a Labour government would abandon not only Britain's nuclear forces, not just the Americans nuclear bases in the UK, but the whole edifice of nuclear deterrence upon which NATO's strategy rests. That can mean only one thing: the end to the European–American partnership based on the American *nuclear guarantee*. The cry 'Yanks go home' has become the official policy of HM Opposition. Mr Bevin must be turning in his grave. We wonder what terse expression Mr Attlee would have used if such a policy had been suggested to him! Mr Gaitskell's courageous stand against the cause of the anti-nuclear left in 1960 has some twenty years later been reversed by a party no longer wedded to Atlanticism. Labour's defence policy has appalled informed European opinion. Why? Because, as Mr Gaitskell pointed out over twenty years ago, a nuclearly-disarmed Britain would be pretending to dissociate itself from the moral discredit of a nuclear policy while continuing to rely on an American nuclear guarantee to give it ultimate protection.

Labour calls for 'a realistic non-nuclear defence policy for Britain in NATO'. And yet its leaders have shown scant interest in or grasp of NATO's flexible response strategy which seeks to delay or control the early use of nuclear weapons in a European war. Instead they talk vaguely of being 'committed to collective security through the United Nations and to the peaceful resolution of conflicts'. Actually they eschew practical measures to deal with the real threat to world peace.

Labour has abandoned realism in defence for an essentially utopian stance which actually ignores the contribution which NATO has made to 35 years of peace in Europe.

The purpose of NATO is to deter any kind of fighting in Europe, nuclear and conventional. It is manifest folly therefore to support a totally non-nuclear (as opposed to a low-profile) strategy for NATO. With no nuclear weapons in the West there would be little or no incentive for the Soviet Union to behave with moderation in a crisis. The Soviets could simply use or threaten to use nuclear weapons at will.

Even the existence of the most proficient conventional forces that money and technology can provide – including the evolving technologies (ET) – cannot cope with nuclear weapons, still less deter their use.

So far, we have examined the arguments put forth by the unilateralists and shown how unilateral disarmament by a medium nuclear power will decrease the security of the country thereby increasing global instability. That is not to say that the goals of the peace movements are not desirable. The main objective of foreign policy and strategic policy in the nuclear age must be the maintenance of worldwide peace and stability. What the unilateralists fail to understand, is the importance of nuclear weapons to the preservation of peace in a global context. Mankind has acquired the knowledge of how to cause irreparable damage to the world and indeed the entire universe. What is more, that knowledge will always exist regardless of the efforts of those who fight for disarmament. Therefore, it is imperative that medium-size nuclear powers learn how to use this knowledge to increase their security.

The importance of maintaining a nuclear arsenal in medium nuclear powers such as Great Britain cannot be over-emphasized. In a nuclear world in which more and more countries will be going nuclear in future years, it is vital that Great Britain maintain a stable nuclear deterrent. The ability to deter Soviet aggression through the fear of punishment will ensure a medium-size power like Britain against the threat of nuclear blackmail. Without a sufficient deterrent force, countries like Great Britain will not only subject themselves to the will of the Soviet Union, but by doing so, they will also disrupt international peace and stability. As we stated earlier, this deterrent force need not be large, all it need do is provide the threat of second strike capabilities against an agressor in order to deter that aggressor. The past thirty odd years of peace between the United States and the Soviet Union indicate that the chances for war go down as the potential costs of war rise. In the words of Thomas C. Schelling, nuclear weapons can serve to deter aggression because of '... the threat that leaves something to chance'.

We conclude this analysis with a warning. Oddly enough, the warning is against the peace movements which are rapidly growing in strength in Western Europe. For, it is they who pose a great threat to world wide peace and security. Their anti-NATO and anti-American sentiments are dangerous in that they undermine the strength of NATO and serve to fuel unreal Soviet ambitions to establish an intimidating correlation of forces favourable to territorial expansionism. The unilateralists fail to examine the potential effects of unilateral disarmament in an international context. Instead of carrying on in this injurious manner, it would be infinitely more productive if these groups would redirect their energies towards discussions of arms control and of how to use nuclear energy to provide a stabilizing deterrent.

11 The Dual Track Decision: the European Dimension

The case for the Dual Track Decision (DTD) was advanced by NATO for reasons of high policy and of principle. It embodied a notion of collective action by the Atlantic Alliance in the name of European security. Its provisions were two-fold: The deployment in Western Europe of 108 US Pershing II intermediate range ballistic missiles (IRBM) and 464 Tomahawk ground launched Cruise missiles (GLCM) in response to Soviet deployment of SS-20 IRBMs targeted at Western Europe, while simultaneously engaging in negotiation for reduction or elimination of these sytems. At the end of 1983 negotiations with the Soviet Union were broken off and full deployment of US systems were gradually implemented. This situation then led to heightened East–West tensions until early in 1985 when both super-powers agreed to negotiate arms control agreements with respect to strategic and intermediate missiles.

The rationale behind NATO deployment was both military and political in nature. The military requirements were for deep strike interdiction of Soviet second and third echelon forces and their supporting command and control networks. It was envisaged that accurate land based theatre nuclear forces (TNF) were necessary for such strike capabilities. Existing systems such as Poseidon (submarine launched ballistic missiles – SLBM) and Pershing I lacked the accuracy and range necessary to accomplish such tasks. The political requirements on the other hand were directly linked to the deployment of the Soviet SS-20 IRBMs. Such deployment constituted, in the eyes of the US, a build-up outside the framework of the negotiated nuclear balance between the two super-powers. It threatened a 'regional breakout' from the delicately negotiated East–West balance, especially for the non-nuclear weapon states of the Western Alliance.[1] It was the unique capabilities of the new Soviet system that brought forth such sentiment.

The SS-20, with its three highly accurate warheads, was viewed in the West as an instrument for nuclear strikes, including limited strikes against key installations in Western Europe. Such strikes could be made without warning and possibly contribute to a first strike option. The political issues which became paramount in NATO's plans for deployment were for the most part conjectural, based on a complex assessment of the inter-relationship between this Soviet capability and the political relationship in Western Europe. The 'psycho-political' theme of coupling between the American nuclear deterrent and Western Europe was put into question.[2] Further, the SS-20 constituted a challenge to NATO (especially the non-nuclear states) in that it raised the issue of selective pressure by the Soviets directed at the countries in the alliance (especially in a crisis). Basically, without deployment, the US (NATO) would only have a limited capacity to launch a similar counterstrike against Soviet targets from European soil.

The US had previously possessed land based intermediate range nuclear forces (INF) in Europe, however, it was considered a short term measure while America completed its ICBM deployment in the 1960s. The US stock of IRBMs in Europe consisted of 60 Thor missiles deployed in Britain (1958), 30 Jupiter missiles deployed in Italy and 15 to Turkey (1959), and 90 Mace-B long range Cruise missiles deployed in the FRG.[3] Upon completion of the build-up of US strategic forces during the Kennedy Administration, these IRBMs were removed. These earlier IRBMs were deployed in the context of American superiority in strategic forces: They could be viewed as elements in a complex balance of imbalances.[4] Soviet SS-20 deployment came, however, in conjunction with the establishment of a rough parity at the strategic nuclear level between the super-powers. Soviet IRBMs, including older SS-4s and SS-5s took on an entirely new significance with respect to the strategic balance in Europe.

With Soviet superiority in Europe and relative strategic parity at the strategic level, there existed a fear that the US would not use nuclear weapons; either because it lacked escalatory option or feared that escalation would leave it worse off *vis-à-vis* the Warsaw Pact. Further, the US might be reluctant to use American Central systems, including Poseidon (Polaris) warheads assigned to NATO for fear it might convey an escalatory signal thus inviting strikes against the US mainland. The requirement for a capacity to strike the Soviet Union would deny the Soviets the position of sanctuary in the event of a further crisis in Europe. The establishment of territorial symmetry with regard to the capacity to threaten nuclear retaliation would prevent Western Europe as being seen as an 'abandoned hostage'.[5] Such an American capability would limit Soviet influence over Western Europe and simultaneously decrease the spectre of limited war in Europe. Moscow's announcement that any attack on the Soviet Union with an American missile would lead to retaliation against the US, created the coupling which NATO was seeking.[6]

Beyond this, the NATO decision to modernize demonstrated its ability to decide on a critical issue. If this had not been established, it would cast doubt on the Alliance ability to act in a crisis. The structure of the NATO deployment was designed to alleviate those fears. In addition, deployment was to have a defensive emphasis. It did not constitute a first strike threat to the Soviets. The limited number of Pershing IIs and the relatively long flight time of the GLCMs was meant to convey this message. Also, it was deemed important to provide visible commitment, thus a land based option was essential.

With respect to deployment, the FRG did not want to occupy a singular position as a basing area for NATO's INFs since it could invite the focused pressure of the Soviet Union during a crisis. Hence it was deemed important that the deployment of new INFs take place in more than one country in Western Europe. It was designated that all 108 Pershing IIs be deployed in the FRG (the 'front line' members of NATO). The GLCMs were deployed throughout Western Europe in the following manner: 160 in Great Britain, 112 in the FRG, 96 in Italy and 48 each in Belgium and the Netherlands.[7] Though in the case of the latter two countries no actual deployment had been agreed by 1985. The new IRBMs would replace existing missiles (i.e. the 108 Pershing IAs in the FRG) on a one-for-one basis.

The Soviet Union followed a different path than NATO in the realm of INFs. The Soviets regarded European IRBMs as separate from its strategic forces, for the US such forces were tied to the overall strategic balance. In light of a presumed American superiority at the strategic level, the Soviets regarded theatre superiority as essential. Therefore their INF deployments were not deemed short term in nature like the initial US IRBM deployment. With the deployment of 600–700 SS-4 and SS-5 IRBMs in the early 1960s, the Soviet Union had long since established a nuclear superiority in Europe. The SS-20 was devised, then, as a more modern and reliable replacement for the older SS-4 and SS-5 missiles.

The SS-20 IRBM first became operational in 1976. It has a range of up to 7000 km and a CEP of 440 ft.[8] It was derived from the first two stages of the unsuccessful SS-16 solid fuelled intercontinental ballistic missile (ICBM); the SS-20 thus was not originally intended to be an IRBM. As from 1983, 243 SS-20s were deployed in 23 sites throughout the Soviet Union.[9] As late as 1984 some 380 SS-4s and 60 SS-5s remained deployed in addition to the SS-20s.[10] They were possibly retained for use as a bargaining chip in the INF negotiations with Europe arising out of the DTD. The number of SS-20s deployed by 1985 exceeded 370.

The DTD blossomed out of NATO as part of a long term balance within the political order in Europe. It gave priority to the political rationale as it coupled NATO deployment to the level of Soviet INFs. The DTD was reached in December 1979. It was a collective decision by the alliance in which the US was entrusted with the management of the negotiations. What was needed – and in fact largely achieved – was a tenable platform for solidarity in NATO thereby increasing Soviet incentive for accommodation. The DTD was formulated with this in mind. It stated that NATO would forgo the option of theatre modernization in light of concrete results from arms control negotiations with the Soviet Union. The DTD was designed then to bring the Soviets to the negotiating table; to have INFs on the agenda, and to elicit Soviet consent on the need to reduce INFs.[11]

Moreover, NATO deployment of these systems was not to be considered irreversible. Indeed the very concept of the negotiations was based on this position; if the balance *vis-à-vis* the Soviet Union was accomplished at a lower level of deployment, so much the better. In addition, collective decision, and the public support necessary for such a decision, was only possible if a link between modernization and negotiation was established.

The DTD did not attempt to create parity in INFs. The proposed deployment of 572 IRBMs by NATO was not meant to match an equal number of Soviet missiles. The primary purpose of possible and then actual deployment would be the ensuing political rather than military balance. Force matching, moreover, suggested a separate European strategic balance conveying a connotation of decoupling which the decision on modernization was designed to counteract. The DTD was preoccupied then with defence equality and alliance unity. NATO was interested in establishing, through negotiations, a right to an equal ceiling rather than actually creating equality in practice. It was decided that 200 to 600 missiles would accomplish these goals; the actual number 572, was on the high end of this estimate as a result of fears that deployment might be scaled down via negotiations with Moscow.

The Americans hoped that negotiations would enhance stability, initiate reduction, be simple in nature and flexible in its provision. The main propositions underpinning the US position in the negotiations were as follows: any future limitations on US systems principally designed for theatre missions should be accompanied by appropriate limitations on Soviet theatre systems; limitations on US and Soviet INF should be negotiated bilaterally in a step by step approach: this reflected the perception that the INF issue should be brought within the structure of the strategic balance between the super-powers; the immediate objective of these negotiations was the establishment of agreed limitations on US and Soviet land based long range theatre nuclear forces (LRTNF); any agreed limitation of these systems must be consistent with the principle of equality between the sides; finally any agreed limitations must be adequately verifiable.[12]

The US envisaged, of course, global INF limitations because of the impossibility of regionalizing the issues in light of the range of the weapon systems involved. Further the US tried to confine the INF negotiations to (LRTNF) missiles rather than the entire range of INFs. In conjunction with this principle the zero-zero or zero-option was proposed by the first Reagan Administration emphasizing the priority of the political purpose of the DTD as it provided for direct coupling between Soviet and NATO INF deployments. Actual negotiations on the zero-option began in November 1981 in that city of lost causes- – Geneva. The zero-option called for the total dismantlement of Soviet SS-4, SS-5, and SS-20 IRBMs in exchange for the non-deployment of the US 572 Pershing II and Tomahawk missiles. The proposal did not include the French and British independent nuclear forces. Further, the zero option put forth the notion that both sides should halt deployment of short range missiles (i.e. the new Soviet SS-21, 22 and 23 systems) as an accompanying measure. It is important to note that the zero option called for 'dismantlement' of Soviet INFs and not just their removal. This took into account the mobility of the SS-20 system and the base in which it could be redeployed in the negotiated theatre at a later date. Modification of the zero option came on 30 March 1983 when President Reagan under pressure from his allies called for a finite, but unspecified equal number of warheads on intermediate range missiles on either side. It included all US and Soviet missiles of this class in the world; it still in deference to Britain and France made no provision for British and French nuclear forces.[13]

For the Soviet Union the introduction of the new American intermediate range missiles in Europe did not constitute a correction of the balance of forces but rather posed a threat to the established force relationship. Pershing II and GLCMs were seen as an additional American strategic option in giving the US the ability to threaten the USSR with nuclear weapons without employing American central systems. The Soviet forces remain – except for those now deployed in Poland and Czechoslovakia – on the homeland, this is the reason they see NATO deployment as altering the balance. The Soviets assert that the SS-20 missiles do not constitute a change in the balance since they are not directed at the US and because they are merely a technical upgrade of existing Soviet Intermediate range systems which the West had previously accepted as outside the central strategic relationship.[14] Thus the Soviet initial reaction to NATO's December 1979 decision was, in light of these views, not surprising: negotiations would only be possible if the US first renounced or at least suspended its own programme.

In response to the zero-option the Soviets asserted that it required them to unilaterally disarm while the present NATO arsenal remained undisturbed. Moreover, they claimed that the decision to produce Pershing IIs and GLCMs was made in 1975, one year before the SS-20 was deployed. Thus the SS-20s were not the real cause of NATO's modernization programme. In addition the Soviets had roughly the same number of missiles in 1975 yet the US did not suggest that any imbalance existed. In a show of flexibility the Soviets on 16 March 1982 froze deployment quantitatively and qualitatively, of medium range weapons in the European part of the USSR.[15] This moratorium would remain in effect until an agreement was reached or until true preparations for US deployment began.[16] In fact the Soviets did not adhere to this act of self-denial and continued to deploy the SS-20s throughout the negotiations.

In the course of negotiations, Moscow insisted on the right to withdraw SS-20s from Europe and redeploy them to the east rather than destroy them as a result of an agreement with Washington. The Soviet Union confined the discussion to forces based in the European theatre. In addition they demanded that the US forward based systems (FBS) be included in the INF negotiations because they threatened the Soviet homeland. The USSR included under the FBS heading US carrier based A-6, A-7 and F-4 aircraft and the 170 US F-111s based in Great Britain.[17] These aircraft are dual capable in that they have the ability to deliver both conventional and nuclear payloads.

Moscow also expressed much concern over the Pershing II IRBM throughout the negotiation process between 1981–83. The Pershing II has the capability to reach its target within Soviet territory in 5 to 7 minutes. Further, with the advanced manoeuverable re-entry vehicle, it is capable of near pin-point accuracy. Thus the Pershing II had, the Soviets contended, all the making of a first strike weapon and as such its deployment was totally unacceptable.

Soviet proposals in these negotiations had always alluded to the 'Nato side', thus implicitly including the French and British nuclear forces. Moscow initially suggested that each side in Europe be reduced to 300 delivery vehicles including British and French missiles.[18] It was insisted that these forces be brought into the calculations because: they presented a clear and continuous threat to the Soviet homeland; the US supplied the technology of a considerable part of the British force and that these forces (warheads) were targeted by the US; finally, because French submarine patrols were also coordinated with the US.

On 21 December 1982 Andropov rather dramatically proposed a sub-level within the proposed ceiling of 300 delivery vehicles. It would permit the USSR as many misiles as in British and French nuclear forces, numbering 162. The number of Soviet missiles could be reduced, even to zero, if British and French systems were likewise reduced. The Soviets referred to this as their 'zero-option'.[19] Inherent in the proposal was the Soviet inclination to count delivery vehicles which contrasted with the American inclination to count deliverable warheads. Though, Andropov did announce on 4 May 1983 that the USSR was prepared to have no more warheads and missiles than NATO and would reduce to the same number of warheads on the British and French missiles.[20] By counting warheads, the Soviets were able to claim that Britain and France had a total of 434 thus Moscow must be allowed 145 SS-20s with three re-entry vehicles each (TOTAL: 435 warheads). Compared with the earlier Soviet proposal the difference based on warheads would be only 17 SS-20 missiles. Further, the new Andropov initiative included both missiles and warheads; but were the French and the British expected to reduce their forces by 17 missiles as well?

The ambiguity was resolved in an amendment to the 4 May proposal stating that if warhead requirements were stricter than that of the delivery systems, Moscow would abide by the warhead limit.

The US perceived Soviet signals primarily as an attempt to pre-empt the then impending decision on deployment rather than as a serious offer to negotiate. Indeed any Soviet attempt to dissuade NATO modernization was seen as an attempt to split the alliance. This was not conducive to the construction of effective arms control agreements. In response to Soviet assertions that SS-20 deployment in the Far East has nothing to do with the European theatre, the US repeatedly stressed that arms control in Europe cannot be purchased at the expense of the security of China and Japan. Large parts of Europe (and Alaska) could be reached by SS-20s deployed east of the Urals. Moreover, the NATO position of including 'all' intermediate range missiles in the talks take into account the prospect that SS-20s aimed at China could be retargeted at (and/or moved to target) Western Europe.

The Soviets wanted to include American FBS, US medium range aircraft based in Europe, in the INF talks. The FBS were supposedly one of the systems that linked the American nuclear deterrent with the defence of Western Europe. There was a fear expressed by America's European allies that a super-power agreement to control or remove FBS would undermine this relationship. The Soviets attempted therefore to include the 340 Carrier based F-4s, A-6s, and A-7s in the negotiations.[21] Yet these systems were dual capable and generally unsuitable for strikes into Soviet territory. Technically it would be difficult to include these systems in an agreement. Verification would necessitate rules as to the patrols and composition of the US 6th fleet in the Mediterranean (a concession wholly unacceptable to the US). Moreover if these systems, along with the 170 US F-111s stationed in Great Britain, were included then the US demanded the inclusion of comparable Soviet systems. These systems include 288 TU-16 Badger (being phased out), 125 TU-22 Binder and the 75 TU-22M Backfire medium range bombers, and dual capable SU-19 Fencer and MIG-23 Flogger C aircraft.[22] The attempted inclusion of such forces in the INF talks shifted the emphasis of the negotiations to the unmanageable position of constructing an overall theatre balance.

With respect to the Pershing II as constituting a first strike threat, the US properly asserted that its flight time was comparable to the SS-20 over a similar distance. The Pershing II has a single, less powerful warhead than each of the SS-20's 3 re-entry vehicles. Further, the Pershings maximum range is 1800 km compared to 5000 km for the SS-20.[23] The Pershing II, with its limited range, would not be able to reach Soviet strategic command and control facilities in Moscow. Of the Soviet strategic forces 90% are beyond the reach of Pershing IIs.

Moreover, 108 Pershings cannot, the US claims, disarm the Soviet Union. Indeed deployment was shaped to avoid such Soviet concern.

One of the most fundamental points of disagreement during the negotiations concerned the British and French nuclear forces. The US proclaimed that the Soviet emphasis on formal equality between the super-powers (via inclusion of the British and French forces) in terms of capability to hit each other, relegated Western Europe to the position of 'an incidental zone of destruction'.[24] Additionally the Soviet demand to include British and French forces was dismissed by America as groundless in military terms, and was calculated to divide the alliance and undercut the US strategic guarantee to Europe. The US also contended it would give the Soviets undue influence over the future evolution of British and French forces, and by blocking deployment of any US missile would give the Soviets a monopoly of land based missiles in Europe. Further, if the Soviets attain equality in terms of nuclear arms with all countries combined (i.e. equality with the US, France, and Britain, and China), it in effect gave them superiority over any one.

On 22 February 1983, in a speech delivered to the American Legion, President Reagan roundly declared that British and French nuclear systems were strategic in purpose.[25] They do not differ from that of American or Soviet forces which are defined as strategic, and thus they should not be included in the negotiations. It was asserted in both London and Paris that British and French forces were for national defence. Both Governments therefore declined to commit them irrevocably to NATO's flexible response. British forces were in fact assigned to NATO but they could only be used on the expressed authority of the government who reserved the right to withhold their use. French forces on the other hand were not assigned to NATO. They were not intended to extend guarantees to the alliance. In fact the existence of the British and French forces was justified by doubts about the credibility of extended deterrence. Britain and France did not want to be included in INF negotiations (nor do they want their forces to be accounted for in an agreement arising in any other fora as laid down by the super-powers in their joint statement issued in January 1985 announcing the resumption of arms talks).

BRITISH MISSILE FORCES *Totals* (in warheads)
2 Submarines – Polaris A3 – 32 Missiles + 3 RVs = 96
2 Submarines – Polaris – Chevaline – 32 Missiles × 6 RVs = 198
Total 4 Submarines – 64 Missiles – 294 Warheads.

FRENCH MISSILE FORCES   *Totals* (in warheads)
5 Submarines – M-4 System – 16 Missiles × 1 RV = 80
18 IRBMs – S-4 System – 18 Missiles × 1 RV = 18
Total 5 Submarines – 18 IRBMs – 96 Missiles – 96 Warheads

Total Warheads British and French Nuclear Forces = 392
162 Missiles – 18 IRBM – 144 SLBM

Both British and French forces were, it was pointed out, being upgraded. The two remaining British SLBM systems were eventually to be fitted with the Chevaline warhead. This in turn was to be replaced by Trident II in the 1990s: 4 Submarines, 16 missiles each, 8 to 13 MIRVs per missile. French modernization plans included re-fitting missiles on 4 submarines with multiple warheads, and for the construction of a sixth submarine. The French IRBM forces were also to be fitted with multiple warheads. Thus there was no basis for including these strategic systems in the INF negotiations. It was also asserted that a balance based on missiles between the USSR and British and French forces would give the Soviets a warhead advantage of 486 to 392. An agreement based on warheads would seem equitable yet the majority of British and French systems were composed of SLBMs (144 out of 162) and were not directly comparable to Soviet land based systems whose readiness was superior. Not all of the French and British SLBMs were on station at one time ready to be fired. At best three subs were on patrol for each nation and usually only two were on patrol.[26] Any arms control agreement must therefore take these factors into account. Britain and France adopted a resolutely negative attitude towards any attempt to include their strategic systems in the abortive INF talks which came to an end with the Soviet walk-out in December 1983. Once the talks broke down a number of conclusions could be drawn about the logic of NATO's decision to deploy the Pershing IIs and Cruise missiles.

Even with the planned deployment, by 1988 NATO will be in 'at least as bad a military position as before the deployment decision'.[27] America and NATO will not in effect have acquired capacity that was 'psychologically reassuring, let alone militarily significant.[28] It was a mistake to conceive of the nuclear issue too narrowly. It should not have been a question of building weapons to counter the SS-20; needs should have shaped forces. Nuclear weapons and nuclear decisions serve in part as political symbols of the alliance yet they should by themselves provide the substance of unity. NATO should have arranged its nuclear forces in a way that made military sense noting that American support for Western Europe was rooted more in political cohesion than military arrangement. Military issues became predominant because the political unity of the alliance was being brought into question. The DTD had come to represent a symbol of alliance that, however unfortunate, could not henceforth be disregarded.

In this respect the DTD established an ill-fated precedent by making an important decision about defence structure, and the alliance as a whole, hostage to negotiations on arms control. A link in arms control requires cooperation by an adversary. Negotiations may fall short of expectations, and this tends to make defence policy more controversial than without the link. The problem was compounded, it is contended by some, by the tendency to establish links between arms control negotiations and the political behaviour of adversaries which makes arms control hostage to global instabilities. Thus the critics of linkage contend that 'this dual linkage has diminished NATO's ability to deal with questions of defence structure, negotiations and the pursuit of arms control by other means'.[29]

The DTD was from the outset full of ambiguities. On the one hand it established as a negotiating objective the attainment of equality through limitation. Yet the actual deployment was not started to establish numerical equality in INF launchers, missiles, or warheads with the Soviet Union. The political purpose of the decision, it appears, would have been clearer if NATO had decided to deploy the number of missiles closer to the lower end of the spectrum. In addition it was a

> mistake to make the DTD a collective decision by the alliance. Even if the decision on deployment of nuclear weapons can be made as collective decisions, ultimately the decision on their deployment rests with the host countries. Participation in decisions concerning nuclear weapons may constitute a burden on social consensus in the small, non nuclear weapons states which may prove detrimental to the support of the alliance in the long run. Further future modernization and adjustments of the nuclear posture in NATO may be made difficult by the *procedure precedent of the dual track decision.* [emphasis added][30]

As a result in the initiation of deployment of American missiles in Europe in November 1983, the Soviets unilaterally broke off the INF talks. They have since slowed removal of SS-4 and SS-5 missiles and have begun new deployments, in arrangement with other Warsaw Treaty Organization Countries, to balance new American FBSs. They have also undertaken other measures to threaten US territory. Moreover the deployment of US and Soviet IRBMs remains unchecked. The Soviets until the end of 1984 made their return to the negotiating table contingent on the scrapping of US deployment and the dismantlement of missiles already in place. Both super-powers agreed that they should try to resolve this situation following the return of President Reagan to the White House for a second term.

The original conception of negotiating INF limitation within the concept of SALT III (now START) was recommended as a new basis for the negotiations were sought in 1985. A new framework for INF and strategic forces was seen to be necessary both to bring about the renewal of negotiations and to prevent the decoupling of the US and the alliance. The US and the Soviets have shown some flexibility, and (i.e.) the principle of verification has been agreed to by both sides. It might still be overly optimistic to state that the grounds for agreement can be found. What both super-powers however envisaged early in 1985 (along with others) was a partial merger of INF and START talks, central and theatre systems, looking for agreement based on a freedom to mix arrangement. This approach should enable the alliance to sort out the proper balance between central and theatre systems without Soviet involvement. Also the issue of defensive weaponry needed to be addressed as a third element in the projected negotiations. So commentators began to argue that in order to form a base for mutual agreement between the US and the USSR and to reopen negotiation channels, an interim agreement could be formulated. It could involve a commitment by NATO to forgo the deployment of Pershing II (the more objectionable US IRBM) and to dismantle those already operational. In return the Soviets could make major reductions (at least commensurate to the NATO withdrawal) in SS-20s deployed in Europe. GLCM deployment could proceed slowly (with Belgium and the Netherlands postponing their deployment of Cruise missiles) but NATO should be willing to accept reductions in planned deployments in return for further reductions of SS-20s. Such an agreement would protect the American right to deploy INFs in Europe. At the same time NATO could express a willingness to consider a mutual freeze on all INF deployments pending an assessment of needs in connection with a single ceiling nuclear force agreement covering both strategic and INFs. The structure of which could be based on the 1982 Nitze–Kvitniski 'walk in the woods' formula.[31] In other words an interim reduction agreement accompanied by a freeze on INF deployment pending outcomes of subsequent negotiations on a single nuclear ceiling in the START framework. The earlier INF talks were entrusted to the US by the alliance, there would be no reason to alter this for the interim agreement or for negotiations on an overall ceiling.

A single ceiling agreement on both strategic and INFs (a separate subceiling could be constructed for short-range nuclear forces) negotiated in START based on a freedom to mix principal could overcome the problem of decoupling and provide a framework for taking into account British and French forces. These forces would have to be taken into account when negotiating a comprehensive nuclear force agreement (and British and French representatives could be present at the negotiations if this was found to be desirable). But whatever the framework for negotiations in the mid-1980s, French and British forces must eventually be taken into account. They represent a clear threat to the Soviet Union. Planned improvements to these systems will significantly increase their damage inflicting potential: Moscow should be permitted some form of compensation. The US has always asserted that British and French forces were tacitly compensated for by concessions made to the Soviets in SALT. Yet no evidence exists to substantiate this (see Statements by under-Secretary of State Lawrence Eagleburger).[32] The US has consistently reiterated that these are strategic systems yet they have not been included in START. They could therefore be included in the START dialogue once the Soviets indicate a readiness to make concessions. Yet the emphasis should be on their reduction and not total abolition. Aircraft of intermediate range (i.e. US F-111s) could also be negotiated in the pursuit of comprehensive agreements with equal counting measures. Dual capable aircraft could be negotiated under a separate single ceiling. A single ceiling would also provide a framework for taking into account SS-20s positioned east of the Urals.

This arrangement could be beneficial for NATO. It is thoroughly coupling in recognizing the strategic unity of the alliance and emphasizing that American nuclear weapons provide a 'continuum of deterrence'.[33] It might be argued that such a merger would force difficult choices for the US between its own national security and that of the alliance. However, the existence of separate negotiations will not prevent links from developing between the two. Moreover it is inherent in the framework of INF negotiations, and in the alliance itself, that US interests are tied to that of Europe. The need for reduction of INFs, indeed all nuclear armaments, has now been accepted by the super-powers. Concession on both sides is necessary for an agreement to be reached. Therefore limiting the arms race and promoting stability and peace are the basics of arms control. We recognize that the question of arms control must be subjected to critical scrutiny (see Chapter 12) and that a thorough examination and evaluation of its rationale is necessary because it carries enormous implications for European defence. In short, the case for regional arms control agreements cannot be divorced from the negotiations concerning the central strategic balance.

Moreover the emergence of a definite European defence consciousness is probably itself dependent upon Europe at some stage taking part in the arms central negotiations as near-equal partner of the superpowers. Be that as it may, the West is on the verge of a series of complicated arms control negotiations in which Western European defence interests must be more clearly defined. Clearly the questions of space weapons and strategic and intermediate-range missiles are interrelated as the joint Soviet–American statement of 8 January 1985 recognized. Moreover this interrelationship by its very nature could raise issues that threaten to undermine European defence requirements. This fear once again underlines the importance of close consultations and solidarity among the Western allies.

12 The Limitations of Arms Control: the Need for a New Beginning?

In its present form, arms control has fallen into serious disrepute. Since this is the case we will consider this first before examining (in the next chapter) new approaches arising from President Reagan's 'Star Wars' speech delivered on 23 March 1983. This is not a surprising state of affairs considering the protracted and periodic nature of the US–Soviet arms limitation negotiations. The Salt II Treaty is still unratified; the START, INF talks were suspended in 1983; initiatives to reduce conventional weapons in the European theatre (MBFR), to arrive at a comprehensive test ban treaty (CTB), to regulate forces in the Indian Ocean, and to control arms transfers have all made little or no progress. Never has so much talk resulted in so little. Hopes rose again in 1985 as East–West arms talks were resumed but critics from the left, right and centre have, however, provided a chorus of condemnation for the process of formal arms control negotiations, rushing forward to explain why, after three decades of talks, the two super-powers are still locked into an unmistakable arms race. Using some of these critiques as a base, we will attempt to examine the fundamental objectives of arms control itself, evaluate its present difficulties in meeting these objectives, and review two popular alternatives and then a radically different approach based on strategic defence which may provide answers for some of Europe's more obvious defence deficiencies. This discussion assumes some relevance given the super-power commitment to negotiate at three international levels: START, INF and on the question of defensive technology in space.

There are three traditional objectives of formal diplomatic East–West arms negotiations: to reduce the likelihood of war by increasing stability; to reduce the damage of war if hostilities break out; and to reduce the economic cost of going to war. The dissatisfaction with arms control stems from doubts about its ability to meet these objectives and from questions concerning the compatibility of the goals themselves.

Beginning with the third objective; we find fairly formidable arguments both supporting and undermining the ability of arms control negotiations to reduce arms expenditures. Though we do recognize that reduction in arms expenditure as such is neither good nor bad. Dr Christoph Bertram, a former director of the International Institute for Strategic Studies, takes the view that 'the tangible economic dividends of arms control have been meagre'.[1] He plays down the promises for defence savings as lip service provided by political leaders to deflect criticism of their arms control efforts. Bertram's argument is strongest when dealing with quantitative arms limitations:

> Quantitative limitations, if they imply reductions at all, are likely to produce only marginal savings, because in the bargaining of mutual concessions both sides will tend to seek the smallest common denominator, which often means the retention of the largest force.[2]

He goes on to argue that if cuts are made they will probably involve phasing out old systems in exchange for new, more expensive ones.

The other important strand of Bertram's argument is more penetrating and subtle. That is, the assertion that arms reduction talks are not only useless in meeting the objective of defence savings, but that they actually spur on the arms race which in turn raises the cost of defence. Bertram makes this argument by citing statistics which claim that American strategic expenditures were decreasing in the decade before SALT I and increasing in the years after. He states '... negotiations and the political ambience they have created have generated at least some dynamics which have favoured arms competition rather than control'.[3] Examples of such dynamics would be the 'bargaining chip' mentality which spurs weapons development for the sole purpose of negotiation leverage, and weapons 'ceilings' which tend to encourage each side to push the military effort to the maximum of what is permitted. More will be said about the present difficulties inherent in arms control, but the argument can definitely be advanced that arms control talks are more than just inadequate to generate defence savings: it can be argued that they generate additional expenditures.

However compelling Bertram's argument is in total, it is not complete enough to allow him the totally negative conclusion he draws.

One criticism of his stance is that it concentrates on savings against actual but not against potential expenditures. It is quite conceivable that without negotiated restrictions the arms race would have spiralled out of all proportion, dragging huge sums of money with it. Bertram anticipates and attempts to counter this line of reasoning by stating that 'it is by no manner of means certain that the absence of arms control would have promoted arms competition more than has the negotiation of formal agreements'.[4] This proposition may be true; but so too might its converse. In a battle of hypotheticals, however, it would seem more sensible to assume that attempts to limit arms through agreement would have a better chance of slowing the arms race and producing some defence savings than would a hands-off policy.[5]

A stronger, less abstract, criticism of Bertram's argument is to point to the ABM Treaty as a preclusive arms control pact in which both sides agreed to forgo the huge investment for a functioning ballistic missile defence, although this self-denying ordinance has since been superseded by the desire to compete in defensive systems (the strategic defence initiative announced by President Reagan is a case in point) exploiting recent advances in technology. Be that as it may, here is where it is especially difficult to agree with Bertram's assessment of the 'meagre' defence savings achieved through arms control negotiations. An operational, fully-equipped ABM system would have cost a large sum to deploy in 1972 and its maintenance for twelve years would have consumed considerable funds. Moreover, this type of preclusive arms control opportunity is once again presenting itself to the super-powers *vis-à-vis* the new anti-satellite and space-based weapons technologies. Agreements in these areas could close off a potential area of military hardware which in strictly economic terms, would undoubtedly be America's most costly endeavour to date. Once again, Bertram recognizes this counter argument, terming the ABM Treaty 'impressive'; yet he chooses to discount the treaty's savings and fails to mention the possibility of other such preclusive arms control pacts.

Therefore a rough balance seems to be struck between the dismal (and possibly counter-productive) contributions of quantitative arms limitations to defence savings, and the definite economic advantages of preclusive arms agreements. Given this balance it is difficult to make any comprehensive judgements about the ability of arms control agreements to accomplish their economic objectives. Perhaps the economic argument in favour of arms control has been over-stated and must be subordinated to other more significant considerations.

The second objective of arms control is to reduce the damage if war should break out. Once again, Christoph Bertram develops a fairly strong argument against the effectiveness of arms control in this area. His main line of reasoning here is that new weapons technology has sometimes been more successful at limiting damage in war than has arms control. Advanced technology has increased the accuracy of both strategic and theatre weapons systems such that collateral damage can be severely reduced. Military installations, instead of population centres, have become primary targets due to precise 'surgical strike' capabilities. Extremely accurate missiles with conventional warheads can now do the job that a nuclear weapon would have previously been used for, thus raising the 'nuclear threshold'. Thus the conventionalization of NATO may be a function of technology rather than the product of the strategy of arms control. Bertram reminds us that this

> is not an argument against arms control; efforts at damage limitation, like the Red Cross talks on incendiary and other weapons, or the negotiations of the United Nations Disarmament Conference in Geneva on chemical weapons, weather modifications, and weapons of mass destruction may also contribute to making war less indiscriminantly destructive.[6]

But his argument does assert that arms control is not always the best way to accomplish this task. Thus the idea that mutual assured destruction is the only way to guarantee peace is replaced by the notion that technology may in the 1990s make mutual societal survivability possible.

The nature of war according to Clausewitz, entails the use of extreme violence. It is a race to extremes, an irresistible force pushing men to absolutes. Yet the only power which can stop the inevitable escalation of war is friction – e.g. chance, social or economic factors, some stopgap which can halt the war's hurtling and chaotic progress. One such stopgap could be the so-called 'fire-break' between conventional weapons and nuclear forces; it could also be the psychological jump between pushing the button on a 'surgical strike' and setting off a weapon which might kill millions. Thus in this view, damage limitation would be increased if high technology arms were controlled rather than procured. The older more powerful weapons would offer starker choices to decision-makers, thus injecting another hopeful element of friction into the accelerating slide toward mass destruction. At one point Bertram writes: 'If war does break out, the new technologies allow for a more discriminating and controlled use.'[7] It would certainly be useful to finish this sentence '... more discriminating and controlled damage per weapon', but it seems that the weapons might be used in a less discriminating fashion precisely because their damage is controllable. More use implies more overall damage, and, in the Clausewitzian world, more danger of total cataclysmic war. It is obvious that emerging military technologies (ET) are likely to be just as lethal as some lower yield nuclear weapon systems.

The first, and most important, objective of arms control, then, is to decrease the chances of war by increasing stability. This objective, unlike the other two, hinges upon a fairly subjective definition. Whereas it is possible to identify defence savings or damage limitation when one sees it, how does one know when 'stability' has been increased? As John C Baker writes:

> Not unexpectedly, defence planners (who tend to be preoccupied with analysing the Soviet threat) portray almost every new Soviet strategic weapon system as sinister and destabilizing but fail to reach the same conclusion concerning similar American weapon systems. And also not unexpectedly, arms controllers (who tend to be preoccupied with the dangers of the arms race) have labelled almost every new U.S. strategic weapon system as both wasteful and destabilizing. Consequently, as many analysts have noted, 'strategic stability tends to be in the eye of the beholder.[8]

One such analyst who carries the subjectivity argument to its most logical extreme is the formidable Richard Burt – the former director of the Bureau of Politico-Military Affairs in the US State Department. Burt claims that the belief that negotiations alleviate sources of military instability is a 'central fallacy' of the existing approach to arms control. He writes that the 'most common result of arms control is not enhanced stability but the registration of reality'.[9] This contention hinges on the view that asymmetries in force structures and military doctrines have precluded any US–Soviet consensus on the meaning of 'strategic stability'; thus what seems stabilizing to one side often appears destabilizing to the other. Burt points to the problem of US ICBM vulnerability during the SALT II talks as a prime example. From the Soviet perspective this development was of a stabilizing nature, thus they had no reason to accept an American proposal to restructure the situation. The resulting SALT II agreement, according to Burt, merely ratified the Soviet advantage. The 1983 INF walkout over the deployment of Pershing II and Cruise missiles underscores the point – that without some semblance of doctrinal convergence on what constitutes 'strategic stability', arms control negotiations may be irrelevant to the entire issue. We find his argument most persuasive and compelling.

Burt further supports his contention by stating that 'there is a common tendency to confuse means and ends when looking at the impact of military programmes on arms control negotiations'.[10] That is, weapons which are viewed as threatening to the progress of arms control talks are automatically considered to be destabilizing, when their impact could be exactly the opposite. For example, the verification and categorization problems presented by Cruise missiles should not (in Burt's view) obscure the fact that deployment of these weapons, in large numbers on both sides, could significantly enhance the stability of the strategic balance. In a most pertinent reflection Burt argues that if the SALT process had been underway in the early 1960s, the Soviet Union and arms control advocates in the US would have jointly maintained that the deployment of the Polaris submarine fleet created verification difficulties, and represented another destabilizing round of the qualitative arms race. However, the deployment of SLBMs can be seen today as a significantly stabilizing step. If arms control is not a substitute for unilateral defence initiatives, 'then the political price of negotiating the fielding of new systems must be measured against the security benefits that will be gained from their deployment'.[11]

Christoph Bertram supports Burt's reasoning that arms control may be irrelevant to issues of stability. He claims that the US–Soviet strategic and theatre balance have shown 'remarkable resilience' over the years despite ineffective arms control talks. He writes:

> Although a very great deal of thought and diplomatic effort, hard bargaining and political courage has been invested on both sides in the process of arms control, it is difficult to prove that without any of it – with the possible exception of the ABM Treaty – the stability of the central balance would be by now seriously undermined.[12]

This is an interesting and relevant point in relation to European defence for it illustrates just how amorphous quantitative 'strategic stability' really is. Bertram, once again, contends the quantitative arms limitation negotiations have been at best, ineffective, and at worst, counter-productive, in their effects on 'strategic stability'. However, he does concede that preclusive agreements – such as the Sea-Bed and Outer Space Treaties, and particularly the ABM Treaty – have made East–West relations more calculable and thus more stable.

Fellow-critic Richard Burt would not agree. From his somewhat hawkish though not false perspective, the ABM Treaty only simplified Soviet nuclear attack problems and enabled them to develop confidence in their ability to destroy the US land-based missile force. At the same time, the treaty imposed constraints on the ability of the US to respond to this dilemma. Additionally, Burt would argue, the ABM Treaty was negotiable only because the US Safeguard ABM system was ready to undergo deployment, thus it was an attractive option for the Soviets to foreclose an area of arms competition in which they were already lagging behind. Certainly the evidence strongly supports this interpretation that the Soviets feared American ABM technology or at any rate its potential. Hence the renewed and determined Soviet opposition to the American search for strategic defence as outlined by President Reagan.

The point is that even among critics of the ability of arms control to enhance stability, there are varying degrees of definitional interpretation. This makes it especially difficult to arrive at an objective evaluation of arms control.

Advocates of arms control attempt to sidestep those swirling mass of arguments over the stabilizing or destabilizing nature of particular agreements or types of agreements. They try to avoid the 'numbers game' by grounding their arguments in the political benefits of the arms control process itself. In other words, advocates will point to the overall act of peacefully negotiating with the other side as a healthy form of communication which is eminently preferable to a provocative silence. This is almost the classic European position; that a dialogue is an end in itself. Now that the Soviet Union has achieved nuclear parity, this type of deterrence management takes on an even more important role. The degree of strategic nervousness will definitely be high over the next decade (so the argument goes), and anything which can reduce the risks of miscalculation or misinterpretation can only be considered beneficial to stability. Treaties such as the Hot Line Agreement and the nuclear accidents agreement are examples of diplomatic pacts which can be used to ameliorate tensions in a crisis. Moreover, such limited agreements can be used as a first step toward further substantive arms limitations pacts.

Arms control advocates also point to the troubling development of nuclear proliferation as a background against which a useful, reciprocal super-power dialogue must be maintained. Arms control negotiations can serve as the cornerstone of a collusive interest between the sides of regulating the spread of dangerous nuclear technologies. Thus the forum of arms control is stressed by advocates not only as a stabilizing factor in present East—West relations, but as the prerequisite vehicle for a future super-power condominium. Without arms control, advocates argue, the world would be even more dangerous than it is now.

Thus arms control draws a mixed impression in its ability to meet any of its three major objectives. However, as mentioned above, arms control *in toto* has been deemed a failure. The reason for this contradiction stems not so much from the inherent deficiencies of arms control, but from the false hopes that are pinned upon it and the essential and inescapable incompatibility of its three objectives. For example, one way of decreasing the likelihood of war, say, through MAD is by making its prospect seem horrible. Mutual fear of a devastating war is the bedrock of deterrence policy, a policy which in turn informs our perception of stability. However, scenarios of 'limited nuclear war-fighting', development of weapons capable of 'surgical strikes' and attempts to construct strategic defence, in short, attempts at damage limitation – conflict with efforts to make war seem horrible, and this one might argue, potentially increases the likelihood of going to war. Thus if one concentrates on the objective of damage limitation, the possibility of hostilities may increase; so the argument runs, if one concentrates, as conventional wisdom has it, on decreasing the likelihood of war by emphasizing its destructiveness, damage limitation is necessarily ruled out. Another tension between objectives can be found in the way notions of defence savings conflict with the two goals discussed above. As argued by Bertram, the best way to limit in war may be to spend defence resources on high-tech systems rather than saving through arms control efforts. Also, substantial savings due to arms cuts may be at odds with trying to decrease the likelihood of war; for the scaling down of weaponry which would produce defence savings might also provide an incentive for the opponent to attack.

Arms control, then, is not a cure-all and should not be looked upon as a process capable of tackling all of Europe's or the West's security problems. Yet in the world of international relations, half a loaf is most often better than none at all; and arms control has arguably advanced each of its three objectives to a certain, not insignificant, degree. However, while arms control may have made some steps to address a complex set of policy objectives, there is no doubt that agreements are becoming harder to come by. The increasing interest in a heightening European profile in the defence of Europe is a recognition of this fact. We now examine the main difficulties precluding arms control pacts and review some options for overcoming these problems before looking specifically at European defence and its relationship to the arms control process with particular reference to the militarization of space.

Two major factors have combined to undercut the effectiveness of the formal negotiations approach to arms control. The first of these factors is the manner in which technological advances rechannel the momentum of the arms race into areas not restricted by negotiations. Efforts to improve the quality of missiles restricted by SALT I (larger throw-weights and MIRVing), and the recent push to develop weapons for use in outer space are good examples here. The impact of technology is also especially felt in the trend toward multi-category multi-mission weapons. Systems such as the Cruise missile and the Backfire bomber pose daunting problems for arms control negotiators because both weapons can theoretically be used in theatre and intercontinental operations. This duality in weapons capability has done much to destabilize the European balance. Technological advances in guidance systems, and the interchangeability of range, yield, and accuracy performance characteristics now make verifiability another extremely sticky and perhaps insoluble problem. These difficulties are compounded by the manner in which technology often outpaces the speed of arms control talks, making their outcome seem irrelevant and perhaps even dangerous: 'Because of technological change and the difficulty of incorporating it in an agreement, it has become almost impossible for arms control negotiators to produce treaties which will be unequivocally fair and equitable.'[13]

The influence of the negotiating process itself is the second factor which undercuts the effectiveness of arms control talks. As mentioned earlier, a premium on equal limit agreements tends to encourage a build-up to symmetry, as higher limits are easier to negotiate than lower ones. Also, negotiating from 'a position of strength' encourages the development of weapons systems as 'bargaining chips'. John Baker writes: 'Many arms control analysts believe that the "bargaining chip" label has led the U.S. to develop and deploy some dubious weapons which otherwise would not have been procured in the absence of the continuing arms negotiations.'[14] This is indeed a sombre conclusion; the 'star wars' project may well be a case in point.

Additionally, the highly formalized negotiating process is often ascribed with undeserved political prominence, transforming arms talks into a bench mark for East–West relations. This aspect can be seen in the blatant and, largely so far counterproductive Soviet exploitation of the peace movement in a bid to undermine the unity of

NATO. Arms control came to be seen as the touchstone of detente in the early 1970s and failure at the negotiating table accelerated a deterioration of super-power relations not worthy of the differences between the two countries at that time or indeed since. Recognition of the linkage between the East–West relationship and arms control has pushed negotiators to make cosmetic arms agreements which have little impact on the arms race, but 'prove' each side's 'peaceful intentions'. Some linkage is inevitable because of the importance of arms talks, but placing the 'need to agree' in the centrepiece role leaves a tenuous relationship balancing on an especially shaky fulcrum. When combined with the difficulty of arriving at equitable agreements due to advancing technology, such linkage erodes any beneficial political effects that an arms control agreement might have achieved. As has been pointedly observed: 'Rather than being a promoter of detente and national trust, inadequate arms control has become a consumer of trust.'[15] Thus NATO's decision to link the Cruise and Pershing II deployments to the progress of the INF talks virtually ensured that those talks would break down. In retrospect it would have been better to have kept the arms deployment separate from the arms control process. The case for deployment of these weapon systems was alway stronger than the case for an arms control agreement affecting their deployment.

The impact of technology and the formal negotiating process itself are two of the major, but certainly not the only, problems undermining the effectiveness of arms control. They do represent, however, the comprehensive nature of the arms control dilemma: both the substance and the structure of negotiations have become a detriment to arms limitations. We now turn to examine two prevalent proposals for overcoming the substantive and structural problems of arms control before considering the case for linking arms control to the search for strategic defence.

Dr Christoph Bertram attempts to solve the major substantive dilemma of arms control by proposing that negotiations concentrate on military missions instead of weapons. Essentially, the argument suggests that quantitative arms restrictions are useless in the face of the qualitative technological onslaught. Thus what is needed is an approach which will 'emphasize agreement on the military missions that neither side should seek'.[16] This strikes us as a fruitful if a somewhat neglected idea. Such missions might include the ability to destroy land-based missiles in a pre-emptive strike, to threaten submarines carrying second-strike missile forces, or to affect satellites housing command and control equipment. Agreements concerning the nature of the forbidden missions and the implementation of restrictions on arsenals and military programmes would constitute the two essential features of this form of arms control.

The author describes a possible scenario:

> Supposing the United States and the Soviet Union had agreed that neither should have the capability to launch a successful first strike against the land-based strategic missile forces of the other. This could be implemented in a variety of ways. It could be effected by reducing the number of MIRVed launchers so that fewer delivery systems possessed the accuracy to destroy a missile silo, or by cutting down the throw-weight of delivery systems so that they could not carry the kind of nuclear yield required for destroying a hardened silo. Another possibility would be to reduce the number of land-based ICBM significantly, both because these are the systems most capable of exact guidance and because they do not pose the command and control problems of the sea-based deterrent forces. In order to implement the basic agreement, both sides could choose the same method of implementation, or they could make different choices if they preferred, within a range of agreed alternatives. Moreover, having made a choice, they could alter it later within an agreed range of options.[17]

Such an approach has three apparent advantages. First, the flexibility of choice offered here would allow each side to adopt a reduction package consistent with its military or strategic doctrine. Such flexibility should make the limitation of forces more palatable, for the contentious quid pro quo aspect of the negotiations would be eliminated. Second, agreements based on the elimination of certain missions could 'incorporate technological change rather than be threatened by it'.[18] 'Grey-area' systems would no longer threaten negotiations: (as at present) problematic attempts to 'count' or 'categorize' multi-mission weapons would be bypassed. All weapons would be viewed only in relation to the missions they could perform. Third, complex verification problems would be significantly reduced under the mission approach. According to Bertram, the differential between the negotiated ceiling in the implementation agreement and the performance requirements for the proscribed capability would be wide enough so that any move to establish a mission competency in a forbidden area would involve a massive build-up – hence easy detection, hence easy verification.

This model is based on the example of the ABM Treaty – an agreement forbidding a certain kind of mission, and any existing or potential technology which has the capability of performing that mission. The approach is an interesting one, mainly because in theory it should alleviate the pernicious impact of technology on negotiations and because it explicitly refers arms control to its heretofor implicit object – to prohibit certain missions which are destablilizing. However, it does appear that agreements concerning which missions to prescribe and what weapons to reduce would be no less troublesome than such negotiations are under the present approach. As Bertram concedes: No new weapons approach to arms control can do away with all the familiar problems of limiting and restructuring military capabilities.'[19] But the shift in emphasis in this approach may well offer an arguable basis for reconciling arms control with the unpredictable impact of technological change.

The mission approach is certainly one of many conceptual answers to the substantive problems facing arms control. Unfortunately, thinking about ways to restructure the arms talks in order to alleviate the problems inherent in the negotiating process suffers from an unmistakable malaise. One of the most prevalent and (sadly) most attractive restructuring notions is the idea of implementing unilateral restraints instead of mutually agreed measures. Informal agreements of this type are similar to formal agreements in that both sides abide by the provisions of the pact as long as it is in their interests to do so. But informal agreements would not be binding in the legal sense, and would therefore provide more flexibility. In a possible scenario, Herbert Scoville, Jr writes:

> one nation could announce that it was not going to proceed with a new weapons development or deployment provided that future events did not indicate that such restraint would prejudice its security. It could then watch the reaction of the other side which, in turn, might exercise reciprocal restraint either in the same or a related area.[20]

There are two arguments on which this proposal is based: Firstly, because armed forces are constituted by unilateral decision, the control of arms should be facilitated by unilateral decision rather than by the search for reciprocity; secondly, the only real sanction against non-compliance in a formal arms agreement is non-compliance on the other side. Therefore, since the sanction is unilateral, why should arms control be complicated by the problems of formal, bilateral agreements?

Such arguments are logically convincing. Their validity is somewhat borne out by the example of the unratified, yet still adhered to, SALT II Treaty. The flexibility inherent in such a structure would undercut the problems of being 'locked into' a suddenly undesirable arms pact. The long, complex negotiations which give rise to 'bargaining chip' weapons systems would be avoided. A reciprocated unilateral decision would also 'create less incentive to find loopholes and limits and place less emphasis on the details of verification'.[21]

However, this approach has some serious and potentially damaging limitations. The most important of these is the fact that informal arrangements are easier to break away from in times of stress and are more likely to create serious misunderstandings. Knowledge of these facts would lead ever-nervous defence planners to spend a great deal in 'hedge' systems to guard against agreement 'break-out'. Thus informal arms agreements would not have much effect on weapons stockpiles. Another considerable problem is that issues subjected to informal procedures would never be truly settled in the fullest sense. Public criticism and debate over any decision could therefore continue indefinitely and at a much more vociferous level than if it was a formal pact. Bertram also argues that the flexibility provided by informal arrangements 'must be reconciled with credibility of response'.[22] It is clear the Soviet Union appears committed to the process that governed SALT and to that inherent in the START negotiations. In short, there are definite problems with the strategy of unilateral restraint which outweigh any advantages it may claim over formal arms control.

The process of diplomatic mutual arms control is therefore, we conclude, the only form for negotiations yet available. This is unfortunate as the aforementioned problems inherent in such a process are quite substantial. It is important to stress that the structural form of the negotiations is as important as the substantive directions taken when striving for successful arms limitation. New proposals for the restructuring of arms control talks in the years that lie ahead will have to be developed so that potentially successful substantive alternatives, such as the mission approach, might have a chance to run their course. Creative thinking in this area, in addition to a lowering of expectations for the ability of arms control to meet a set of difficult and often contradictory objectives are two essential factors for the revival and future success of any arms control agreements.

We are not optimistic. This sensibly brings us to the question of the militarization of outer space and arms control which we need to discuss separately in order to establish the background to the so-called 'star wars' controversy. Obviously, this question carries enormous implications for European defence which need also to be carefully considered.[23] The idea of strategic defence, should it prove possible, would require a different approach to formal arms control negotiations which actually implies the need for quite radical strategic arms reductions. Herein lies a totally new approach to the negotiations in which strategic defence would become as institutionalized in the years that lie ahead as has the idea of the supremacy of offence over defence in the past. Such a defensive capability might indeed be more compatible with the defence of Europe.

13 European Defence and the Strategic Defence Initiative

It is clear that Britain is the NATO ally most sceptical about President Reagan's 'Star Wars' initiative. The proposal in our view could involve spending approximately $60 billion over the next ten years on research into a possible two-layer defence against nuclear attack. The overwhelming reason for British doubts is a fear of the consequences it might have for Britain's own independent nuclear deterrent. It is disputed in Whitehall that ballistic missile defence (BMD) will be within the possible state of the art in the form of a layered defence system, using conventional kinetic energy, laser and particle – beam weapons. Yet the formation of a defence system against the threat of nuclear ballistic missile attack may no longer be a remote or unattainable goal. Indeed technically, these defensive capabilities are within the state of the art and but for the constraints imposed by the 1972 ABM Treaty could be in place today.

Clearly, substantial progress has been made in related activities such as developments in anti-satellite, anti-missile, anti-aircraft, anti-ship and anti-personnel technologies. It is also recognized that it is not ultimately meaningful to distinguish between 'total' and 'partial' anti-missile defence. As Dr Cockcroft has observed in this context: 'what must be described as a "partial" system today [e.g. F-15 launched anti-satellite missiles] may well become part of integrated overlay systems of the future, whether land or space-based or both'.[1] The President and his closest advisers believe that the Strategic Defence Initiative (SDI) might eventually lead to a more comprehensive defence system which replaces the reliance on assured survival as the basis of deterrence.

But cautious observers emphasize more modest 'intermediate' objectives involving the protection of military rather than civilian targets.

Critics suggest that SDI suffers from the debilitating weakness associated with over-estimated capabilities and under-estimated costs. Moreover, it is suggested by Professor Lawrence Freedman that

> the critical question in assessing the potential of all the various proposals in this area to shift the balance away from the offence to the defence is whether the cost of introducing the new defences is more or less than the cost of introducing effective counter-measures.

Previous experience was not encouraging: 'the last push for strategic defence in the 1960s ended in failure'.[2] Air Vice-Marshal Stewart Menaul believes this view to be seriously mistaken and stresses that the 'Star Wars' defence would be a reality within ten years. He asserts that 'ballistic missile defence offers the prospect for assured survival. The arguments in favour of a strategic defence system, ground and space-based are overwhelming on political, moral and military grounds.'[3] Professor Freedman's critical question concerning the cost of SDI is not in fact the real test. Rather, it is whether the cost incurred is worth the diminution of the risk of a first-strike against the US ICBM bases. The 'costs' of achieving this are irrelevant. The gain is beyond calculable cost.

It is indeed arguable that a deterrent based on damage limitation and denial of victory could prove to be more effective than a deterrent threatening a condition of mutual societal vulnerability. It would also be more consistent with a credible arms-control strategy. Thus there is a compelling logic to a policy which permits reductions in offensive weapons and which encourages unfettered strategic defence. Moreover, the evidence is clear that significant reductions in offensive-force levels will not be achieved under the rubric of mutual assured destruction (MAD). So-called strategic equivalence resulting in mutual deterrence, has proved to be a sterile basis for radical arms-control measures. Clearly, a victory-denial strategic doctrine and force posture can be rendered compatible with arms control.

Therefore the first successful missile intercept, on 10 June 1984, in space achieved by the US provided an opportunity for a more realistic arms-control policy. Nothing was more calculated to bring the Soviet Union to the negotiating table – as events in 1985 strikingly confirmed – than a technological breakthrough in defensive capabilities. The need for a strategic doctrine compatible with a serious commitment to strategic defence became more urgent. A victory-denial strategic doctrine should encourage the United States to pursue real and radical reductions in offensive weapons through the START negotiations. Clearly, a strategic posture based on real strategic defence would be more compatible with the extended deterrent responsibilities placed on US strategic forces.

Yet this optimistic view initially carried little conviction in Europe as well as amongst its well-entrenched critics in the US. The concern also initially expressed in Paris echoed the British critique that if the United States pushes ahead, the Soviets will redouble their own efforts to militarize outer space. That, so it was feared, could lead to the Soviets deploying an anti-ballistic (ABM) which, in an updated version of their present systems, though not yet sophisticated enough to neutralize a huge attack by America, could annihilate the nuclear forces of Britain and France. If such a Soviet investment in ABMs went ahead, these secondary nuclear forces possessed by Britain and France would therefore lose their credibility, and the two countries would become vulnerable to nuclear blackmail or worse. The British government it was asserted is acutely aware of this prospect since it has just spent £1 billion on modernizing its Polaris nuclear submarine force by adding warheads and decoys. It is also planning to spend, as we have noted, in an earlier chapter, over £10 billion on the new Trident submarine system, to replace Polaris.

But Britain also articulated a wider concern which related to the impact that SDI might have on NATO strategy. This concern arises from the very nature of defensive systems which envisage a world where nuclear missiles are unable to reach their targets. Such a capability would, it was alleged, undermine the whole basis of deterrence and increase the chances of a conventional war in Europe. These fears were for a time also echoed in other European capitals, particularly Bonn.

Thus, Mrs Thatcher during her three-and-a-half hours of talks at Camp David, the presidential retreat in Maryland, just before Christmas 1984, set out a number of conditions for her continued support for SDI. The British position clearly is that it will continue to support the research programme, while keeping its options open on testing and deployment of space weapons. The Government recognized that the Soviets strides in space probe development made research by the United States not only prudent, but necessary. The two governments agreed on four specific points involving arms control as well as the 'Star Wars' plan.

Firstly, the United States and Western aim was not to achieve superiority but to maintain balance, taking account of Soviet developments. Secondly, that SDI related deployments would, in view of treaty obligations have to be a matter of negotiation. Thirdly, the overall aim is to enhance, and not to undermine deterrence. And fourthly, East–West negotiations should aim to achieve security with reduced levels of offensive systems of both sides.[3] These somewhat bland conditions were drawn up in anticipation of the Geneva talks which were held on 7 and 8 January 1985 and which were conducted by Mr George Shultz, the US Secretary of State, and Mr Andrei Gromyko, the Soviet Foreign Minister. It soon became apparent that these four conditions were not all compatible and that subtle differences existed between the British and the Americans over the matter of SDI. Clearly this reflected to some extent the difference of view between the European-members of NATO and the United States itself. As *The Times* editorial stated on the matter of the four Anglo-American principles:

> on the first two points, Britain and the United States are in fact profoundly divided in their strategic philosophy. The Third is also relevant to this difference, not of emphasis but of view ... [the] fourth was somewhat inconsistent with her [Mrs Thatcher's] own vigorous opposition to SDI whose consequences, should its research prove effective, would be to tilt the balance substantially in favour of defensive systems for the first time in the nuclear age.[4]

Thus we see here a clash between the British, and to a lesser extent, the European view of deterrence based on the logic of mutual assured destruction and the American view which is now passing into a post-MAD phase. The US is thus anxious to offer the Europeans the benefits of SDI when and if it becomes operational. They wish to head off any initiative undertaken by the Western European powers to promote an agreement to ban the testing and deployment of space-based weapons systems. A series of negotiations did, in fact, take place between the USA and the USSR from June 1978, to August 1979, on the feasibility of banning anti-satellite systems. They were, of course, interrupted by the Afghanistan crisis. However since the talks ended the Soviets have been working flat out on their own research into anti-missile technologies. They are even better placed than America to build an ABM system quickly. Indeed, the Soviets have spent more on strategic defensive forces since the anti-ballistic missile (ABM) treaty was signed in 1972 than on strategic offensive forces.

The most striking and alarming confirmation of this came in the summer of 1983 with the Americans' discovery that the Russians are building a huge new radar near the village of Abalakovo, in the heart of

Siberia. The evidence was regarded in other NATO capitals with reserve, but President Reagan believes the construction amounts to the most blatant case so far of Soviet violation of existing arms control agreements. The significance of the radar which had been in construction for almost three years is still fiercely contested. But intelligence analysts in Washington are convinced that the radar complex is in a good position to enable the Soviets to build a second inland ABM system (they are permitted one, round Moscow, under the Treaty). The radar covers a pie-shaped wedge facing towards the Pacific – precisely the flight path American submarine – launched missiles have to take if aimed at the Soviet missile fields in the south. Moreover, US defence planners see the radar as the latest in a series of developments that cause concern. The Soviets, for example, tested a modern anti-aircraft system, the SA12 at heights of about 100 000 ft. This capability exceeds the height achieved by any aircraft yet developed. These developments should not be seen in isolation however. For the militarization of outer space covers both Asat (anti-satellite) and 'Star Wars' weaponry. Asat weapons are intended to kill military satellites; 'Star Wars' weapons are intended to kill incoming missiles.

Unlike the United States, the Soviet Union already has an Asat weapon ready for use, though the effectiveness is questionable. Perched on top of a large SS9 rocket, the 4400 lb satellite killer would make one or two orbits around the Earth before destroying its target about three hours after launch by exploding like a grenade and showering the satellite with shrapnel.

The Soviet Asat can reach about a third of the 40 or so US satellites now in space, but cannot reach the important early-warning and communications satellites in orbits of 12 000 miles or higher.

The United States first test-fired a trial Asat weapon in January 1984, using an F-15 fighter as the launch vehicle. The weapon, a small 33 lb cylinder, would use eight telescopes to home it on an enemy satellite and ram, meanwhile the US Air Force is commencing work on a second generation of Asat weapons which would involve ground-launched satellite killers and laser beams. So-called 'Star Wars' weapons on the other hand form part of President Reagan's strategic defence initiative which he launched originally in March 1983. This constitutes a costly and complex programme. In fact 'Star Wars' is a four-stage programme which would not be operational (even assuming it receives congressional backing) until well into the next century at a cost of billions of dollars. The ultimate aim of a 'Star Wars' system would be to provide the United States with a protective umbrella against a surprise Soviet first strike, involving tens of thousands of nuclear warheads.

Initial research is taking place into ways of destroying as many missiles as possible (the 'boost-phase' defence) in the first five minutes after their launch. Direct energy weapons, mounted on space-based battle stations, would fire thin laser beams to burn holes in the missiles, either collapsing them or detonating their fuel tanks. Researchers are trying to harness the X-rays generated by a nuclear explosion for conversion into missile-killers. But an early report from the Office of Technology Assessment (OTA) in Washington has severely criticized the feasibility of such weapons. The OTA report says that 'the prospect of a near-perfect defence against nuclear missiles is so remote that it should not form the basis of public policy'.[5] This assertion prompted the head of the 'Star Wars' initiative, James Abrahamson, to claim that the OTA report was inadequate since it contained 'technical errors, unsubstantiated assumptions and conclusions that are inconsistent with the body of the report'. The OTA report however contends that the development of fast-burn missiles may thwart a 'Star Wars' defence. The OTA has even gone so far as to say that the deployment of fast-burn missiles could be a 'potent, even decisive' counter-measure against laser weapons.[6]

Yet it is as well to remember that so far the US intercept on 10 June 1984 was merely a demonstration of the low-technology aspect of a 'Star Wars' defence. But this test was a significant achievement in its own right because it brings to the US the capability to intercept incoming missiles with a non-nuclear warhead. The Soviets, incidentally, have had the ability to intercept incoming missiles with a nuclear bomb for some eight years. However the 'Star Wars' initiative is more than just a low-tech destruction of satellites and missiles by impact. It embraces a whole new technology designed to intercept nuclear missiles. These include laser beams and charged particle weapons to be used from stations on earth or in space in conjunction with interceptor missiles. In view of these prospective developments, Mr Caspar Weinberger, the US Defence Secretary, in April 1984, assured NATO that any US–'Star Wars' missile defence would protect Western Europe as well as the US.[7] Mr Weinberger was asked if the defence would protect Western Europe along with the US. The Secretary of Defence gave a firm, unequivocally positive answer, according to a NATO official.[8] If a medium-range missile was to be knocked out as it approached its target, a defence would have to be based in Europe. Mr Weinberger agreed that this would indeed be so.

There was no discussion of who would pay for any such defensive deployment in Europe.⁹ However, a recent report accepted by the NATO Assembly carried a clear implication that the European members of the alliance would be called on to share the cost of such a system. The likely bill was estimated by a NATO scientific committee at between $100 billion and $600 billion. This would be a mere fraction of the amount to be spent on the project over the next ten years. The Defensive Technologies Study team, for example, suggested that in the next five years the Pentagon would need to spend $7.7 billion on developing equipment capable of spotting, tracking and targeting newly launched Soviet missiles, $6.2 billion on particle beam and other directed-energy research, and $5.2 billion on conventional anti-ballistic missiles to fire against those threatening America.¹⁰

Thus the cost-factor is of some importance for NATO even though the real costs are to be born by the US. Yet it would not be wise for the Europeans to conclude that any benefit the SDI might yield would be only to America's advantage. Though there is the residual fear that such defensive technology could foreshadow a return to some form of isolationism in America the principal anxiety in Western Europe in the 1990s could be the colossal danger that the Soviet Union itself might obtain a workable 'Star Wars' weapons capability.¹¹

Of course the military aspects of European defence arising from the development and possible deployment of defensive technology are crucial given the present contradictions inherent in the strategy of flexible response. As Gerald Frost has noted in this context:

> indeed, it may provide the answer to problems, inherent in the NATO strategy of flexible response, which have long been perceived by a number of those with a professional interest in strategic issues – weaknesses which politicians have generally not been keen to expose to public scrutiny. These weaknesses flow from the nature of the ultimate step in the flexible response strategy: the use of U.S. intercontinental missiles in retaliation against a Soviet attack on Europe.¹²

We have noted the relevance of this argument earlier in the book; and in our analysis of the declining credibility of the American nuclear retaliatory threat in an age of strategic parity. Again, as Frost trenchantly observes:

an effective Western anti-ballistic missile system in space, however, could transform this situation by performing the inestimably valuable task of reducing the scale of the risks to the United States in providing nuclear protection to its European allies. If the risks are judged to be fewer, it follows that United States readiness to accept them is likely to be much enhanced, and the Soviet Union will have to take account of this in its strategic calculations. This is an important argument, but so far no European public figure appears even to have taken it into account.[13]

But whether such a defence capability can be achieved still remains the question. Which interpretation of the facts is preferable when contemplating policy options over the next decade? We juxtapose some very different views of the matter, before attempting an evaluation which also takes up the issue of arms control. Professor Lawrence Freedman remains a distinguished critic of the strategic defence initiative (SDI), whose views are broadly those of the strategic studies establishment in Britain. His position is that

> there is no such thing as a 'purely defensive system' in the nuclear age. If both sides could achieve a perfect defence simultaneously that might take us out of the condition of mutual assured destruction, although it is highly unlikely that Western Europe would also be protected.[14]

He clearly regards the 'Star Wars' project as a technological chimera.

Two distinguished military figures who have contributed to Britain's defence debate over the last decade or so far are Air Vice Marshal S. W. B. Menaul and Colonel Jonathan Alford. They disagree fundamentally on so-called 'Star Wars'.

First, Colonel Alford, who, in a letter to *The Times*, stated that

> even if one accepts the most optimistic judgements of the President's advisers (none above 90 per cent effectiveness overall for a multilayered system) and even if that figure is applied (again optimistically) to a START – limited offensive arsenal of 5,000 strategic warheads could still be assumed to reach their targets. By every count that still amounts to 'assured destruction' and must raise doubts about the value of such a tattered umbrella'.

Col. Alford sees five difficulties with the project:[15]

There would seem to be a number of quite simple counter-measures available (penetration aids) to reduce effectiveness still further.

Second, the exclusive concentration on defence against ballistic missiles leaves uncovered a large (and, because of Cruise missiles, increasing) number of nuclear delivery systems with strategic consequences.

Third, it is almost certainly the case that it will be cheaper to build still more warheads than to deploy effective defences.

Fourth, (and of the greatest concern), any system devised will be very vulnerable to pre-emptive destruction, especially the satellites and communications links which are assumed to be an integral part of that system. If war threatens, the temptation to degrade the defensive system at once will be very great and that is hardly conducive to strategic stability.

Finally, there are bound to be very substantial opportunity costs involved and I am far from convinced that this is the most sensible way to dispose of what are bound to be distinctly finite resources for defence.

In short. I do not believe that the case for SDI has been established beyond doubt even if it can be made to work to the level of 90% effectiveness. I doubt if it is worth the huge cost that is likely to be involved.

I cannot see that it will lead to greater strategic stability and it could have profound consequences for Western Europe which have hardly been explored.[16]

This is a telling, if a slightly self-important, analysis of SDI and its implications.

However Air Vice-Marshal (Paddy) Menaul characteristically took a different view (which he advanced attacking an article by Lord Kennet entitled, 'Shoot Down This Perilous Idea').[17] He regretted that Lord Kennet should add his name

> to the growing number of ill-informed critics of the United States strategic initiative. Most of those who have so far ventured an opinion on the concept of defending against attack by ballistic missiles have demonstrated a remarkable lack of knowledge of what SDI is all about, the technology that makes such a defence system possible and how it could contribute to stability and a reduction in the nuclear arsenals of the superpowers.[18]

Air Vice-Marshal Menaul pointed to certain in-house presidential study groups which between 1980 and 1982 had studied the matter of strategic defence and which finally resulted in the SDI under the direction of General James Abrahamson. He concluded firmly:

> the SDI is simply a research programme into a new concept of non-nuclear defence against ballistic missiles, whether nuclear or conventionally armed. The best scientific brains in the United States believe that an effective BMD (ballistic missile defence) system can be developed, but whether or not it would be deployed would depend on the outcome of discussions with the Soviet Union on the future military use of space.

The West spends millions on surface-to-air missiles and manned interceptor aircraft to bring down manned bombers. Ballistic missiles and manned bombers were simply different means to achieve the same objective. Menaul concluded that 'Missiles travel through space on their trajectories to their targets; bombers travel through the air on a similar mission. It is just as logical to defend against ballistic missiles as it is to provide elaborate defences against manned bombers.'

The SDI was in his view an imaginative and progressive research project 'which has so far received little recognition in Europe, due largely to ignorance and lack of interest, even though a ground and space-based system would provide defence for Europe as well as the United States'.[19] Well, apart from Paddy Menaul's tendency to dismiss those who disagree with him as ill-informed, this is a reasoned analysis of the case for SDI. There is much truth in what both men have to say on the subject (as well as their obvious agreement about the connection between the project and arms control). Indeed as Col. Alford asserts:

> given what is known about Soviet research and development programmes in this area, it probably is necessary to hedge against their possible success. If the SDI has the effect of producing better and more durable arms control agreements to fence off this area of competition, it could turn out to have been worth it.[20]

But what if arms control is at a dead end? Quite so. In the light of this, we now relate SDI to the arms control process itself with reference to the strategic arguments involved concerning the true purpose of deterrence as it may evolve well into the next century. Indeed this debate about the merits and demerits of strategic defence mirrors the importance of the much earlier debate in the late 1940s over whether America should proceed to develop a thermo-nuclear bomb. As in both cases it vitally affects European defence.

It is clear that SDI could in certain circumstances favour the defence of Europe and assist in the process of the Europeanization of NATO. First, a deterrent focusing on damage limitation and denial of victory is likely to prove more effective than one endorsing a condition of mutual destruction in promoting arms control. Clearly, the ability to wage war successfully and survive is best consistent with the real purpose of arms control. Therefore, a capacity for strategic defence would allow reductions in offensive weapon systems to take place. Mutual assured destruction (MAD), of course, depends on a large offensive capability. The formula that SDI would permit *vis-à-vis* arms control can be summed up as unconstrained strategic defences for constrained offensive force levels achieved through negotiated reductions. This formula would deny the Soviets a theory of victory should deterrence fail. Thus both the United States and NATO-Europe could exploit the Soviets' fear of a protracted war with the Western powers (the Soviets simply favour a short-war scenario as things stand at present), which given the West's potentially superior forces constitutes a more viable deterrent strategy than the present commitment to a forward strategy dependent on deliberate controlled nuclear escalation which might prove too difficult and complex to control. The logic is clear: a Western capacity to execute a threat of an immediate victory denial, accompanied by recovery and mobilization made possible by a partial SDI system should constitute a more effective deterrent than NATO's contemporary strategy.[21] Moreover, the strategic defence system is expected to be at least as effective against the SS-20s aimed at Western Europe as it is against ICBMs.

We accept that this new strategy depends on the fulfilment of three conditions which would, in our judgement, prove to be a more adequate basis for effective defence than the illogical and irrational commitment implicit in the doctrine of mutual assured destruction (MAD). Firstly, the US in particular – and NATO-Europe in general – must deploy a counterforce – capable strategic posture;

Secondly, the US must develop a capacity to threaten the Soviet command, communications and control (C3) targets – even given BMD emplacements – in a bid to disrupt and destroy their capacity to coordinate a war-winning strategy. Also America should retain a capacity to threaten political targets, designated as command centres at both the military and political levels;

Thirdly, the US must develop in particular, and NATO-Europe in general, a more credible post-attack and mobilization options more consistent with a real capability to wage a protracted war.[22]

These three conditions, then, constitute a radical departure from the current approach to deterrence theory, strategic doctrine and the START process. It has to be emphasized that these changes are necessary because technology now makes – or will make – such options more feasible but also because the nature of current Soviet strategy appears to embody a theory of victory in war. As we have noted elsewhere, the Soviets are committed to a military strategy which seeks to achieve four objectives in a bid to secure military victory:

(1) they seek the early destruction of the US and NATO's capacity to carry through a powerful retaliatory attack;
(2) they seek the rapid achievement of a dominant nuclear capacity following the opening phase of the war, and particularly following pre-emption;
(3) they seek the quick seizure of the West's critical strategic assets (particularly in Western Europe); and
(4) they seek if necessary – depending on how the war progresses – the partial or total destruction of the American political, military – industrial complex.[23]

Now given the above Soviet military objectives, through the pursuit of a strategy of denial, the West requires a 'denial of victory' deterrent which ensures that America (and NATO-Europe) has a high degree of survivability for its strategic forces achieved under the rubric of the strategic defence initiative (SDI). This means that America at the strategic level (and NATO at the nuclear-theatre level) must be capable of sustaining an escalation process as part and parcel of the threat of a victory denial strategy. The essential corrollary of such a posture is the need for NATO-Europe to have the capacity to deny the Soviets in all circumstances any pre-war or postwar preponderance of nuclear capability. Thus both SDI and FOFA are complementary strategies. America, as the centrepiece of the alliance, must possess this capacity to an even greater extent. This calls for the 'point defence' of the American missile silos. It is particularly necessary to protect the 550 silos containing US Minutemen 3 ICBMs, of which 300 have the highly precise mark-12A warheads. Therefore we conclude that a fundamental commitment to damage limitation cannot – and must not – be separated from the threat of victory denial. In other words, SDI could provide the means whereby damage limitation is rendered consistent with a capacity to prevent a Soviet military victory. The clear advantage which an emphasis on strategic defence confers (as opposed to strategic offence) is that it deals with the real danger that the West faces over the next ten years and beyond. Thus, the effect of SDI on deterrent theory should be to provide a conceptual basis for defence planning which actually gives the United States and a Europeanized NATO (in the sense defined in earlier chapters) the capacity to achieve four principal objectives:

(1) the capacity to deter the Soviet Union from executing nuclear attacks against the United States *and its European allies*;
(2) the capability to influence Soviet behaviour in a crisis that might provoke American strategic nuclear strikes;
(3) the ability to induce the Soviet Union in all conceivable circumstances to pursue rational targeting procedures in the event that deterrence fails (to reinforce Soviet counterforce priorities); and
(4) to develop some form of strategic defence as envisaged by the strategic defence initiative compatible with US war survival and Western European capacity to endure and overcome even the effects of a counterforce nuclear war.[24]

The above requirements will not be easy to meet, though to some extent already the Soviet Union itself has pursued a similar set of objectives embracing the notion of survival and damage limitation. To the extent to which both the Soviet Union (and its allies) and the United States (and its allies) have the capacity to survive (mutual survivability), then reason and restraint in the conduct of war would have been partially restored.[25]

It is a curious comment on thinking about nuclear strategy and theories of deterrence that the well-established (in theory) Soviet potential for national survival in war has been regarded as acceptable (even to some reassuring), but that a similar Western capacity is seen to be potentially (if not actually) destabilizing and therefore a threat to peace. However given the changes envisaged above, *both* superpowers would be committed *not* to mutual destruction but mutual survival. Moral purpose would thus have been restored to war in the nuclear-missile age. Also, real defence planning in Europe could begin, and with it a genuine basis for the creation of the twin-pillar concept of Western defence which can alone ensure a sound basis for a stable East–West *détente*.

14 Conclusions

The formation of NATO, as we have repeatedly said, some 36 years ago was the result of the perceived need felt by both Western Europe and the United States to form some sort of alliance to protect Europe while it was recovering from the Second World War. The structure formed prior to NATO, the European Recovery Programme, was instituted by the US in 1947 to prevent economic collapse in Europe during the postwar years – a time when collapse could have meant a complete, non-military infiltration and full exploitation of Europe by the Soviet Union. It was not long, however, before the United States noted that if the Soviet Union was stymied in its non-military attempts to gain control over badly needed agriculture and industry, it might be tempted to use military force to attain its goals. At that time, this threat was not particularly plausible, yet the North Atlantic Treaty Organization was formed in 1949. A US military presence was 'permanently' established in Western Europe and the two areas of the world became coupled as the United States pledged to defend her allies. In essence, this relieved Western Europe of all military pressure so that they could concentrate on economic recovery.

That was 36 years ago. Since then, Europe has made a full-scale recovery economically, industrially and socially. Politically, Europe (that is, the individual nation-states) was fated never to be as strong as it was prior to the 1900s, yet some significant measure of political recovery resulted in the postwar years. However, the situation has now gone beyond the control of the status quo NATO posture. European dependence upon US aid and military commitment has resulted in a Europe plagued with a wide variety of doubts. Europeans fear, as we have seen in a various context, a US–USSR conspiracy to wage war on European soil, and, at the same time, they see their own military weakness, inability to cope, and disunity leaving them unable to handle the situation. They recognize that they have no control or very little control over the use of the nuclear missiles deployed on their land. They have a diminishing fear of a Russian attack despite an increase in

Russian power; but are more terrified of a nuclear war resulting from a miscalculation by the West. European nations are currently beset by anti-nuclear demonstrations and peace movements who fervently believe the US should take its bombs and go home; while many other Europeans believe and fear that the US is planning to return to isolationism – abandoning its North Atlantic allies. Europeans also see that they disagree with the US in many areas outside of the NATO alliance; the Americans have apparently opposing interests in Latin America, Africa, the Middle East, and other Third World Nations. They fear even the suggestion of German unity and/or possible nuclear-armed West Germany. Finally, Western Europe feels uneasy or even perhaps humiliated at its continued dependence upon the US. Yet in spite of its ability to remedy that situation through increased defence expenditure and conventional defence, there is a debilitating unwillingness among the Europeans to do so. Within the present ossified framework of NATO, these problems seem inescapable, yet some changes could be made before disaster strikes. In dividing the problems into two central areas of change, we have attempted in this book to provide at least a direction in which the changes could take place; we no longer doubt the need for change. The advocates of no early-first-use define the central issue as the need to increase European responsibility for its own defence. The obvious, most feasible direction they argue for Western Europe to turn is towards the formation of a conglomeration of nations with a heightened conventional defence. European nations they assert currently have the resources and the manpower to provide themselves with this defence. Fears of US withdrawal need not be realized as increased European armament does not require the withdrawal of American troops or munitions. There would be little incentive to withdraw the troops since protection of Europe will always be in the best security interests of the United States. They further go so far as to suggest that with the increase in European NATO troops providing for the defence of such a vital area, US soldiers would be more likely to remain. The US congress would be more willing to support their deployment.

The European fear of turning the continent into an armed camp also they contend need not be realized. To seek to maintain a more than adequate conventional army need not put an unnecessary strain on the economy and the fabric of society. Turning Europe into an armed camp would only be necessary if the goal were to win a decisive conventional attack against the USSR, which is not – nor should it be – the objective of the proposed military policy. NATO should only aim for a policy of initial conventional retaliation in the event of a Soviet attack. A state of greater military preparedness at the conventional level they argue, would have two very important advantages over the status quo.

First, they say, it would diminish the gap which presently exists in the defence arrangements of Europe. Now, the Western allies do not adequately provide conventional defence for their own defence; US and other troops stationed in Europe act simply as major impediments to a Soviet attack. Yet, as we have argued for the US to provide adequate additional conventional protection is not only unfeasible in terms of cost and manpower, but it would be unwanted by the European nations that would have to quarter the soldiers on their homeland. However it is argued that if the Europeans provided their own strong, essentially non-nuclear defence this could relieve a large part of the European dependence on the United States; it would reduce the need for US troops in Europe and therefore reduce the gap in the present static linear defence system.

More importantly, they assert, a properly conventionally equipped Europe would go a long way in deterring a conventional Russian attack. Europe's defence potential they say is enormous because European wealth and population are higher than that of the Soviet Union. The Soviets would find themselves at a 3:1 disadvantage in terms of troops when faced with the temptation to invade. That in turn provides for a more stable environment in which to deter aggression. However supplying some if not all NATO forces with Emerging Technologies and training as they become practical would in our view be a better option than increased reliance on present conventional capabilities. It could deter a conventional invasion and therefore decrease the risk of uncontrolled nuclear escalation. Although the use of Emerging Technologies may not decrease the number of casualties the battle would cause, an inherent advantage lies in the absence of radiation – future generations would not have to suffer genetic mutations. A frightening advantage, but an advantage none the less.

It may also be wise, once again, to re-emphasize the importance of dual control over the nuclear weapons themselves. The obvious disadvantage in dual control for the US lies in its loss of control over the use of nuclear warheads which must result in a diminution of its power. On the European side, however, as we have argued, there is potential for great advantage. Dual control has the potential to lessen a major source of tension and discontent experienced by the NATO allies. Dual control would allow NATO member governments input on two levels:

a negative input in that a veto could be cast with respect to their use, and a positive input in that NATO – Europe could shape future nuclear and non-nuclear strategy in a manner more in keeping with their interests.

A decline in anti-American sentiment and a reduction of fear concerning American policy could also result from a greater feeling of control over such a threatening menacing technology. This decline in fear also applies to fear of miscalculation, misjudgements of the situation and/or mistakes made in haste, since dual control would require European approval on use of NATO missiles. Dual control, then, equals alliance unity.

Dual control would also shift the burden of responsibility off the shoulders of the US and on to those of the alliance. Along with the responsibility would go the right for Europe to have a large sphere of influence both inside and outside of NATO. Europe after all has a vested interest in international order. European input and importance during arms negotiations would also increase. American hegemony would become recessional: this would then lead to genuine alliance equality.

There is also a great possibility that dual control would have a dramatic defusing effect on the peace movements which currently plague the nations of Western Europe. Anti-nuclear demonstrations seem to be aimed principally at US nuclear weapons in Europe and not at those of Britain or France. The French have experienced very limited discontent from their own citizens concerning their missiles. However, the rest of Europe is not so fortunate and, as Dr Henry Kissinger noted in *Time* magazine in 1984, one of the dangers of the protest movement in Europe is that they have managed to pull some governments: '... in the general direction of their policies, even though those governments disagree with their premises'.[1] The effect of the protect movement on opposition parties is equally insidious in that the opposition are changing their policies to gain electoral support from the increasing numbers of people attracted by simplistic policies promising world peace. The shifts in policies as Kissinger notes: '... amount to unilateral nuclear disarmament for their countries'.[2] Both effects present a destabilizing force within the nations involved. Although it is not certain what dual control of nuclear missiles would do for the situation, it can probably be expected that a wider acceptance of the nuclear weapons would result, as in the example of France. (Dual control of nuclear weapons with Germany presents its own unique opportunities.)

To provide for a smoother transition from dependence on US military protection to dependence on European forces, European influence within the Eurogroup should be heightened within NATO and a separate, exclusively European defence group should also be set up to provide a forum for specifically European defence issues. Defence ministers in Europe should be made members of this European non-NATO group which should meet regularly to present ideas calculated to enhance a sense of European consciousness in strategic matters. This group could act as a link between the individual governments and the Euro-group within NATO, where policies could be formulated and submitted for approval. This structure would signal a decided shift from Europe's current *secondary* role in its own defence to that of a *primary* role. The rise of European defence could then become a fact.

Increased communication and co-operation would result in the advancing of goals in the area of standardization and the 'interoperability' of armaments throughout the West insofar as this is regarded as desirable. A broader set of political goals which could be discussed include methods of maintaining US defence commitments to the mutual agreement of both sides and the strengthening of a European identity. Simply by relying less upon the US, Europe will be able to voice more effectively its opinions on Third World and non-NATO issues without being over-shadowed by American power.

This suggestion (i.e. European groups to provide fora for discussion) is now supported by a wide section of defence opinion in Western Europe.

Although we do not believe that a totally self-sufficient Europe or super-power is possible, or that the Europeans could survive without US bombs and soldiers, we do perceive that heightening contact and more organization in Europe is vital to the future stability of the region. However, there is much less agreement over the second central issue which we wish to face: tampering with the structure and strategy of the North Atlantic Treaty Organization. This brings us to the issue of the local strategy of NATO.

Current NATO strategy, flexible response, in its present form, is (as we have stressed many times in this study) in need of restructuring and of radical change. It is partially outdated, it no longer serves the same goals as were intended at its creation in 1962, and it never really answered any of the basic questions which a sound policy should seek to encompass. For example, defence planners should have been able to determine from the policy how long a conventional war was to be fought before nuclear missiles are launched, what targets were to be struck, when the targets were to be struck and with what weapons were the targets to be struck. If nothing else, these questions should be answered by the restructuring so that a definite policy could replace the vague, general policy which exists today. General Roger's Follow-on-Force attack concept has considerable potential for the future as does the US army's concept of the Air–Land battle. But reworking the policy to include a modestly enhanced European conventional force and dual control of the NATO nuclear long-range theatre weapons is palpably necessary. During these discussions, a large debate over West Germany's surrogate nuclear status will inevitably take place.

A surrogate nuclear West Germany would solve a great deal of problems in the defence of Europe. We argue reasonably that Western Germany deserves to be a nuclear power having a capacity to shape nuclear strategy since its exposure to danger lies on three fronts: it currently possesses no national nuclear weapons of its own, it is a country which borders Warsaw Pact held territory, and if war breaks out in Europe, it is quite likely to begin on German soil. Thus West Germany should be allowed to lease the Pershing II and Cruise missiles currently deployed by NATO and also be allowed to lease from the US a sea-borne second-strike retaliatory system. This we call a surrogate nuclear status because unlike either Britain or France, West Germany will be deemed to have leased its nuclear warheads and missiles from America. She will not therefore need to test nuclear weapons nor flight-test missile systems. The rest of Europe, however, is apparently terrified at the suggestion of a surrogate nuclear Germany in spite of the advantages for protection that such an option would afford. Clearly, a national deterrent even of this tenuous character, would be a more effective deterrent to a direct attack on Germany than an exclusively conventional response. Compromise will have to solve this impasse – the concession made in exchange for Germany's surrogate nuclear status could be the acceptance that the nuclear release would have to be a joint decision with Britain and France which both possess an independent nuclear status. Moreover they themselves should possess dual-control over American nuclear warheads. This seems to be a reasonable way to deal with both the needs and the fears of an alliance which depends for its credibility on a consensus about the use of nuclear weapons. But we recognize the political impediments that remain to conferring on Western Germany such a nuclear status.

However, we do not see why allowing Germany to have first dual control and then in the fullness of time absolute possession of nuclear missiles should automatically heighten the anxieties of the rest of

Europe. The Soviets will no doubt try and orchestrate virulent anti-German sentiment over the issue.

All in all, this basic approach to restructuring NATO provides only a starting point. We must also pay attention to the new direction in conventional defence which has been promulgated in SHAPE's Follow-on Force attack concept and the US army's Air-Land Battle doctrine for NATO's strategy of flexible response which were briefly discussed in earlier chapters. We believe that one of the by-products of the Western debate about NATO nuclear weapons and strategy has been to reinforce the case for the Europeanization of NATO. If this Europeanization implies a strengthening of NATO by increasing the importance of the European pillar of the alliance then it must be encouraged. Moreover, it is clear to us beyond preadventure that the European influence within NATO can be enhanced by the introduction over the next decade of so-called 'Deep attack' concepts based on both emerging military technologies and existing capabilities. An increasing number of defence specialists now see the possibilities of emerging technology as a way of diminishing NATO's dependence on nuclear weapons. This issue and its relationship to the Europeanization of defence will prove to be of vital importance in the years that lie ahead together with the vexed question of the military and arms control aspects of so-called 'Star Wars' anti-missile defence. Europe therefore stands on the threshold of being able to defend itself and with the rise of this capability achieve a more proportionate and balanced relationship with super-power America.

Notes

INTRODUCTION

1. Collins, John M., *United States/Soviet Military Balance*, Library of Congress, Congressional Research Service, Issue Brief Number 1B78029.
2. Ibid.
3. *Time*, 21 Mar. 1983, p. 16.
4. *The Economist*, 1 Sept. 1983.
5. *Report of the President's Commission on Strategic Forces*, Apr. 1983.

1 : BRITAIN AND THE THIRD FORCE SYNDROME

1. See Jacob Javits, 'The Second Battle of Britain', Congressional Record. US Congress, Washington, DC, vol. 111, no. 148, 12 August 1965, pp. 19421–5. Also see Edward English 'Atlantic Trade Policy: the Need for a New Initiative', Moorgate & Wall Street, London, Autumn, 1965.
2. For an early analysis along these lines see Lionel Gelber, 'A Marriage of Inconvenience', Foreign Affairs, Council on Foreign Relations, New York, Jan. 1963; reprinted in *Survival* (London Institute for Strategic Studies, Mar. 1963).
3. For a clear statement of a Eurocentric viewpoint see Alastair Buchan, 'East of Suez: Why Dangle Vain Hopes'? *The Sunday Times*, London, 18 Aug. 1968.
4. Geoffrey Lee Williams, *Natural Alliance for the West* (London: Atlantic Policy Research Centre, 1969) p. 21.
5. See a penetrating study of maritime strategy in L. W. Martin, 'The Sea in Modern Strategy' (London: Institute for Strategic Studies, Chatto & Windus, 1967).
6. Michael Wells, 'Russian Build-Up in Middle East Oil', *The Sunday Times*, 28 July 1968.
7. See *The Times*, London, 17 Aug. 1968, for a belated editorial interest in the fate of the Persian Gulf.
8. See, for instance, *The Times*, 15 Aug. 1968.
9. For a perceptive analysis of American arguments for a US withdrawal from Asia see Gelber, 'History and the American Role', Orbis, Foreign Policy Research Institute, University of Pennsylvania, Philadelphia, Spring, 1967. Also see Gelber, 'The American Role and World Order', *The Yale Review*, Yale University Press, New Haven, Conn., Summer, 1967.

Regarding the debate in Australia over the future of defence policy, and in particular the controversy over a possible off-shore strategy, there was continuous coverage in *The Australian*, the *Sydney Morning Herald* and *The Bulletin*, Sydney, and *The Canberra Times*, Canberra, throughout 1968.
Also see A. D. Robinson, 'Australia–New Zealand Defence', *Australian Outlook*, Australian Institute of International Affairs, Canberra, Apr. 1966, for a discussion of Australian forces serving overseas.
10. Geoffrey Williams, *The Permanent Alliance: the European–American Partnership, 1945–1984* (Leyden: Sijthoff, 1977) p. 216.
11. Ibid., p. 219
12. Gavin Kennedy, *Defence Economics* (London: Duckworth, 1983) p. 71.
13. Geoffrey Lee Williams and Alan Lee Williams *Crisis in European Defence*. (London: Charles Knight, 1978) p. 219.
14. Geoffrey Williams, op. cit., p. 211.
15. Guido Vigeveno, *The Bomb and European Security* (London: C. Hurst & Co., 1983) pp. 7–23.
16. See a detailed discussion in Neville Brown, *Arms without Empire* (Harmondsworth: Penguin, 1967).

2: THE GROWTH OF THE STRATEGIC DICHOTOMY

1. Robert McNamara, when US Secretary of Defence, at press conference, San Francisco. 17 Sept. 1967. (See USIS Press Release, 19 Sept. 1967.)
2. This was one of the reasons for the anxiety expressed by Sir Alec Douglas-Home, Opposition spokesman in Britain on foreign affairs, at the time of the United States decision in the spring of 1968 to halt the bombing of North Vietnam and begin negotiations with Hanoi. See *The Times*, 1 Apr. 1968. For a discussion, though not a condemnation of the risks the United States has taken in opening discussions with North Vietnam.
3. Henry Kissinger, 'The Nth Country Problem', *The Reporter*, New York, 28 Mar. 1963.
4. Press Release issued after press conference held by President de Gaulle in Paris, 14 Jan. 1963.
5. Geoffrey Williams, *The Permanent Alliance: the European–American Partnership, 1945–1984* (Leyden: A. W. Sijthoff, 1977) pp. 178–98.
6. Ivor Richard, *Europe or the Open Sea?* (London, Charles Knight, 1971) pp. 20–6.
7. Ibid., pp. 20–6.
8. Geoffrey Williams, op. cit., p. 216.
9. See a perspective study by L. W. Martin *British Defence Policy: the Long Recessional*, Adelphi Paper no. 61 (IISS, 1969).
10. Geoffrey Williams *Natural Alliance for the West* (Atlantic Trade Study, 1969) pp. 16–22.

3: THE RISE OF EUROPEANISM

1. Henry Kissinger, 'A Plan to Reshape NATO', *Time*, 5 Mar. 1984, p. 15.

2. Michael Howard, 'Deterrence, Consensus and Reassurance in the Defence of Europe', p. 23.
3. Samuel P. Huntington, 'Broadening the Strategic Focus', p. 31.
4. John D. Steinbruner & Leon V. Sigal, *Alliance Security* (Washington: The Brookings Institution, 1983).
5. Rainer W. Rupp, 'Sharing the Defence Burden' in *NATO Review*, Dec. 1982, p. 24.
6. Ibid., p. 24.
7. McGeorge Bundy et al., 'Nuclear Weapons and the Atlantic Alliance', *Foreign Affairs*, Spring 1982, p. 763.
8. Guido Vigeveno, *The Bomb and European Security* (London: C. Hurst & Co., 1983) p. 130.
9. Ibid., p. 130.
10. Henry Kissinger, 'A Plan to Reshape NATO', *Time*, 5 Mar. 1984, p. 16.
11. Henry Kissinger, 'The Realities of Security', *AEI Defence Review*, 1982.
12. Hedley Bull, 'European Self-Reliance and the Reform of NATO', *The Atlantic Quarterly*, Summer 1983, p. 36.
13. Geoffrey Lee Williams, *The British Nuclear Defence Option* (London: British Atlantic Publications, 1983) p. 14.
14. Ibid., p. 14.
15. Ibid., p. 16.
16. Andrew J. Pierre, *The Global Politics of Arms Sales* (Princeton University Press, 1982) p. 34.
17. T. B. Millar, *The Strategic Balance* (London: Allen & Unwin, 1983) p. 58.
18. Pierre, op. cit., p. 34.
19. Alexander H. Cornell, 'Collaboration in Weapons and Equipment', *NATO Review*, Aug. 1980.
20. Ibid.
21. Mark Blacksell, *Post-War Europe* (London: Hutchinson, 1981) p. 52.
22. Gavin Kennedy, *Defence Economics* (London: Duckworth, 1983) p. 41.
23. Geoffrey Williams et al., *Crisis in Procurement: a Case Study of the TSR-2* (London: RUSI, 1969) p. 27.
24. *NATO—Facts and Figures* (Brussels, 1975) pp. 7–20.

4: THE FRAGMENTATION OF ALLIANCE

1. Henry A. Kissinger, 'Strategy and the Atlantic Alliance', *Survival*, no. 5, 24 (1982).
2. Ibid.
3. Henry A. Kissinger, *The Necessity For Choice* (London: Chatto & Windus) pp. 75–81.
4. Robert W. Kower, 'Ten Suggestions For Rationalizing NATO', *Survival*, ISS, no. 2. 19 (1977) p. 67.
5. Ibid. Spain now brings NATO to Sixteen members.
6. Ibid., p. 67.
7. Ibid., p. 67.

8. Steven Canby, 'NATO: Reassessing the Conventional Wisdoms', *Survival*, ISS (1977) p. 164.
9. Ibid., p. 164.
10. Ibid., p. 166.
11. Boyd D. Sutton *et al.*, 'New Directions in Conventional Defence?', *Survival*, ISS, no. 2, 26 (Mar./Apr. 1984) p. 164.
12. Ibid., p. 164.
13. Sam Nunn, 'Conventional Forces And Alliance Strategy', *Survival*, ISS, no. 5, 24 (1982) p. 234.
14. Sutton, op. cit., p. 53.
15. Ibid., p. 68.
16. Karl Kaiser, Georg Leber, Alois Mertes, Franz-Josef Schulze, 'Nuclear Weapons and the Preservation of Peace', *Foreign Affairs*, 1982.
17. Ibid.
18. Phil Williams and William Wallace, 'Emerging Technologies and European Security', *Survival*, ISS, no. 2, 26 (Mar./Apr. 1984) p. 75.
19. Sutton, op. cit., p. 68.
20. C. F. von Weizsacker, *The Politics of Peril* (New York: Seabury Press, 1978) pp. 228–33.
21. Lawrence Freedom, *The Evolution of Nuclear Strategy* (London: Macmillan 1981) p. 327.
22. von Weizsacker, op. cit.
23. Guido Vigeveno, *The Bomb and European Security* (London: C. Hurst & Co., 1983.) pp. 83–5.
24. Freedman, op. cit., p. 100.
25. Bernard Brodie, *War and Politics* (London: Cassell, 1974) p. 378.
26. Vigeveno, op. cit., p. 87.

5 : EUROPEAN DEFENCE

1. Lenin, *Collected Works*, vol. 28 (Moscow: Progress Publishers, 1964) p. 3.
2. Guido Vigeveno, *The Bomb and the Security of Europe* (London: C. Hurst & Co., 1983).
3. The calculation of the correlation of forces constitute an objective assessment of the international situation which then determines policy in a scientific way. All decisions based on this calculation are tactically expedient and do not consciously affect ultimate aims or intentions.
4. Gordon Craig, *Europe Since 1945* (New York: 1966).
5. Lt Col. Ye Rybkin, 'On The Nature of a Nuclear Missile War' in W. R. Kintner & H. F. Scot, *The Nuclear Revolution In Soviet Military Affairs* (University of Oklahoma Press, 1968) p. 109.
6. Dimitri Simes, 'Deterrence and Coercion In Soviet Policy', *International Security*, vol. 5. no. 3. 1981, p. 88.
7. Colin S. Gray and Keith Payne, 'Victory is Possible', *Foreign Policy*, Summer 1980, no. 39, pp. 14–28.
8. Konrad EGE et Martha Wenger, La Nouvelle Doctrine ' "Airland Battle":

Ce Que Serait Une Guerre en Europe,' *Le Monde Diplomatique*, Feb. 1983, pp. 12–13.
9. Dimitri Simes, op. cit., p. 88.
10. Franklin D. Holzman, 'Are the Soviet Really Outspending the U.S. on Defence'?, *International Security*, vol. 4., no. 4, Spring 1980, p. 86 ff.
11. Konrad EGE, 'L'Effort de Rearmement Aux Etata Unis: Budget de Defence ou Budget de Guerre'?, *Le Monde Diplomatique*, 1983, p. 6.
12. Konrad EGE, op. cit.
13. Ibid.
14. *SIPRI Yearbook 1981* (London: Taylor & Francis) p. 152.
15. Douglas T. Stuart, 'Prospects for Sino-European Security Cooperation', *Orbis*, vol. 26, Autumn 1982, p. 721.
16. Douglas T. Stuart, op. cit., p. 273.
17. David Yost, 'Ballistic Missile Defence and the Atlantic Alliance', *International Security*, vol. 7, no. 2, Autumn 82, p. 143.
18. David Yost, op. cit., p. 145.
19. Epstein, *Measuring Military Power: the Soviet Air Threat* (Princeton University Press, 1984).
20. Fen Osler Hampson, 'Groping for Technical Panaceas: The European Conventional Balance and Nuclear Stability', *International Security*, vol. 8, no. 3, Winter 1983/84, p. 57.
21. Nino Pasti, 'Euro-Missiles and the General Balance of NATO and Warsaw Pact Forces'(Helsinki World Peace Council, 1979).
22. *NATO Review*, NATO Inf. Sers., June 1979, p. 31.
23. *International Herald Tribune*, 27–28 June 1981, p. 1.
24. *New Statesman*, 31 Oct. 1981.
25. *Newsweek*, 30 Nov. 1981, p. 12.
26. International Institute for Strategic Studies, 1982–83 (London).
27. Jonathan Steele, *World Power: Soviet Foreign Policy Under Brezhnev and Andropov*, In 'Power Without Influence', *Guardian*, 28 Sept. 1983, p. 9.
28. It must be said that nuclear threats are not peculiar to the Russians. The US is known to have threatened to use them at least 19 times, e.g. Eisenhower, Kennedy, Nixon and Carter threatened to use them respectively during the Korean War; the Cuban Missile Crisis; the Vietnam War and the Missile East war of 1973 when all US nuclear forces were put on alert; and during the Iranian crisis.
29. Brodie, US Senate, Committee on Foreign Relations, *Perceptions: Relations between the US and the USSR* (Washington, Government Printing Office, 1978) p. 329.
30. Lawrence Freedman, *The Evolution of Nuclear Strategy*. (London: Macmillan, 1981) p. 336.
31. Sh.P. Sanakoyev and N. I. Kapchenko, *Socialism: Foreign Policy in Theory and Practice* (Moscow: Progress Publishers, 1976) p. 126.
32. David Holloway. *The Soviet Union and the Arms Race* (New Haven, Conn: Yale University Press, 1983) pp. 81–2.
33. Stephen M. Meyer. 'Soviet Theatre Nuclear Forces, Part 1: Development of Doctrine and Objectives', Adelphi Papers no. 2, 187 (London: IISS, 1983) p. 4.

34. D. a. Volkogonov et al. (eds), *Voina i Armiya* (Moscow: Voenizdat, 1977) p. 354.
35. Holloway, op. cit., p. 82.
36. Vernon V. Aspaturian, 'Soviet Global Power and the Correlation of Forces', *Problems of Communism* (May–June, 1980) p. 9.
37. A. Sergiyev, 'Leninism and the Correlation of Forces as a Factor of International Relations', *International Affairs*, May 1975, p. 103.
38. Aspaturian, op. cit. p. 10.
39. Ibid., p. 10.
40. Ibid., p. 11.
41. Ibid., p. 11.
42. Ibid., p. 2.
43. Ibid., p. 2.
44. Ibid., p. 3.
45. Aspaturian, op. cit., pp. 1–2.
46. Zbigniew Brzezinski, 'Tragic Dilemmas of Soviet World Power, the Limits of a New-Type Empire'. *Encounter*, pp. 12–13.
47. Holloway, op. cit., p. 102.
48. Brzezinski, op. cit., pp. 10–15.
49. Aspaturian, op. cit., p. 9.
50. Holloway, op. cit., p. 102.

6: THE TRANSFORMATION OF THE SOVIET NAVY

1. David Fairhall, *Russian Sea Power* (Boston: Sambit Inc., 1971).
2. Barry M. Blechman, *The Changing Soviet Navy* (NY: Brookings, 1973).
3. John Erikson et al., *The Role of Maritime Forces in the Security of Western Europe*, RNA Conference Proceedings, 21–24 Sept. 1971.
4. Sergei G. Gorshkov, *The Seapower of the Sea* (Oxford: Pergamon Press, 1979).
5. Geoffrey Williams, *Global Defence: Motivation and Policy in a Nuclear Age* (New Delhi: Vikas, 1984) pp. 14–37.
6. Bryan Ranft and Geoffrey Till, *The Sea in Soviet Strategy* (London: Macmillan, 1984).
7. Robert G. Weinland, 'Soviet Naval Operations – Ten Years of Change', Centre for Naval Analysis, Professional Paper 125, Aug. 1974.
8. *Power at Sea*, Part III: *Competition and Conflict*, papers from IISS Seventeenth Annual Conference, spring 1976.
9. Geoffrey Till (ed.), *The Future of British Sea Power* (London: Macmillan, 1984).
10. Ibid.
11. Geoffrey Williams, op. cit., p. 17.
12. Ibid., p. 17.
13. David Fairhall, op. cit., p. 24.
14. John Erickson, op. cit., p. 72.
15. Geoffrey Williams, op. cit., p. 36.

16. Geoffrey Williams and Alan Williams, *Crisis in European Defence* (London: Charles Knight, 1971) p. 84.
17. Global Defence, op. cit., pp. 11–22.
18. Ibid., pp. 11–22.
19. Ibid., pp. 11–22.
20. David Fairhall, op. cit., p. 17.

7 : NATIONAL PERSPECTIVES WITHIN THE ALLIANCE

1. Karl E. Bimbaum, *East and West Germany: Modus Vivendi* (Lexington Books, 1973) pp. 1–43.
2. Michael Palmov, 'The Prospects for a European Security Conference', European Series, no. 18 (London: Chatham House PEP, 1971).
3. Ross A. Johnson, 'The Warsaw Pact's Campaign for European Security'. Rand Report, Nov. 1970.
4. Philip Windsor, 'Germany and the Western Alliance: Lessons from the 1980 Crisis', Adelphi Papers no. 170, IISS, 1981.
5. Geoffrey Williams, *Global Defence: Motivation and Policy in a Nuclear Age* (New Delhi: Vikas, 1984) pp. 117–25.
6. David Botton (ed.) *Campaigns against Western Defence: NATO's Adversaries and Critics* (London: Macmillan, 1985).
7. Geoffey Williams, *The Permanent Alliance: the European–American Partnership, 1945–1985* (Leyden, Sijthoff, 1977).
8. Peter van den Dungen, *West European Pacifism and the Strategy for Peace* (London: Macmillan, 1985).
9. Willian Gutteridge, *European Security, Nuclear Weapons and Public Confidence.* (London: Macmillan, 1982).
10. Geoffrey Williams, op. cit., p. 77.

8 : DIFFERING PRIORITIES

1. *Keesing's Contemporary Archives: Record of World Events*, vols XXVIII, 1982 and XXLX, 1983 (London: Longmans) p. 31965.
2. Ibid., p. 31965.
3. Stan Woods, *Pipeline Politics: the Allies at Odds* (Centre for Defence Studies, 1983) p. 27.
4. Ibid., p. 13.
5. Ibid., p. 14.
6. Jonathan Stern, *Soviet Natural Gas Development to the 1990's* (London, 1983) pp. 179–180.
7. Ibid., pp. 179–80.
8. Woods, op. cit., p. 28.
9. Ibid., p. 28.
10. Ibid., p. 29.
11. Ibid., pp. 30–1.

12. Ibid., p. 48.
13. Ibid., p. 48.
14. Ibid., p. 48.
15. Ibid., p. 49.
16. Keesing's op. cit., p. 31965.
17. Gavin Kennedy, *Defence Economics* (London: Duckworth, 1983) pp. 177–9.

9: THE BRITISH NUCLEAR DEFENCE OPTION

1. Coral Bell, *The Debatable Alliance* (London: Oxford University Press, 1962). This book deals with the nature of the special relationship on p. 35.
2. R. N. Rosecrance, *The Defence of the Realm: British Strategy in the Nuclear Epoch* (New York: Columbia University Press, 1967). Present evidence of British subserviency to United States arms.
3. *Statement on Defence, 1962: the Next Five Years*, Cmnd 1639, Part I. (London: HM Stationery Office, 1962) ch. I, para 2. p. 3.
4. David Rees, *The Age of Containment* (London: Macmillan, 1965) p. 44.
5. Lord Avon (memoirs of), *Full Circle* (Cambridge, Mass., Houghton Mifflin, 1960) p. 166.
6. *Statement on Defence, 1954: Annual White Paper*, Cmnd 9075, Part I. (London: HM Stationery Office, Feb. 1957) ch. 2, para. 3, p. 5.
7. *Statement on Defence, 1957: Report on Defence*, Cmnd 363, Part I. (London: HM Stationery Office, Feb. 1957) ch. 2, para. 2, p. 4.
8. Geoffrey Williams, *Global Defence: Motivation and Policy in the Nuclear Age* (New Delhi: Vikas, 1984) p. 134.
9. Ibid., p. 134.
10. Ibid., p. 134.
11. Sixth Report from the Expenditure Committee. *The Future of the United Kingdom's Nuclear Force Policy*, 3 Apr. 1979, pp. 23–4.
12. Ibid., p. 23.
13. Ibid., p. 24.
14. Ibid., p. 24.
15. Ibid., p. 24.
16. Ibid., p. 24.
17. Ibid., p. 24.
18. Ibid., p. 23.
19. Ibid., p. 29.
20. Ibid., p. 29.
21. Ibid., p. 29.
22. Ibid., p. 27.
23. Ibid., p. 27.
24. Ibid., p. 27.
25. Ibid., p. 27.
26. Ibid., p. 27.
27. Ibid., p. 27.
28. John Strachey, *In Pursuit of Peace*, Fabian Pamphlet, 1960, pp. 27–9.

10 : THE UNILATERALIST THREAT TO PEACE

1. Lord Hill-Norton, Sir Frederick Sowrey, Sir David Wills, *Defence Begins at Home* (The Sherwood Press: London) p. 1.
2. Zbigniew Brzezinski, 'Tragic Dilemmas of Soviet World Power', p. 1. Hill-Norton, op. cit., p. 1.
3. Boutwell, 'Politics and The Peace Movement in West Germany', *International Security*, vol. 7. no. 4, p. 75.
4. Peter Nailor and Jonathan Alford, 'The Future of Britain's Deterrent Force', Adelphi Paper, no. 156, 1983, p. 2.
5. John Strachey, *The Pursuit of Peace* (The Fabian Society: London, 1980) p. 2; *Guardian*, 19 Nov. 1982; Peter Nailor, op. cit., p. 35.
6. John Strachey, op. cit., p. 2.
7. *The Times*, 17 Jan. 1983.
8. Bertrand Russell, 'The Case For British Unilateralism', *Arms and Arms Control* (Frederick A. Praeger: New York, 1982) p. 152.
9. Thomas C. Schelling, *Arms and Influence* (Yale University Press: 1966) p. 231.
10. Kennth N. Waltz, 'Toward Nuclear Peace', *The Use of Force* (London: University Press of America, 1983) p. 585.
11. McGeorge Bundy, 'To Top The Volcano', *Foreign Affairs*, Oct. 1969.

11 : THE DUAL TRACK DECISION

1. Johan Holst, *INF and Political Equilibrium in Europe* (Oslo: Norwegian Institute of International Affairs, June 1983) p. 1.
2. Johan Holst, *The Dual Track Decision Revisited*, (Oslo: Norwegian Institute of International Affairs, Apr. 1983) p. 4.
3. Ibid., p. 3.
4. Ibid., p. 3.
5. Ibid., p. 8.
6. Ibid., p. 21.
7. Karl E. Birnbaum, *Arms Control in Europe: Problems and Prospects* (Austrian Institute for International Affairs, Mar. 1980) p. 34.
8. David Carlton and Carlo Schaerf (eds), *The Arms Race in the 1980's* (London, The Macmillan Press, 1982) p. 241.
9. Ibid., p. 241.
10. Ibid., p. 241.
11. Holst, *Dual Track*, p. 6.
12. Carlton, op. cit., p. 238.
13. Charles R. Gellner, *British and French Nuclear Forces in the INF Negotiations* (Washington US GPO, July 1983) p. 1.
14. George Treverton, *Nuclear Weapons in Europe*, Adelphi Papers no. 168, (London: International Institute for Strategic Studies, 1981) p. 16.

15. Institute for Defence and Disarmament Studies, The Arms Control Reporter, *A Chronicle of Treaties—Negotiations—Proposals* (Brooklyn Mass., IDDS, 1983) p. 403.
16. Ibid., p. 403
17. Freedman, op. cit. p. 22.
18. Yellner, op. cit., p. 1.
19. Ibid., p. 1.
20. Ibid., p. 1.
21. Ibid., p. 1.
22. Carlton, p. 242.
23. Holst, *Dual Track*, p. 8.
24. Ibid., p. 17.
25. Yellner., op. cit. p. 3.
26. Ibid., p. 4.
27. Arms Control Reporter, William van Cleave, *Chicago Tribune*, 1 Jan. 1984.
28. Treverton, op. cit., p. 22.
29. Holst, *Dual Track*., p. 11.
30. Treverton, op. cit., p. 16.
31. Holst, *Dual Track*., p. 22.
32. Yellner, op cit., p. 68.
33. Guido Vigeveno, *The Bomb and European Security* (London: C. Hurst & Co., 1983) pp. 88–119.

12: THE LIMITATIONS OF ARMS CONTROL

1. Christoph Bertram, 'Arms Control and Technological Change: Elements of a New Approach,' in Bertram (ed.), *Arms Control and Military Force* (1980) p. 160.
2. Ibid., p. 160.
3. Ibid., p. 158.
4. Ibid., p. 159.
5. Bertram's statistics are somewhat misleading here for US defence spending in 1980 discounting inflation was the same as it was in 1960, and fluctuations in strategic expenditures between 1965–75 can be as much attributed to American reaction to Vietnam, Watergate, and domestic social problems as they can to arms control.
6. Bertram, op. cit., p. 159.
7. Ibid., pp. 158–9.
8. John C. Baker, 'Alternatives to Formal Negotiations', in William Kinkade (ed.), *Approaches To Arms Control* (1979) p. 27.
9. Richard Burt, 'Defining the Problem', in Richard Burt (ed) *Arms Control and Defence Postures in the 1980's* (1982) p. 6.
10. Ibid., p. 9.
11. Ibid., p. 7.
12. Bertram, op. cit., p. 157.

13. Ibid., p. 153.
14. Baker, op. cit., p. 29.
15. Bertram, op. cit., p. 154.
16. Ibid., p. 170.
17. Ibid., p. 171.
18. Ibid., p. 176.
19. Ibid., p. 176.
20. In Bertram, op. cit., p.167.
21. Joseph S. Nye, 'The Future of Strategic Arms Control', in Barry M. Blechman (ed.), *The U.S. Strategic Posture* (1982) p. 237.
22. Bertram, op. cit., p. 168.
23. *Strategic Survey 1984–85* (London: ILSS, 1985) p. 122.

13: EUROPEAN DEFENCE AND THE STRATEGIC DEFENCE INITIATIVE

1. Dr A. E. Cockcroft, 'Facing the realities', letter to *The Times*, 19 June 1984.
2. Professor Lawrence Freedman, 'Star Wars Initiative', letter to *The Times*, 26 June 1984.
3. Air Vice-Marshal S. W. B. Menaul, 'State of the art in "Star Wars" ', letter to *The Times*, 15 June 1984.
4. 'Mrs Thatcher gives backing for critical Geneva meeting', *The Times*, 24 Dec. 1984.
5. *The Times* editorial, 28 Dec. 1984.
6. 'Compliance Diplomacy', *Survival*, vol. XXVI, no. 3, May/June 1984, pp. 127–35.
7. David Whitehouse 'The Burn-Up that Could Beat Star Wars', *The Times*, feature article 13 June 1984.
8. Ibid.
9. 'Reagan Told: So Far Super Defences', Harold Jackson, 19 Oct. 1983, report from the *Guardian*'s Washington correspondent.
10. 'Reagan's Star Wars – the Force Is not with Them', 30 Nov. 1983, Harold Jackson's report in the *Guardian*.
11. Gerald Frost, 'Soviet Reaction to SDI Programme' letter to *The Times*, 20 Dec. 1984.
12. Ibid.
13. Professor Lawrence Freedman, 'A "Star Wars" Challenge to Peace', letter to *The Times*, 13 June 1984.
14. Colonel Jonathan Alford, 'Deficiencies in "Star Wars" programme', letter to *The Times*, 14 June 1984.
15. Ibid.
16. Air Vice-Marshal S. W. B. Menaul, 'Rationale of U.S. Defence Study', letter to *The Times*, 29 Dec. 1984.
17. Ibid.
18. Ibid.
19. Ibid.
20. Ibid.

21. Col. Alford, op. cit.
22. Dr Geoffrey Lee Williams, 'Arms Control Up in the Air' letter to *The Times*, 13 June 1984.
23. Ibid.
24. Dr Geoffrey Lee Williams, 'Striking a Balance on Defence', letter to *The Times*, 18 Dec. 1984.
25. Keith B. Payne, 'Deterrence, Arms Control, and US Strategic Doctrine', *Foreign Affairs*, Autumn 1981, pp. 147–469.

14: CONCLUSIONS

1. Henry Kissinger, 'A Plan to Reshape NATO', *Time*, 5 Mar. 1984, p. 16.
2. Ibid., p. 16.

Selected Bibliography

Ball, M. M., *NATO & European Union Movement* (London: Stevens & Sons Ltd, 1959).
Baylis, J., *Alternative Approaches to British Defence Policy* (London: Macmillan, 1984).
Beer, Francis A. *Integration and Disintegration in NATO* (Ohio University Press, 1960).
Godson, J. (ed.), *Challenges To The Western Alliance* (London: Times Books, 1984).
Kissinger, Henry A., *The Troubled Partnership* (New York: McGraw-Hill, 1965).
Kennedy, K., *Defence Economics* (London: Duckworth, 1983).
Liska, George, *Nations in Alliance* (Baltimore: Johns Hopkins Press, 1968).
Myers, Kenneth A. (ed.), *NATO: the Next Thirty Years* (Boulder: Westview Press, 1980).
Osgood, Robert E., *NATO: the Entangling Alliance* (University of Chicago Press, 1962).
Rose, C., *Campaigns against Western Defence: NATO's Adversaries and Critics* (London: Macmillan, 1985).
Vigeveno, G. *The Bomb and European Security* (London: C. Hurst, 1983).
Williams, Geoffrey, *The Permanent Alliance: the European-American Partnership, 1945-1984* (Leyden: A. W. Sijthoff, 1977).
Williams, Geoffrey, *Global Defence: Defence Thinking in the Nuclear-Missile Age* (New Delhi: Vikas Publishing House, 1984).
Williams, G. and Read, B., *Dennis Healey and the Policies of Power* (London: Sidgwick & Jackson, 1971).
Williams, G. and Williams A., *Crisis in European Defence* (London: Charles Knight, 1974).

Index

Abalakovo (Siberia), 203–4
Abrahamson, General James, 209
Afghanistan, 5, 39, 79, 92–3, 123, 130, 203
Afheldt, Horst, 73–6
Africa, 214; Southern, 38, 98; *see also* South Africa; West Africa
aircraft carriers: US, 104–5, 178–9; Soviet, 106
Airland Battle 2000, 82
Air–Land Battle (ALB), 1, 65–6, 87, 104, 218–19
Alford, Colonel Jonathan, 207, 209
Algeria: gas supply, 136
Andropov, Yuri, 150, 178
Angola, 39, 79, 93–4
Anti-Ballistic Missile Treaty (ABM), 1972, 188, 191–2, 197, 200, 203
anti-ballistic missiles, 8, 200, 202–9
anti-satellite weapons, 6, 9, 204
Anti-Tank Guided Missile Launchers (ATGMLs), 87
Arbatov, G. A., 83
'area munitions', 140–1
Argentine, 17, 151
arms control, 71–3, 89, 148–53; regional and strategic, 185; objectives, 186–93; and economic savings, 187–8; and war damage limitation, 188–9; and increased stability, 190–3; implementation problems, 193–7; and SDI, 209–10
Arms Limitation accords, 6
Asat weapons (anti-satellite), 204
Aspaturian, Professor Vernon, 95–6
Athens guidelines, 1962, 46
Atlantic Council, 89
Attlee, Clement, 142, 170
Australia, 20

B-IB (US bomber), 7
B-52 (US bomber), 7, 143
Backfire (Soviet bomber), 102, 104, 106, 155, 178, 194
Badger (Soviet bomber), 104
Baker, John C., 190, 194
ballistic missile defence (BMD), 200–1, 209–10
ballistic missile early warning system (BMEWS), 144
Basic Principles of Relations Between the USA and the USSR, 97–8
Battle of Britain, 1940, 143
Bavaria, 32
Beira patrol, 17
Belgium, 174, 183
Belize, 157
Berlin, 31–2, 124
Bertram, Christoph, 50, 187–9, 191, 193, 195–8
Bevin, Ernest, 168, 170
Blackjack (Soviet bomber), 8
Blair House Agreement, 1948, 142
Blinder (Soviet bomber), 104
Blue Steel ('standoff' weapon), 144
Blue Streak (British ICBM), 143–4
Boeing Aerospace Corporation, 88
'boost-phase' defence, 205
Borneo, 17
Bradford University School of Peace Studies, 140
Brandt, Willy, 123
Brazil, 165
Brezhnev, Leonid, 5, 80, 90–2, 95
Britain: military resources, 1; and third force doctrine, 15–17; membership of EEC, 15–17, 117, 125, 146; abandons East of Suez role, 15, 19–20, 116, 125;

Index

Britain – *cont.*
Eurocentric defence policy, 15–20; military operations (1950–66), 16; naval forces, 18–19, 108, 115–18, 156; global commitments, 23; technological capacity, 23; submarines, 24, 118–19, 141, 156, 180–1; co-operation with France, 24, 53, 130; independent nuclear capability, 29–30, 53–4, 110, 118, 120, 141–3, 148–53, 155–9; in McNamara Committee, 31; troop numbers in Europe, 32; conscription abolished, 51, 72, 128–9; and standardization, 55; total war economy, 67; relations with USA, 113–17, 125, 130, 142–7; and flexible response, 115; defence allocations, 115–18, 156; imperial role, 116; attitude to NATO and defence, 116–17, 120, 125, 130; US missiles and forces in, 119, 178; vulnerability to nuclear attack, 118–19, 158; peace movement in, 119, 127–8, 164–71; opposes German nuclear arms, 129; oil and gas supply, 136; and non-nuclear option, 141, 152–9; post-war weapons development, 142–6; in multi-lateral force, 146; in arms control negotiations, 148, 150; and proliferation, 150–3; civil nuclear programme, 152; defence spending, 156–7; cruise missile deployment, 174; and INF negotiations, 176–8, 180–1, 184; views on SDI, 200, 202–3; fear of Soviet ABM, 202
British Army on the Rhine (BAOR), 116, 120, 156–7
British Nuclear Force, 147, 156
Brodie, Bernard, 75, 93
Brookings Institute, 103
Brzezinski, Zbigniew, 99
Bull, Professor Hedley, 49, 52
Bundy, McGeorge, 50, 165
Burt, Richard, 190–2

Callaghan report, 54

Callaghan, James, 147
Campaign for Nuclear Disarmament (CND), 128, 153; *see also* peace movement
Canada, 31, 108
Canberra (British strike-reconnaissance aircraft), 143
Canby, Dr Steven, 64–5
Caribbean, 40
Carter, Jimmy, 5–6, 36
Carver, Field-Marshall Michael, Baron, 50, 140
Casey, William, 84
Central America, 40
Central Intelligence Agency (CIA), 83
China: deterrent, 30; Reagan visits, 41; strength of forces, 86; relations with USSR, 86, 93; non-participation in Test Ban talks, 148; and US arms control, 179
Churchill, Sir Winston, 142–3, 157
CINCAFMED (Commander-in-Chief Allied Forces Mediterranean), 18
Circular Error Probability (CEP), 5
Clausewitz, Carl von, 80, 118, 189–90
Cockcroft, Dr A. E., 200
Cominform, 92
Command–control–communications (C3), 8
Commonwealth, British, 20, 116
Communist Party of the Soviet Union (CPSU), 80
Comprehensive Test Ban Treaty (CTB), 148, 186
Conference on Security and Co-operation in Europe, 148
Cornell, Alexander H., 55
correlation of forces, 96–7, 100–1
counter-force strategy, 73
crisis diplomacy, 33
Cruise missiles: US, 7–8, 35, 52, 79, 85, 89–91, 119, 126–7, 140–1, 150, 168, 218; Soviet naval, 104–5; as theatre weapon, 155; and stabilization, 190–1; and arms control, 194–5

Index

Cuba: Missile crisis, 4, 92, 103, 125, 145; and Soviet power position, 21, 93; troops in Africa, 79, 98
Cyprus, 18
Czechoslovakia, 21, 28, 32, 34, 92

Deep Attack, 65–6, 70, 219
'Defence Guidance' (US document), 86
Defence Intelligence Agency (DIA), 84
Defence White Papers (British), 142, 143
détente, 46, 93, 212
dual control, 215–16, 218
Dual Track Decision (DTD), 172, 175–6, 182

ERW (neutron bomb) anti-tank weapons, 73
Eagleburger, Lawrence, 184
East–West trade, 45–6, 56
Egypt, 93, 153
Eisenhower, Dwight D., 144–5
Emerging Technologies (ET), 66, 69–70, 190, 215
energy resources, 134–6
English, Professor Edward, 16
Epstein, J. M., 87
Ethiopia, 39, 94
Europe, Western: integration of, 2, 25–6, 45, 58; nuclear missile capability, 23–5, 53; dependence on USA, 25–6, 48–9, 109–12, 114, 213–14; as Third Force, 23, 26–7; economic power, 39, 51; danger of war in, 48, 68, 110–12, 213–14; neutrality in, 44, 47; peace movements, 53, 111; nationalism in, 77; and Siberian pipeline, 132–7; views on SDI, 200, 202–3; and US anti-missile defence, 205–7, 210; proposed increased influence, 215–17
European Defence Community (EDC), 40, 117, 130
European Economic Community, 15–17, 25, 46, 58, 124–5, 146

European Recovery Programme, 15, 213
European Theatre of Nuclear Forces (TNF), 46, 53
evolving technologies, *see* Emerging Technolgoies

F-15 (US fighter aircraft), 8, 200, 204
F 111 (US bomber), 154–5, 178–9, 184
FB 111 (US bomber), 154–5
FRG, *see* Germany, West
Falklands War, 1982, 17, 46, 116–18, 151, 156–7
Field Manual 100/5 (USA), 82
'fire-break', 189
first strikes, 35, 37, 42, 66; *see also* No-First-Use
flexible response, 23, 28, 32–3, 43–5, 50, 55–6, 62, 115, 118, 122, 141, 204, 217
follow-on force attack (FOFA), 1, 38, 65–6, 82, 104, 211, 218–19
Ford, Gerald, 36
Foreign Affairs (journal), 165
Forward-Based Systems (FBS), 155, 177, 183
forward strategy, 38, 121, 140
France: military resources, 1; withdrawal from NATO, 15, 30, 118; global commitments, 23; technological capacity, 23; submarines, 24, 181; co-operation with Britain, 24, 53, 130; and Third Force Europe, 25–6; relations with USA, 26, 118; independent nuclear capability, 29, 49, 53–4, 110, 118, 130, 149–50, 154, 159; ground forces, 33; confidence in dealing with USSR, 48; and standardization, 55; and stronger Germany, 57, 122; strength of forces, 86; and naval resources, 108; post-war position, 114; resents British relations with USA, 116; alliance with Germany, 124–5, 130; in EEC, 124–5; opposes German nuclear arms,

France – *cont.*
129; energy imports, 133; non-participation in Test Ban talks, 148; non-signatory of Non-Proliferation Treaty, 165; and INF negotiations, 176–8, 180–1, 184; and ABM systems, 202; limited anti-nuclear protest movement, 216
Freedman, Professor Lawrence, 94, 201, 207
Frost, Gerald, 206

GLCMs, *see* ground-launched Cruise missiles
Gaitskell, Hugh, 168, 170
gas pipeline, *see* pipeline (Siberian)
Gaulle, Charles de, 15, 26, 118, 146
Gaylor, Admiral Noel, 50
Germany, West (FRG): military resources, 1; technological capacity, 23; and Third Force Europe, 25–6; requests response to SS-20s, 42, 88; confidence in dealing with USSR, 48; availability of nuclear forces, 49, 53, 74, 121–2, 127, 129–31, 216, 218; proposed deterrent system, 53–4, 57, 129, 218; and standardization, 55; and NFU, 67–8; and Soviet threat, 68, 117, 121; as armed camp, 72, 126, 129; security of population, 74; and naval resources, 108; post-war position, 114; involvement in NATO, 114, 121–2, 124–6, 130; questions US commitment, 115; peace movement in, 119, 126–8; defence policy and doctrine, 120–6, 129; relations with USA, 121–3, 125–7; and reunification of Germany, 123–4, 214; relations with France, 124–5, 130; in EEC, 124–5; energy imports, 133; and British nuclear abandonment, 154; Cruise missile deployment in, 173–4, 218; and dual control, 216, 218–19; surrogate nuclear status, 218

Gorshkov, Admiral Sergei G., 102–3
Graham, Daniel, 84
Gray, Colin, 43, 82
Greenham Common, 128
Green Party (W. Germany), 128
Greenwood-Davignon report, 26
Grenada, 46, 125
'grey area' weapons, 154–5, 196
Gromyko, Andrei, 97, 203
ground-launched Cruise missiles (GLCMs), 172, 174, 177

Hackett, General Sir John, 32–3
Haig, Alexander, 90
Healey, Denis, 34, 168
Heath, Edward, 19, 24
Holland, *see* Netherlands
Holzman, Franklin D., 83
Howard, Professor Michael, 36, 47, 50
Hyde Park Agreement, 1944, 142

Iceland, 17
India, 22; nuclear device, 151, 153; non-signatory of Non-Proliferation Treaty, 165
Indian Ocean, 105, 186
Indonesia, 17, 93
inter-continental ballistic missiles (ICBMs), 5–9, 81, 173
Intermediate Nuclear Force (INF): negotiations over, 40–2, 52, 57, 118, 140, 149–50, 154–5, 175, 177–84, 186, 190, 195; deployment, 173–4, 180–4; and START, 183
intermediate range ballistic missiles (IRBMs), 6, 56, 111, 172–7, 182–3; *see also* Cruise; Pershing; SS-20
International Institute for Strategic Studies (IISS), 86, 91
International Peace Research Institute, Stockholm, 84
Iran, 5, 71
Israel, 151, 153, 165
Italy, 18, 23, 31, 108, 174
Ivan Rogov class (Soviet amphibious ship), 105

Japan, 179

Index

Jaruzelski, General Wohciech, 133
Javits, Senator Jacob, 16
Jupiter missiles, 173

Kampuchea, 39
Kennedy Round, 16
Kennedy, John F., 81, 92, 145–6, 173
Kennet, Wayland Young, 2nd Baron, 208
Kent, Monsignor Bruce, 91, 127
Khrushchev, Nikita S., 34, 80–1, 92
Kirov (Soviet cruiser), 107
Kissinger, Henry, 50, 52, 61, 98, 111, 115, 121, 216
Klepsch report, 26
Kohl, Helmut, 25
Korea, North, 21
Korea, South, 151
Korean War, 102
Kosygin, Aleksey, N., 92
Kower, Robert W., 63–5

Labour Party (British), 47, 111, 119, 128–9, 147–8, 167–70
Laos, 39
Latin America, 151, 214
Lebanon, 102
Lehman, John, 106
Leopard II (German tank), 87
Liberal Party (British), 128
Libya, 153
Lisbon Force agreement and goals, 1952, 48–9, 114
Long-range theatre nuclear force (LRTNF), 176
Luxembourg Agreements, 1966, 16, 25

M-1 (US tank), 87
MX (US missile), 7
McDonald, Admiral Wesley, 108
Mac-B (long-range Cruise missile), 173
McMahon Act, 1946 (USA), 142
Macmillan, Harold, 15, 144, 147
McNamara Committee, 31
McNamara, Robert, 15, 23, 31, 37, 66–7, 73, 115, 145

Malacca Straits, 17, 19
Malaysia, 17, 19–20
Malta, 18
Manhattan Project, 113, 142
Marshall Aid, 15, 45, 92, 113
Martin, Professor Laurence, 19
Marxism–Leninism, 79–80, 94, 96
Mason, Roy, 148
massive retaliation, 28, 30, 114–15
Mediterranean, 105, 116
Menaul, Air Vice-Marshal Stewart B., 201, 207–9
Middle East, 18, 38, 42, 151, 214
Midgetman (US ICBM), 7
Milshtein, 83
mini-nukes, 74–6
Minuteman (US ICBM), 6, 211
Mitterrand, François, 25
Mountbatten of Burma, Admiral of the Fleet Louis, 1st Earl, 140
Mozambique, 93
multilateral force (MLF), 40, 73, 146
multi-national force (MNF), 146
multiple individually-targeted re-entry vehicles (MIRVs), 30, 147, 194, 196
mutual assured destruction (MAD), 35–7, 189, 207, 210
mutual balanced force reduction (MBFR), 148–9, 154, 186

NFR 90 (NATO frigate replacement), 108
Nassau Agreement, 1962, 117, 146–7, 154
national security memorandum 242 (USA), 36
Nerlich, Professor Uwe, 73
Netherlands (Holland), 31, 108, 136, 174, 183
neutralism, 3, 44, 47–8, 50, 56, 111; see also peace movement
neutron bomb, 73, 75
New York Post, 86
New Zealand, 20
Nicaragua, 46
Nitze–Kvitniski talks, 183
Nixon, Richard M., 5, 98

No-First-Use (NFU), 66–9, 127, 140, 214
non-nuclear options, 140–1
Non-Proliferation Treaty, 1968, 148, 151–3, 164
North Atlantic Treaty Organization (NATO): twin-pillar concept ('Europeanist'/'Atlanticist'), 1–4, 10–11, 26, 35, 40, 44, 49–58; local strategy, 1; vulnerability, 2; France withdraws from, 15, 30, 118; dependence on USA, 21, 26, 29–30, 34, 39, 42, 44–5; and national nuclear capacity, 26; Defence Planning Committee, 29–30; deterrence doctrine (flexible response), 29–30, 37–8, 43, 45, 56, 62, 72–3, 81, 110, 141, 217; Nuclear Planning Group, 31–2, 38, 89, 119; strength of conventional forces, 32–4, 45, 50–2, 59, 62, 86–7; and limited war, 37; policy options, 44–58; standardization of weapons, 44, 51, 54–5, 57, 65; and Third World, 46; dissension in, 45–7; costs and contributions, 49, 51, 63–5, 206; commanders and administration, 52, 55–7; control of nuclear forces, 52; Eurogroup, 58; Charter, 58; mixed nuclear/conventional strategy, 62–70, 73–6, 128, 215; rationalization proposals, 64–5; reserves and mobilization, 65, 85; and central control, 73–4, 109; war-fighting capacity, 82–3; defence spending, 84; and SS-20 threat, 88–9, 91; and naval power, 103–4, 106–8; forward offensive strategy, 108; conflict of national and community interests, 110, 115, 123, 125; formed, and goals, 114, 213; German membership, 114, 121–2, 124–6, 130; proposed alternative strategies, 128–9, 213–14, 217–18; policy affected by events, 134; and Siberian pipeline conflict, 137–9; and arms reduction, 150, 180–2, 184; and unilateralist arguments, 167–70; and Cruise missile deployment, 172–7, 184; and new technology, 189; and SDI, 212; and dual control, 215–16, 218; heightened European influence proposed, 217–19
Northern Army Group, 157
Northern tier, 33
Norway, 107, 136
Norwegian Sea, 102, 107
nuclear strategy: assessed, 61; limited, 75–6
nuclear threshold, 2, 38, 45, 48, 75–6, 189

Office of Technology Assessment (USA), 205
Olympic Games, Moscow, 1980, 46
OPEC (Oil Producing and Exporting Countries), 134
Oscar class submarines (USSR), 104, 106
Ostpolitik, 43, 122–4
outer space, 199, 202, 204
Outer Space Treaty, 191

pacifism, *see* neutralism; peace movement
Pakistan, 153, 165
Paris Agreements, 1954, 121–2, 129
Partial Test Ban Treaty, 1963, 148
peace movement, 53, 111–12, 126–8; dangers of, 159, 163–7; exploited by USSR, 194–5; and dual control, 216
peaceful co-existence, 80, 92, 123
Pershing I (US missile), 6, 172
Pershing II (US missile): deployment, 7–9, 35, 40, 52, 79, 85, 89–91, 119, 126, 140, 150, 183, 190, 195, 218; and Dual Track Decision, 172, 174, 176, 178–9; range, 179–80
Persian Gulf, 19, 38–9, 42, 116
Pierre, Professor Andrew J., 54
pipeline (Siberian), 43, 46, 123, 132–9

Index

Pipes, Richard, 43
'point' targets and defence, 24
Poland, 21, 40, 93, 130, 133–5
Polaris (nuclear submarine), 118–19, 141, 146–50, 154, 156, 168, 173, 191, 202
Poseidon (US submarine-launched missile), 147, 172–3
Presidential Directives (USA): PD 53, 36, PD 57, 36; PD 58, 36; PD 59, 36–7
proliferation (nuclear), 150–2, 164–5, 192; see also Non-Proliferation Treaty

Quebec Agreement, 1943, 142

Race-Trace proposal (Carter), 6
Reagan, Ronald (and Reagan administration): and arms race, 6, 10; and deployment of missiles, 7, 176, 183; 'Star Wars' programme, 8, 186, 200; visits China, 41; attitude to USSR, 43, 46; disparages neutralism, 47; and NFU, 68; defence policy, 82; on use of tactical nuclear weapons, 90; 1981 'four point agenda for peace', 90–1; build up of naval forces, 108; modifies Polish sanctions, 133, 137; and energy supply to W. Europe, 136, 139; on British and French nuclear systems, 180; strategic defence initiative, 188, 192, 204; on Soviet violation of control agreements, 204
release procedures, 76
Reykjavik Conference, 1968, 28
Rogers, General Bernard William, 88, 140, 218
Rome, Treaty of, 25; see also European Economic Community
Rose, François de, 50
Royal Air Force, 142–5
Royal Navy, 18–19, 115–18, 156
Rusk, Dean, 28
Rybkin, Colonel Ye., 80

SA-12 (Soviet anti-aircraft system), 204
SS-4 (Soviet missile), 88, 90–1, 173–4, 182
SS-5 (Soviet missile), 88, 90–1, 173–4, 176, 182
SS-11 (Soviet missile), 155
SS-16 (Soviet missile), 89, 175
SS-17 (Soviet missile), 81
SS-18 (Soviet missile), 5, 7, 9, 81
SS-19 (Soviet missile), 9, 81, 104
SS-20 (Soviet missile), 6, 8–9, 35, 40, 42, 56, 79, 88–91, 126, 140; and arms reduction talks, 150, 155, 181, 183–4; deployment, 172–9, 184; and SDI defence, 210
SS-21 (Soviet missile), 176
SS-22 (Soviet missile), 176
SS-23 (Soviet missile), 176
SSBN (nuclear firing submarines), 103, 106
Sabroski, Alan Ned, 92
Safeguard ABM system (USA), 192
SALT I, 1972, 22, 35, 52, 97–8, 148, 155, 194
SALT II, 6, 35, 53, 149, 155, 186, 198
SALT III, see START
Sanakoyev, Sh. P., 94
Sanity (CND magazine), 164
Schelling, Thomas C., 171
Schlesinger, James, 36
Schmidt, Helmut, 90, 119
Schultz, George, 203
Schwarz, Hans-Peter, 54
Scoville, Herbert, Jr., 197
Scowcroft Commission: Report on Strategic Nuclear Forces, 6, 9
Sea-Bed Treaty, 191
'second centre of deterrence', 1, 3
second strike capability, 165–6
Sergiyev, A., 96
Simes, Dimitri, 82–3
Singapore, 19–20
Skybolt (missile system), 144–7
Smart, Ian, 74
Somalia, 93
South Africa, 151
South Vietnam, 39

South Yemen, 39, 93
Soviet Military Power (US publication), 86
Sovremenny class (Soviet guided missile destroyer), 107
Space Shuttle programme (USA), 6, 10
Spain, 108
Sputnik, 115
'Star Wars', 8, 45, 186, 194, 200–8, 219; *see also* strategic defence initiative
START (Strategic Arms Reduction Talks), 91, 148, 150, 154, 183–4, 186, 198, 202, 211
'Stealth' technology, 7
Steele, Jonathan, 92
Stern, Jonathan, 135
Stevens, Senator Theodore, 50
Stockholm, *see* International Peace Research Institute
Strachey, John, 157
Strategic Air Command (USA), 143–4
Strategic Arms Limitation Talks, *see* SALT I *and* SALT II
Strategic Arms Reduction Talks, *see* START
strategic defence initiative (SDI), 24, 188, 192, 200–5, 207–12
Strategic Nuclear Force (British), 141, 145
Strategic Reserve (British), 146
Stuart, Douglas T., 86
submarine launched ballistic missiles (SLBM), 181, 191
submarines, 7, 24, 88, 104, 108, 178, 181; *see also* Polaris
Suez crisis, 1956, 17, 40, 92, 102
Summer, Theo, 50
Supreme Allied Commander Atlantic (SACLANT), 18, 52, 55
Supreme Allied Commander of Europe (SACEUR), 52, 55, 154
Supreme Headquarters Allied Power Europe (SHAPE), 18, 219
Sweden, 22, 119, 169

TSR-2 (British strike-reconnaisance aircraft), 146

tactical nuclear weapons, 30–3, 73–4; *see also* neutron bomb
Taiwan, 151
Task Force 10 on Theatre Nuclear Modernization . . . , 149
Taylor, General Maxwell, 50
Teamwork naval exercise, 1984 (NATO), 107
'techno-commando' squads, 73–4
Thatcher, Margaret (and Thatcher administration), 130, 149, 153, 155, 202
theatre nuclear forces (TNF), 172
Third Force Europe, 23, 25
Third World, 39, 43, 45–6, 56, 71, 77, 93, 214
Thor rockets, 144, 173
Times, The (newspaper), 203
Tito, Josip Broz, 92
Tomahawk (US missile), 172, 176
Tornado (US aircraft), 55
Trenchard, Hugh Montague, 1st Viscount, 143
Trident II (submarine missile system), 7, 24, 54, 141, 150, 153–4, 156–7, 166, 168, 202
Turkey, 31

Udaloy class (Soviet guided missile destroyer), 107
unilateral disarmament, 111, 119, 158, 163–71; *see also* peace movement
Union of Soviet Socialist Republics (USSR): pre-emptive strikes by, 2, 22; military planning, 3; superiority in conventional forces, 3, 74; and Cuba crisis, 4–5; and military balance, 5, 9–10, 22, 41, 79, 84; missiles, 5–6; respect for power, 8; economic weakness, 8, 10, 99; and arms control, 9, 73, 150, 155, 180–4; as global power, 19; fear of losing E. Europe empire, 21–2; deterrence policy, 22; threat to W. Europe, 24, 29; and NATO deterrence, 29–31; and mutual destruction, 29; intervention outside Europe, 30; conventional warfare capacity,

32–4, 68–9, 84–6; and revised US counterforce strategy, 36–7; American/European analyses of, 41–2; attains nuclear parity, 45, 91, 192; and Europeanised NATO, 57; war fighting and winning, 65, 80–3; total war economy, 67; and NATO's NFU, 68; and emerging technologies, 70; ideology, 78–81, 93–6; superiority in theatre nuclear forces, 78–9; navy, 78, 88, 102–8; deterrence through denial, 80–2; defence spending, 83–4, 163; reserves, 85; rejects Reagan's 'four point agenda', 91; aggression in Europe questioned, 92; post-war foreign policy, 92–4, 96, 98; military doctrine (and 'correlation of forces'), 94–7, 100–1; superpower status, 97–100; develops nuclear arms, 114–15; fear of W. Germany, 124, 129; Siberian pipeline and energy exports, 132, 134–6; and Polish crisis, 134; technological dependence on West, 135–7; and Anglo-French nuclear deterrents, 149–50, 180–1, 184; as threat to West, 163; deployment of IRBMs, 172–4, 176–9, 182–3; and outer space anti-missile technology, 202–4, 206; strategic objectives, 210–11; and SDI policy, 212

United States of America (USA): relationship with W. Europe, 1–4, 8, 25–6, 27, 34, 39, 44–5, 48–9, 109–11, 115, 214–19; global strategy, 2; weapons production, 5; continental air defence, 8, 10; nuclear arsenal, 9, 108–10; and arms control, 9, 84; economic strength, 10; and Far East/Pacific defence, 20; alliance system, 22–3, 43–4; and flexible response, 23, 28, 32; and mutual destruction, 29; disposition of fleets, 31, 34–5, 39; in McNamara Committee, 31; withdrawal of troops from Europe, 32, 131, 214; reinforcement capability, 32–3; revised counterforce strategy, 36–7; domestic political constraints, 40; decline in strength, 41; analysis of Soviet decline, 41; and Third World, 45–6; and war in Europe, 45, 48, 68; defence costs and contributions, 49, 97–100; isolationism, 50, 111, 214; NATO-committed forces, 51–2; and NATO command, 52, 55–7; view of warfare, 65, 82–3; total war economy, 67; and European nationalism, 77; and limited war, 90, 112; and Soviet superpower status, 97–100; as global power, 99–100; naval forces, 104–6, 108; relations with Britain, 113–17, 125, 130, 142–7; initial nuclear dominance, 114; commitment to German defence, 121–3, 125–7, 130; conscription, 128; and Siberian pipe-line, 132–9; forces and equipment in Britain, 144; Non-Proliferation Act, 152; separation from Europe, 155, 157; possible reaction to British unilateral disarmament, 167; and INF negotiations, 174, 180–4; and strategic defence initiative, 200–3, 209–11; and dual control, 215–19

United States Arms Control and Disarmament, 84

Urengoi (Siberia), 132

Uzhgorod, 132

'V' bombers (British), 141, 143–4

Vietnam, 5, 7, 23, 71

Vigeveno, Guido, 75

XV-2 and XV-3 (US infantry fighting vehicles), 87

Warsaw Pact: and strategic balance, 3; and first use, 30; military strength, 32, 38, 50–1, 56, 64, 74, 84–6; as threat to West, 45–6; reduction of tension in, 52; efficient use of resources, 63; views of conventional warfare, 64–6;

Warsaw Pact – *cont.*
  defence spending, 84; reserves and mobilization, 85; aircraft and forces, 87; naval strategy, 104–5; and missile deployment, 183
Weinberger, Caspar, 205
Weizsäcker, Carl Friedrich von, 72, 73

West Africa, 105
Wilson, Harold, 15, 17, 147, 152
Windscale, 152
Woods, Stan, 133, 136

'zero-option', 90, 176–7